SHADOWS OF OUR ANCESTORS

Map by Gue Pilon

Shadows of
Our Ancestors

READINGS IN THE HISTORY
OF KLALLAM-WHITE RELATIONS

EDITED AND
WITH COMMENTARIES BY
JERRY GORSLINE

ISBN-13: 978-1523989935
ISBN-10: 1523989939

TABLE

PREFACE

At the time of first Euro-American contact the Klallam people occupied the area on the Olympic Peninsula, Washington State, along the south shore of the Strait of Juan de Fuca, from the Hoko River east to Discovery Bay.

Their first "contact" was with the English and Spanish explorers who penetrated these inland waters in the last years of the 18th century seeking the legendary Northwest Passage. Following the explorers came fur traders, missionaries, gold seekers and then settlers.

In the winter of 1855, their numbers decimated by disease and alcohol, dependent on a mercantile economy, their culture and resource base devastated, the remaining Klallams gathered to negotiate a treaty with Isaac Stevens, Governor and Indian Superintendent of the Washington Territory.

From the time of white settlement until the reaffirmation of their treaty rights in the 1970s, the Klallam nation faced a fundamental challenge to its existence.

This collection is intended to document that ordeal and to convey the flavor of Indian-white relations on the north Olympic Peninsula during that crucial phase when the Coast Salish way of life was completely overturned and modern patterns ingrained.

The readings are drawn from diverse sources: journals and letters, oral testimony and the research of historians and anthropologists.

Throughout the book I have provided commentary on the text to help the reader appreciate the historical context and some of the implications of each selection.

In most cases I retained the original spelling in historical documents. Exceptions are references to Klallams and their 19th century chief Chet-ze-moka, which were standardized to conform to modern usage.

I assembled this collection of readings to illuminate the background of present Indian-white relations on the north Olympic Peninsula, and with the hope that it could contribute toward cleansing and clarifying that relationship.

I would like to thank the following people whose support and inspiration made the book possible:

Finn Wilcox and Pat Fitzgerald for their loyalty and friendship.

Peter Simpson, whose work inspired this book and added substantially to its content.

Jim Dodge, Finn Wilcox and Tom Jay, who raised a significant portion of my limited budget out of their conviction the book was worth supporting.

Agropyron, for her exceptional generosity.

Marian Taylor, one of the "strong people," who gave so generously of her time and knowledge of the Jamestown S'Klallam.

Tree Swenson: her elegant design sense and typographic vocabulary rendered a complicated manuscript into a graceful and readable book.

The Jefferson County Centennial Committee and the Jefferson County Historical Society for their financial assistance.

The many others that helped in significant ways: Michael Daley, Morris Graves, Robert Yarber, Gary Snyder, Joe Waterhouse, Jr., Mary Jane Knecht, Helen Byers, Steve Johnson, Bruce Brown, Robert Steelquist, Lanie Johnson, Steve Wang, Cy Frick, Ross Hamilton, Virginia Keeting, Carol Cahill, Nelsa Buckingham, Autumn Scott, Fred Sharpe, Diane Doss and the crew at the Salal Cafe.

Thanks to the Jefferson County Historical Society, and to Marsha Moratti in particular, for giving this book a new lease on life.

Acknowledgements:

"Earliest Expedition Against Puget Sound Indians," reprinted from *The Washington Historical Quarterly*, Vol. I, No. 2.

Letters from Fort Vancouver reprinted from *The Publications of the Hudson's Bay Record Society: McLoughlin's Fort Vancouver Letters. First Series*, 1825-38.

"Mystery Solved," "Point No Point Treaty," "Smallpox Ship," "Circumstantial Evidence" and "The Hangman's Tree" from *The Dungeness Massacre and Other Regional Tales*, by Mary Ann Lambert.

Excerpts from *The Records of the Stevens Treaty Commission in Western Washington by Barbara Lane, Ph.D; Treaty of Haud-Skus or Point No Point by*

George Gibbs; A Case of Post Contact Reform Among the Clallam by L.L. Langness and the text of the Point No Point Treaty, all courtesy of Jamestown Klallam Archives, Sequim, Washington.

"The Great White Father" by Kent D. Richards excerpted from *Isaac I. Stevens: Young Man in a Hurry*, courtesy of Brigham Young University Press.

"Indian Policy-Treaties on Puget Sound" excerpted from *The Life of Isaac Ingalls Stevens by Hazard Stevens*. 2 Vols. (Boston: Houghton, Mifflin & Co., 1900).

"Testimony of See-Hem-ltza Regarding the Point No Point Treaty" from a letter to A.N. Taylor dated Feb. 20, 1922, National Archives, Seattle.

"Ten Years of Missionary Work" excerpted from *Ten Years of Missionary Work Among the Indians at Skokomish, Washington Territory*, 1874-1884 by Rev. Myron Eells.

"Seam-Itza" and "Commentary: An Anthropologist's View" reprinted from *Dalmo'ma V: Digging for Roots*, Empty Bowl Press.

"The Prince of Wales" excerpted from "The Prince of Wales, Present Chief of the Clallams, Jefferson County." Unpublished manuscript from the Washington Pioneer Project.

The title for the book is adapted from a poem by Dee Koester, a Lower Elwha Klallam, "The Sleep of Whispering Echoes."

Cover photo by Anders Beer Wilse.

PRELUDE

KLALLAM PREHISTORY

The Klallam belong to the Salishan linguistic family whose range extended from the central British Columbia coast to northwestern Oregon and, in the interior, the Fraser and Columbia drainages (Suttles, 1987).

Archaeological evidence suggests that the Salish people were relatively recent arrivals to the Puget Sound area from the interior by way of the Skagit and Fraser rivers (Drucker, 1963). Excavations reveal that they were well established by 1300 A.D. (Carlson, 1960). Estimates by Mooney (1928) and Kroeber (1939) indicate the Coast Salish population at the time of European contact was around 30,000 people. The Klallam tribe may have moved from Vancouver Island into their historic range on the Olympic Peninsula, wedging themselves between the Chemakuan speaking Quileute and Chimakum tribes (Swadesh 1949).

Early population estimates for the Klallam suggest there were approximately 1,500 to 2,000 in 13 villages along the south shore of the Strait of Juan de Fuca (Taylor 1963; Gunther, 1927).

FIRST CONTACT

The earliest record of Klallam contact that I have been able to locate occurred in July 1788, when the Englishman Robert Duffin, one of John Meares' officers, was sent from the west coast of Vancouver Island on a longboat expedition. Duffin was sent out from Port Effingham on July 13th and returned July 20th with several badly wounded in a boat pierced "in a thousand places with arrows." The crew had penetrated as far as present-day Port Townsend and had been preparing to land west of there in Discovery Bay when they were attacked in their boats by Indians in canoes paddling to meet them. These Indians, presumably Klallams, were armed with clubs, barbed arrows and stone "bludgeons" (Meares, 1790).

During the four year interval between Duffin's longboat expedition and the arrival of the Vancouver expedition, Spanish explorers were active in the area. Bricks from the Spanish/Mexican outpost at Neah Bay, in Makah territory west of the Klallam, are the oldest remnants of local Euro-American material culture extant in Washington (Gamboa, 1989). In 1790, the Spanish explorer Manuel Quimper also reached Discovery Bay. The peninsula on which Port Townsend is located is named after him.

In 1792, the Vancouver expedition entered the Strait of Juan de Fuca to explore and map the Puget Sound area for the first time. Evidently, by now, the Klallam were quite used to European vessels. While in the vicinity of New Dungeness, near the mouth of the Dungeness River, Vancouver from a distance observed the inhabitants of a Klallam village through his glass and commented on their "utmost indifference and unconcern; they continued to fish before their huts as regard less of our being present, as if such vessels had been familiar to them, and unworthy of their attention" (Meany, 1957). Later, while anchored in Discovery Bay (which Vancouver named for his ship "The Discovery") some Klallams came from a small village along the shore to barter venison and fish for trinkets and copper. The inventory of collections made by the expedition include two bows, some arrows, a war club, two halibut hooks, a scoop or dipper, a rattle and a necklace of bird beaks (Gunther, 1960).

DISEASE

Members of the Vancouver expedition noted the ravages of smallpox on the faces of the Puget Sound tribes. It is important to understand that contact between Europeans and North American aboriginals also represents contact between two previously separate eco-systems. One disastrous consequence of this fact, for the Klallam as well as all other North American Indians, was the introduction of exotic diseases. Like trade goods, disease had diffused inland from the coast and northwards from the Columbia River. Alfred Crosby, in his study of the biological and cultural consequences of what he terms the "Columbian Exchange," writes:

The American Indians developed their ways of life in a very nearly complete isolation. That isolation weakened their defenses against the major diseases of mankind. In the first place, the climate of Siberia, the land bridge, and Alaska screened out many diseases: the cold killed the germs and, more important, the cold and the rigor of the life in those latitudes eliminated all humans suffering from debilitating diseases. In the crudest sense, the life of the earliest Americans was a matter of the survival of the fittest. These first emigrants carried few diseases with them and found no humans in America, diseased or healthy. They lived, died and bred alone for generation after generation, developing unique cultures and working out tolerances for a limited, Native American selection of pathological micro-life. When the isolation of the New World was broken, when Columbus brought the two halves of this planet together, the American Indian met for the first time his most hideous enemy: not the white man but the invisible killers which those men brought in their blood and breath.

Disease raged across the continent from the time of Columbus, devastating first South and then North America. In 1782-83, a smallpox epidemic was unleashed among the Indians of the northwest coast by contact with sailors on board vessels engaged in the maritime fur trade. Wayne Suttles (1987) records traditions in the strait area according to which whole villages were wiped out by white-borne disease before the first whites themselves arrived.

Death from disease caused profound social and political disruption of native societies by destroying the lives of key figures, creating holes in the social fabric, and generally demoralizing the Indians.

The mode of treatment employed by native people, the steam bath and cold plunge, merely increased the virulence of smallpox, and communal living habits hastened the spread of disease. Smallpox was not the only disease that cut deeply into the Indian population: epidemics of measles, influenza, tuberculosis and others took heavy tolls. In 1830, malaria broke out near Fort Vancouver in the lower Columbia Valley and in three years wiped out about three-quarters of the native population (Cook, 1955). George Gibbs (1855), writing in 1854 of the Chinook tribes of the lower Columbia River and the Makah tribe at Cape Flattery at the mouth of Juan de Fuca Strait, notes:

Trails now partially obliterated and overgrown connect different points on the Columbia, with the people of which the inhabitants kept up a trade...at present very few Indians remain here, the smallpox having nearly finished its work during the past year. In the winter and spring it spread with great virulence along the coast as far north as Cape Flattery. During the last year the smallpox found its way to the [Makah] region, and, it is reported, reduced them to one hundred and fifty, their famous chief, Flattery Jack, being among the number who died.

Dr. J.G. Cooper (1859), writing about the Willapa Bay region in southwestern Washington in 1853 quotes the following entry from his journal:

On the 18th of July ... I went with a party to explore a route through this valley to the sound. Very few of the Indians knew anything of the trail, as it had not been used for twenty years, or since the whole tribe of Willopahs inhabiting the valley were exterminated by smallpox.

This situation greatly aided white settlement of the Pacific Northwest, which otherwise may have met strong resistance.

ALCOHOL

The earliest visitors to the northwest coast found no intoxicating liquor, or any taste for it, among the natives, but initial dislike of strong liquor broke down as Russian, Spanish, French and English explorers and traders introduced it into native society. The first recorded sale of liquor by maritime traders was in 1792, when the French ship "La Flavie" arrived at Nootka Sound loaded with brandy:

The evidence shows that in the 1790s the Indians everywhere on the coast had acquired a taste for intoxicating liquor....By about 1800 the keen competition for sea otter skins had led to the general introduction of intoxicating liquor as an article of barter....The trading ships now carried an assorted cargo of European manufactures; they were a combination of liquor store and modern department store....On board every trading vessel as a part of her goods for barter were arms and ammunition, and casks - many casks - of New England and West Indian rum. We have now traced the stream of liquor amongst the natives of the Coast from its source in the friendly glass of wine given by the explorer simply for good fellowship, or by the maritime trader to ingratiate himself and enable him more easily to do business with the Indian; we have seen the Indians' original antipathy and disgust change rapidly to fondness for and intense desire for intoxicants; and we have seen the casual friendly glass replaced by thousands of gallons of liquor sent out as the best trade medium (Howay, 1942).

The Hudson's Bay Company, with permanent trading posts and a long-term perspective, strictly limited the flow of alcohol, but whiskey dealers thrived after American settlement. At the time of the post-treaty annuity distributions, agents called in troops to check the whiskey peddlers who "waited like crows or ravens on the perimeters of potlatch grounds to snatch government Indian issues in exchange for a few bottles of whiskey" (Ruby and Brown, 1981).

Special Agent J. Ross Browne observed the practice of the whiskey trader a few miles from the Squaxin Reservation (about ten miles from Olympia on Klackemin Island at the entrance to Budd's Inlet). Whenever he got a new supply of spirits, he would descend to the beach and blow a horn, "at which signal they paddle off in their canoes and enjoy a general debauch, which only ends when the whiskey gives out. In this way, their blankets, clothes and earnings are sacrificed, and they return, naked, sick and dispirited" (Dillon, 1965)

Puget Sound District Indian Agent R.C. Fay, in charge of the Penn Cove Indian Agency on Whidbey Island, wrote in 1858:

...the Indians have had liquor from some quarter at times, but from where it is impossible definitely to ascertain; they invariably say, however, that they get it through their friends who visit them from Port Townsend. They all say they would prefer not having it, as they cannot desist from using it when they have it, hence the consequences. There have been instances since my last annual report where difficulties have occurred in which eighteen lives have been taken that I know of, and, upon an investigation as to the causes of these difficulties, have found them wholly attributable to the use of liquor (Fay, 1858).

I
The
Fur Trading
Years

HUDSON'S BAY COMPANY

Commentary

Chartered in 1670, The Hudson's Bay Company was the first dominant presence in Oregon country, that vast region which included all of present-day Oregon, Washington and Idaho, plus substantial portions of Wyoming, Montana and British Columbia. The company was of such historical lineage that the American fur trappers used to joke that the initials HBC stood for "here before Christ."

In 1825, the company established Fort Vancouver on the north shore of the lower Columbia River. Following is a description of that early outpost by Carlos Schwantes (1989):

Fort Vancouver constituted a small, almost self sufficient European community that included a hospital; thirty to fifty small houses where employees (engages) lived with their Indian wives; storehouses for furs, trading goods, and grains; and workshops where blacksmithing, carpentry, barrel making, and other activities were carried on. A small sawmill provided lumber for repairs and the construction of buildings and equipment. The company also operated a shipyard, gristmill, dairy, orchard, and farms of several hundred acres where employees planted crops and raised herds of cattle and other domestic animals. Ships from distant ports called at Fort Vancouver bringing news, books and periodicals to stock the post's library.

An unusually cosmopolitan population collected around Fort Vancouver: Delaware and Iroquois Indians from the East, local Chinooks, Hawaiians, mixed-blood Métis from the prairies, French Canadians, Scotsmen, and presiding over them all was the imperious John McLoughlin, harsh, brooding and given to occasional temperamental outbursts. More than profit and loss were involved in a Hudson's Bay post: each enclave was a visible link in a truly imperial system joining London with the vast hinterland of the Pacific Northwest.

Unlike the missionaries and settlers to come, the Hudson's Bay Company left the Indians to their own devices. They did not care to change their traditional patterns and were interested in only trading with them. Of course this in itself began to alter aboriginal patterns: it changed their relations towards animals, giving them a new mercantile value, which ultimately devastated beaver and sea otter populations, nearly driving the latter to extinction. It also changed aboriginal demographic patterns and trade routes and introduced into the native economy new items such as the famous Hudson's Bay blanket, goods which would ultimately replace native artifacts. And the Hudson's Bay Company introduced the musket.

Although the "Honorable Company" maintained a laissez faire policy toward the natives, it also extended protection to the lives and property of its clientele, whether Indian or white. This brings us to our first reading: "Earliest Expedition Against Puget Sound Indians: Notes Connected with the Clallam Expedition."

Frank Ermatinger, a clerk at Fort Vancouver in 1828, recorded this narrative of a punitive expedition against the Klallams ostensibly to avenge the murder of some Company men by the Klallams. I have appended a commentary by Dr. John McLoughlin, Chief Factor with the Hudson's Bay Company at Fort Vancouver.

Eva Emery Dye wrote the following introduction to the original January 1907 publication of Ermatinger's account in the Washington Historical Quarterly:

These "Notes connected with the Clallum Expedition" by Frank Ermatinger, a well known clerk of the Hudson's Bay Company, were copied from the original document for me by Mr. R.E. Gosnell, private secretary of the Premier of British Columbia, and more recently editor of the Victoria Colonist. For more than three quarters of a century this earliest record of Puget Sound lay unnoticed and unread, until at my repeated and urgent request Mr. Gosnell obtained a loan of this and other matters connected with old Hudson's Bay days, and kindly sent me this transcript, the only copy, I believe, in the United States.

EARLIEST EXPEDITION AGAINST PUGET SOUND INDIANS

Frank Ermatinger

Notes connected with the Klallam Expedition fitted out under the
command of Alex. R. McLeod, Esquire, Chief Trader at
Fort Vancouver on the 17th of June, 1828.

FRIDAY 13TH, 1828: Since the unfortunate murder of Mr. Alex McKenzie and the four men under his charge, by the tribe called the Klallams, in Puget Sound, on their way back with an express from Port Langley, in January last, it appears to have been a decided impression of all that an expedition to their quarter would be most necessary, if not as a punishment to the tribe in question, at least as an example, in order, if possible, to deter others from similar attempts in future...this morning affairs appeared more determined and a muster was made of all the effective men upon the ground, both free and hired and they were told by Chief Factor McLoughlin, of the necessity of going off in search of the murderous tribe, and if possible, to make a salutary example of them, that the honour of the whites was at a stake, and that if we did not succeed in the undertaking it would be dangerous to be seen by the natives any distance from the Fort hereafter....

MONDAY, 16TH: The most of the day Messrs. McLeod and Dease equipping the men with their arms and a little ammunition, each, to try them with. The party will, independent of the vessel which extra manned for the occasion, consist of upwards of sixty men, headed by Mr. A.R. McLeod and Mr. Dease....

TUESDAY, 17TH: At 4 o'clock all Mr. McLeod's arrangements were completed and the Vancouver Local Militia put in motion....

WEDNESDAY, 18TH: We were upon the water this morning at half past three, were more than two hours ashore for breakfast, reached the mouth of the Cowlitz River at noon and encamped for the night....

THURSDAY, 19TH: We commenced our march at half past four and continued on at a brisk rate until the usual hour for breakfast, when we put ashore and remained two hours. We then resumed and reached the Cowlitz Portage at half past two. We here saw a solitary native, from whom, I believe, for I cannot speak positively (as we are seldom advised with, altho' I was requested by Mr. McLeod to keep notes of the Voyage I am never told what is going on, but collect what little information I possess how and when I can), that a few horses can be hired a small distance from this, that the Klallams have divided, those who wish to stand neutral having separated from those who wish to resist, and that we may possibly find and punish them with much less trouble or danger than was at one time anticipated. FRIDAY, 20TH: At eight o'clock this morning the interpreter Laframboise was sent off to Indian Lodges to hire what horses we could collect, and Mr.

Dease, without orders accompanied him. At ten they returned with a few Natives, who had four, and after some trouble and bargaining they were hired for the Trip, and in course of the day some more were added to the number, which with two here belonging to the company made fourteen that we have to commence the march with. Two and a half skins, I am told, is the stipulated price for the voyage to and fro, and some altercation proceeded from a wish to obtain five skins for each horse, which the natives say was the price they had from Mr. McMillan for the trip merely across, and again they wished to obtain Blankets or ammunition in payment. However, Mr. McLeod would not give either and threatens if they were not contented with Stronds, etc. he would send back his provisions to the Fort and feed his men upon horseflesh whenever he found any....

Old Towlitz, alias Lord St. Vincent, was amongst our visitors today and is to be added to the party, as assistant Interpreter.

SATURDAY, 21ST: We this morning commenced operations by hauling up our Boats and putting them en cache. The first of the party then got under way at half past seven and stopped for breakfast at nine. The rest started as they got ready and continued to arrive at our resting place until half past eleven. We then began to make a few more saddles, as it appeared that only four new ones were got ready last night. We resumed our march in the same order again at half past one, and encamped for the night at six o'clock. Our march this day looked more like that of gypsies than a force collected for the purpose we are. A light shower or two about noon, but the weather upon the whole fine and fresh. We hired a few more horses today, of which there appears to be no want on our road....

SUNDAY, 22ND: Our horses were loaded and we off at half past four, and at eight we stopped for breakfast, but like our order of yesterday it was nine before the last of our men arrived....We resumed our route at twelve and encamped at five o'clock. This night a watch was commenced to consist of four men and a gentleman for four hours each watch, and in crying "All's Well," which they were required to do, at intervals....

MONDAY, 23RD: We were under way at half past five, were the usual time at breakfast, arrived at the end of the Portage at half past one. We found here a canoe of the Company's left by Mr. Hanson and hired two more from the natives. The men of their own accord immediately commenced making their paddles. The watch of the men altered from four to two hours but ours stands at four....

TUESDAY, 24TH: At seven o'clock this morning Laframboise and a party of men were sent off in two small Canoes, to trade or borrow some of the larger kind, and Le Etang, our guide, with another party went overland, on horseback, to meet them at an appointed place, where, after giving the horses in charge to an Indian, who is to keep them until our return, they are to assist in working the Canoes here. At a small distance from the Camp Le Etang killed a Deer, which he brought to us and immediately took his departure again. It was thought unnecessary that any gentleman should accompany either party, confidence being put in Laframboise for the purpose.

This afternoon two Indians arrived from Cheenook with a letter from the "Cadboro," Capt. Simpson, dated as late as the 20th, so that we have now a consolation for our lost time, for, had we got on as we ought our chance of seeing her in the Sound would have been small. All I fear is that this confounded note will be made an excuse for more tardy movements. One of the free Iroquois killed us another deer. I pass over further notice of our practice of firing and it may be considered a regular turnout every day, however, it may not be amiss to note that the most of the shooting is rather from pride than the want of practice, for it is the good marksmen only who do it, and when their own ammunitions runs short they assist the diffidents to get through theirs. 8oo shots at least, an average of ten per man, were fired today to the danger of those who found it necessary to go a few yards from the camp. Mr. Dease has the stores in charge, and intimated that the stock would not stand out, if we continue on at such a rate.

WEDNESDAY, 25TH: At five o'clock p.m. Laframboise and Le Etang returned in eight canoes, including the two they took off, but four men short, whom they left as it appeared to me in rather a curious manner with the natives, looking after another canoe. They had very little trouble in obtaining six, and could possibly, so the guide says, have got a few more. Would not a great deal of time have been saved by our all going where the canoes are instead of remaining inactive here? The distance is short. The news is that the Klallams expect us and have collected at their farthest village, that they have formed many plans to ward off our balls, wetting their blankets is the most approved amongst them, and the natives of this quarter wish to accompany us in order to revenge the death of four of their Tribe, whom they have killed....

THURSDAY, 26TH: This morning the four men left behind yesterday, after some misery, returned to the Camp with a good large Canoe, and Laframboise with eight men, was sent off again. At five o'clock he returned with four more canoes. Heavy rains throughout the day.

For want of other amusement, during the rain, Mr. Work's

Chart of Puget Sound was produced and something like a plan, for the first time laid open, which was merely this: When we see the murderers, said Mr. McLeod, we must endeavor to come to a parley, and obtain the woman, who, by the by, I had scarcely ever heard mentioned before today, that was taken by them when our people were killed, and after we have her in our possession - What then? said I. Why then to them pell mell. Messrs. Yale,

Dease and I at once admitted it to be a most laudable wish to set the poor woman at liberty, which we thought could always be done at the price of a few Blankets and without so many men coming so far, but to make it the primitive object of our expedition, we never understood, nor could we, we added, ever agree to it. The business was then wound up with a short account of the influence her father had amongst his tribe to do mischief to the whites, upon whose account her liberty was at any consideration to be obtained by us.

FRIDAY, 27TH:....The canoes were in the course of the morning allotted, they are of a small kind for our purpose, but will, I trust, make a shift....At two o'clock P.M. we got under way in eleven Canoes of different sizes, and proceeded on for three hours and a half, when we encamped. No Indians accompany us, except Lord St. Vincent...

SATURDAY, 28TH: We got under way at five o'clock, but before breakfast we were merely running about for canoes, that we hired, and left two of our mall ones. At 10 we embark again. Mr. Yale and I together, and with us a native to act as a Klallam interpreter. We continued on in fine, calm weather until six o'clock when we encamped. Just below where we stopped for the night, we saw a few of the Puy-ye-lips Tribe, but they were so much frightened, by the continued firing of our men firing at the Eagles that they paddled off, and it was with great exertion that our canoe could approach them and come to a parley. Our guide told Mr. Yale and I, as a great secret, that the information obtained, was, that the Klallams had

withstood some liberal offers for the woman in order to restore her and that they wish to compromise the murder of our men.

SUNDAY, 29TH: We were upon the water at five this morning, stopped three hours to breakfast, and encamped opposite, or rather between, two small villages of the Soquarmis. Several small canoes of these fellows came to our encampment, but did not debark, and one of them having a Powder Horn upon him, belonging to one of our deceased men, little ceremony was used by Laframboise in dispossessing him of it. We received little or no information, but they offer themselves to us as auxiliaries, and were told, I believe, that we fought our own battles. However, the chief received a present and was told that he might embark with us, alone. They had heard the Vessel's Guns. Just before we encamped the Interpreter went off to one of the villages, and some of the men following in order, I suppose, to trade themselves a few shellfish....

MONDAY, 30TH: We left our encampment at four o'clock this morning, crossed to the Village, when we exchange two of our small Canoes for a larger one, the chief then embarked and four canoes of his tribe followed us, at a small distance. We took breakfast at the usual time, but were much shorter about it. At one o'clock we saw two small canoes of the same Tribe, and the one Mr. Yale and I were in gave them Chase. They debarked upon a point and hid themselves amongst the Woods, but upon the old Indian who was with us calling to them, they made their appearance. We learnt from them, that a few Klallams are at a small distance upon a portage over which we have to cross. We at once, upon the advice of our Indian Interpreters, &c., put ashore and were to remain all very quiet in order, if possible, to take them by surprise during the night. The Iroquois, Owhyees, and Cheenook slaves painted themselves ready for battle. But all the ceremony must be rendered a burlesque by our men, at least, one or two of them discharging their pieces and behold, we to mend the matter, send off rockets!!! Really one would think it was purposely done to warn the natives.

We heard the Vessel's guns just about Dark.

JULY, TUESDAY 1ST: At one o'clock this morning we embarked, and took with us one of the natives we saw yesterday noon, for what purpose we did not know.   He was in our canoe with the Klallam interpreter.   Our crew consisted of one young Canadian (Canada dit Encan) one half breed (Canotte), two Iroquois (Little Michel and Louis Frize), two Owhyees

(Tourawhyheene and Cawinai) and two Cheenook slaves (Antoine and Nastee). Mr. Yale and I passengers.   With Mr. Mcleod was Laframboise and with Dease, Old Towlitz, so that from the Interpreters being thus separated, it was necessary when the most trifling question was to be asked by Laframboise, that we should get near to each other, and even then speak louder than could be wished.   We continued on slowly with the greatest caution of more than two hours; occasionally, however, stopping for consultations amongst the interpreters, (which were kept entirely secret from us, nor repeated to Mr. McLeod, in French while we were near, lest I presume, we should understand) as we thought, to a portage, but all at once we found our canoe alone, and the Indians changed their places to immediately behind Mr. Yale and I, and appeared to solicit us to advance by signs, occasionally holding up seven of their fingers and uttering the word Klallams.   I thought they wished to debark and told Michel the foreman so, who no sooner put the canoe ashore than out they got, and with them Yale and five of the crew, and were instantly making along the shore.   When I saw this, I also left the canoe and ordered the Canadian to remain with it, while with the other two I ran after the rest.   We overtook them just as they were in sight of two Indian Lodges, (there might be more at a distance) situated close to the woods, to one of which the Indians without pointed and said Klallams.   It was the furthest off and far the smallest of the two.   Mr. Yale and I got upon a large fallen tree, close alongside of it, behind which I proposed we should get and fire, if we found ourselves outnumbered or worsted.   The Indians were evidently asleep when we arrived, the day was just breaking, but upon hearing the noise we made, awoke, and a man put his head out of the Lodge, and upon seeing us (however he could not, I think, distinctly distinguish who we were) hove a most piteous sigh.   Tirer Dessus was called out and four or five shots were immediately off.   I saw two men, I thought, fall, but whether dead I could not say.   The rest took the edge of the woods, but some of our men were there before them and the firing became general.   Eight or ten shots were discharged in rapid succession.   I remained stationary and saw Mr. Dease, Laframboise, Le Etang and a few of the men had joined the party from the canoes behind.   The confusion was great and we were apprehensive that the men would kill each other by shooting in opposite directions.   From the natives, there was now no danger, as those in the other Lodges remained quiet. In vain did we call out to the men to spare the women; take care of yourselves. They continued on in the same order until they thought the whole of the inmates were killed. In fact, one half could not understand us when we did call. Two families, I believe, were killed, three men, two or three women, a boy and a girl. To this point I cannot speak positively, as I saw none after they were down, but have the information from those who killed them, however, it was made a doubt whether the men were dead or not, as they were not seen after, but I am almost positive that I

was not mistaken almost positive that I was not mistaken in the two I saw drop. The truth is we did not lose time to look after them, but went off to the other Lodge, and remained there few minutes, for Mr. McLeod, who surrounded by the remains of the party, joined us.

Well, really, Gentlemen, said he, what is the meaning of all this confusion? Why, Sir, answered I, with some warmth, for I was piqued such equivocating conduct, it proceeds from you not letting us know, that we were so near the Klallams; we were led to understand that they were upon a portage, and here we find our canoe alone and amongst them before we are aware of it. If, added I, Mr. Mcleod, you will only let us know your plans, you have young men with you ready at any risk to execute them for you. My dear Sir, replied he, I do not doubt it, but how can I form plans? I know no more what is going on than yourselves!! Mr. Dease now observed that we ought to know the arrangements, as a few of the men appeared to be aware of them, and if, added he, if we get any information it is from them. This touched Mr. McLeod, and he told Dease that it was not the first time, he had heard this same remark from him, and that he should answer for it hereafter. Really Mr. McLeod, said I, this is not a time or before these men, for altercations amongst ourselves. If we have done wrong – I do not say you have done wrong, it is all well as it has happened, and after a few more casual observations preparations were made to continue en route.

We found a fine large canoe, said by the Indians to be the one in which the murderers followed Mr. McKenzie, able to contain 20 Men; it appeared too new; This we took and embarked, without once enquiring who was in the other Lodge. I saw a good many men there and it was well for them that a council did not sit to determine their fate, for I should have voted hard against the whole as I thought it more than probable that they were Klallams also, and betrayed the other Lodge to save themselves. We could at all events have been justified in using them as such. The head of one of the families killed is said to be the brother-in-law of the principle murderer and the spot of the Camp near where Mr. McKenzie was killed.

Having given a brief account of what I was myself witness to, I shall now note a few observations which passed at the Canoes. Mr. McLeod, I am told, reached our canoe just as the first shots were fired. There, said he, is four shots, the four Indians are dead, and one or two of the men were occasionally running off to the Lodge, but were called back, however, some

would not return, observing that they did not come to look on. But when the last shots were heard, then cried Mr. McLeod is treachery. One of the men told him that if he thought so they had better go to our assistance. Oh! no, was the answer, surely eight men were enough for so few Indians. In the meantime he heard all was over and left the canoes. When along the road to us he observed, here I who ought to have been the first find myself the last. We got to the portage just after sunrise. The Klallams we expected to find, were off, but their fires still alight. We passed on until we got off Cape Townshend, where we put ashore for Breakfast and saw the Cadboro'. All the Indians except Interpreters left us. Messrs. McLeod and Yale went on board, and we proceeded on for a mile, to a better spot for our camp. The Gentlemen returned at 4 o'clock. Mr. McLeod in much better spirits from the arrangements of Capt. Simpson, who he told us had nearly succeeded in getting the woman, at least he has Hostages on board for her, said he. In the evening I was sent to tell the Captain that the land Party would be ready to get under way with him tomorrow morning. The men were sent back, who accompanied me, to the camp, but I avail myself of an invitation to remain on board for the night.

WEDNESDAY, 2ND: This morning the captain was prepared but lost part of the Tide waiting for the men from shore, when they joined, the Vessel got under way and the canoes were towed for a few miles. Anchored off Protection Island and opposite a bay, where we saw a village of Klallams. The men encamped upon the island and were watered from the vessel.

Two women came to us from a Village, but what their object was I could not learn.

I remained on board until next night and before going ashore I told the Captain that I would propose an attack upon the village off us, to which he said he could soon run us close in, but upon mentioning it to Mr. Mcleod, he merely observed, without consideration, that Captain Simpson was aware his object was to proceed on.

Mr. Yale very ill.

THURSDAY, 3RD: We again kept close to the vessel and followed with the Tide until we came to New Dungeness, where we cast anchor, as near to a large Village of Klallams as the Vessel could be towed. Mr. Dease was sent with the men having water from the vessel, to a sand bank some

distance off, to cook and ordered to return at night. A chief came off to us and received every attention, in order that he might, I suppose, return again. He promised to use his influence in restoring the woman and to visit us tomorrow. In the evening before Mr. Dease had returned, a large body of Indians collected, armed, singing and yelping before us. The Captain put the Vessel in a posture of attack, and being apprehensive of the safety of our men ashore, he would immediately have commenced upon some large Canoes that were making off in their direction, two cannons were leveled and every preparation made, without a dissenting voice, but the seamen had no sooner got the lighted match over the touchhole ready, than Mr. McLeod run to the Captain and said, here a fellow of yours Captain wishes to send the whole to Hell, not at all, Sir, he will do nothing without orders, then turning to the man who had the match called out to him to lay it down. Here was a fine chance lost. The Indians went off in triumph and Mr. Dease after seeing the men well surfeited with pea soup at the expense of the Captain's water returned and we all slept on board. Much talk, to procure the woman, but not a word of the ostensible cause of our Trip. This Helen of ours, said I, will cause another siege as long as that of Troy.

FRIDAY, 4TH: Everything remained in much the unsettled state as yesterday and bore evident marks of indecision. This led to an altercation between our commander and the Captain. The latter having alluded upon deck, to something that Mr. McLeod had previously told him with respect to his plans, I did not myself hear correctly what it was, the former denied it, but the Captain was positive and said he could appeal to any gentleman present, whether it was not so, all were silent as the appeal was not directly made, and Mr. McLeod still persisting that he had not said any such thing, ultimately irritated the Captain, who with some warmth repeated you did, Sir, upon my honour, you did and my honour I hold sacred, and then left the deck. Mr. Dease and I were ordered to escort the men to the same bank again, to cook their peas, but returned immediately they had done. They made application to go to the main shore, observing the natives would think they were afraid, however, were not allowed.

The little chief was off again, and a Sinahomis chief called the Frenchman, with a few of his followers also visited us, the bringing of the woman still evaded. Much was said about her, to which I paid no attention. Mr. Dease intimated to me that in a conversation he had with Mr. McLeod today, the latter had said he would presently drive him mad, and told Mr. Dease to beg

of me, for God's sake to let him alone. This quite surprised me, as I am not conscious of a single observation having fallen from me that ought to have given the slightest offence [sic]. I have certainly said that I wished the business was brought to a point, as by our measures we were giving the

Indians too much time to collect if they wished to resist, or to go off if they do not, and upon one occasion I remarked that it was too far to come to see the Cadboro' fire a gun. At another time I told Mr. McLeod that Mr. Connolly would be anxious to be off for the interior. Let him go was the reply, how the deuce can he go, Sir, said I, and his men here. Well then let him stop. If these casual remarks have tended to distract Mr. McLeod I am sorry that I make them, but it was with no view to do so. Mr. Dease went further, for he proposed to him, so he told Mr. Yale and I to take the command and go ashore with the men, if Mr. McLeod felt any reluctance to go himself.

This morning the little chief and another Indian of considerable importance in the village, the former primly dressed in a tinsel laced cloth coat, came off in a small canoe by themselves to the Vessel and were as usual kindly received, but after strutting the deck for some time the Frenchman's canoe was seen coming alongside, when from some cause or other they took an abrupt departure. Mr. McLeod called out to them *arreter, arreter, le donc,* and all was in an uproar, but the Indians seeing the bustle only made the more haste to get away. He then called to the men *Tirer dessus* and guns were immediately presented *arreter* they were lowered. *Tirer donc* and six or seven shots are immediately off, one after the other. The report of the guns brought the Captain upon deck, who had only a few minutes before left it, and asked who had given orders to fire. It was I, said Mr. McLeod. Well,

Sir, you had no right so to do on board this Vessel, I am commander here. Why did they not stop when I called to them, was the reply. Sir, said the Captain, with some warmth, they were under the protection of the ships, and if you had told me that you wished to detain them I would have made the smallest boy I have do it. In the meantime a canoe of the Iroquois were off to the bodies, the Little Chief they found dead, and he was stripped of his clothes and scalped in an instant, and the latter, was placed upon a pole. They were then about to commence upon the other, who we perceived was not dead, and at the request of the Captain, they were ordered to desist. He was brought on board, and it was found that the ball had only slightly grazed his skull. The wound was dressed, he received a Blanket, and a guard was

placed over him. As the business has begun it is necessary now, said the Captain, to make the most of it, to which purpose the ship was a second time prepared and without further ceremony a cannonading commenced upon the Village, which appeared instantly deserted. There, said the Captain, now is your time, Mr. McLeod, to land and destroy it. *Embarque* was called out in all quarters and the canoes were immediately manned. Mr. Yale (still

seriously ill) and I were just getting down the side of the Vessel, when Mr. McLeod put his head over the gunwales and faltered *Oh nos gens ce ne vaut pas la peine*, and we ascended again. Well, then, said the Captain, all we have done is useless. We ought now to destroy the Village, and after some few words, that I did not distinctly hear Mr. McLeod said, well, Sir, since you insist upon it – No, No, Mr. McLeod, I do not, called out the Captain. However, we embarked and went ashore. When just landing a few hundred yards above the village three cannons were fired upon it and we destroyed the whole. There were about thirty good canoes of which we took four for our return and the rest were broke or Burnt. A large quantity of provisions, train oil, etc., etc., which after the men had helped themselves to what they chosed [sic] was with the buildings also set fire to. A musket, Mr. McKenzie's bedcloth, together with a few trifling articles belonging to his Party were found. Upon the whole the damage done to their property is great, and will, I trust, be seriously felt for some time to come, but I could wish we had been allowed to do more to the rascals themselves. In their hurry to decamp when the vessel's guns were fired, they left two small children whom we have on board, until some arrangements can be made. On our return to the Vessel we saw a body of natives a little distance from us, but when it was proposed that we should go and make them retreat Mr. McLeod said the men must have time and no further notice was taken of them during the day, yet they remained stationary, and in the evening a few of them came opposite us and fired two or three shots.

Our commander is evidently pleased with the day's success, and is in the highest spirits. However, little credit is due us for the destruction of the property.

SUNDAY, 6TH: We remained on board, inactive, and the natives showed themselves upon the point. A negotiation was commenced. The Frenchman acting for us, to exchange the man taken yesterday for the woman so much has been said about. The two children were put on shore this morning, and we saw a native come and carry them off....

MONDAY, 7TH: This day our heroine was brought on board, and the prisoner set at liberty. The news from the natives that the friends of the seven they make out to have killed upon the first instant had to revenge the cause of their deaths, killed two of the principal murderers of Mr. McKenzie, &c., and that the shot from the Vessel killed eight, that one native is missing, which will, according to their computation, make twenty-five. This, I believe, to be a made-up story amongst themselves, however, as so little has

been actually done, it is as well that the report should get to Cheenook and be made the most of.

TUESDAY, 8TH: Early this morning the Vessel, in consequence of Mr. McLeod's arranging of last night, got under way, and seen [sic] us back to the place. About noon we took an abrupt departure, without having come to any settlement with the natives, either for war or peace, or ever having, to my knowledge, once mentioning to them the object of our coming through the Sound, at least the murder of Mr. McKenzie and his men was never enquired into, nor their names once mentioned. However, we commenced our march, leaving the Captain to shift for himself. At the village where the natives were said to have followed them from we debarked and burnt it. But I here note my candid opinion that, if a single individual had been seen about, even this would not have been done. A promise was made to pass at the Frenchman's Camp, who had not yet been settled with for the interest he took in our Cartel, yet this was not observed. The watch altered from four to ten men, this time as before.

TUESDAY, 15TH: We reached the Fort this morning, without having met with anything worth observation on our return.

LETTERS FROM FORT VANCOUVER

Dr. John McLoughlin

The following profile of this larger-than-life figure (probably the most important man in the Oregon country during the first half of the 19th century) is excerpted from Carlos Schwantes' *The Pacific Northwest: An Interpretive History* (1989):

> *A man of dominant and vivid personality... McLoughlin (pronounced McLocklin) left a lasting imprint on Pacific Northwest history. He was born in Quebec in 1784 and at the age of 14 was apprenticed to a physician. After four years he earned a license to practice medicine and surgery. Young Dr. McLoughlin entered the service of the North West Company, first as an assistant to the regular physician and later as a trader east of the Rockies.*
>
> *Little is known of McLoughlin's persona/life: he was of mixed Irish, Scottish, and French-Canadian ancestry and became a Roman Catholic late in life. He married the half-Swiss, half-Indian widow of a fur trader who bore him four children in addition to the four she brought to the marriage from her first husband. McLoughlin was a man of striking appearance, standing six feet, four inches tall, raw-boned, well proportioned, and strong. His eyes were piercing; a flowing mane of prematurely white hair hung down over his massive shoulders. Local Indians called him the White Headed Eagle. McLoughlin ruled the sprawling Columbia Department from 1824 until 1846. Given the tenuous nature of British and American authority in that region, this single Hudson's Bay Company official wielded extraordinary power. (J.G.)*

Fort Vancouver 10th July 1828

To The Governor, Deputy Governor & Committee
Honble. Hudsons Bay Compy.
Honble. Sirs,

...5. I presume long before your Honors receive this you have been informed of the murder of Mr. Alexr. McKenzie & four of the Companys Engages by the Natives of Hoods Canal; from every information I have been able to collect, they committed this crime without having had the least difference with our people & murdered them merely for the sake of their apparel &

Arms & the murderers had Dances among themselves to celebrate the deed, & sent us word to come & revenge it, that they were ready. To pass over such an outrage would lower us in the opinion of the Indians, induce them to act in the same way, and when an opportunity offered kill any of our people, & when it is considered the Natives are at least an hundred Men to one of us it will be conceived how absolutely necessary it is for our personal security that we should be respected by them, & nothing could make us more contemptible in their eyes than allowing such a cold blooded assasination [sic] of our people to pass unpunished, & every one acquainted with the character of the Indians of the North West Coast will allow they can only be restrained from Committing acts of atrocity & violence by the dread of retaliation.

6. To punish those Murderers two modes could be adopted, either to employ Indians or act ourselves.

7. All the Indian Tribes on the Columbia from the Dalls to the Sea, offered us their Services, but accepting their offer would be kindling war among them, cause a great deal of innocent Blood to be shed, give them a claim on us & lower us in their opinion, as they would consider by our employing them that we were unable without their assistance to protect ourselves, for these reasons we declined accepting their offer.

8. In acting by ourselves, the best plan we could follow would have been to embark our people on Board the "Eagle" (the "Cadboro" is too small for such a purpose) and go in her to the Village of the Murderers. A Vessel of the size of the "Eagle" would have a very imposing appearance in the eyes of the Natives, & add much in their estimation to our respectability & prevent Indians from accompanying us.

9. For these reasons I proposed to Capt. Graves to embark our people on board the "Eagle" & take them to Hoods Canal, at the same time observed I did not wish him to assume more responsibility than his instructions warranted. He answered he could not of himself agree to my proposal as his Instructions were only to come to the Columbia & added if I would take the responsibility he was willing to go, but as his Instructions are to come to the Columbia & Return direct to England-going to Hoods Canal would be such a deviation as I was afraid would vitiate the Insurance - I could not therefore assume so great a responsibility.

10. It only remained for us to send the party by land and let the "Cadboro" wait them in Admiralty Inlet.

11. On the 17th June Mr. Chief Trader Alexr. Rodk. McLeod accompanied by Messrs. Ermatinger, Dears & Yale & fifty nine labourers started; it is supposed they will be twenty or twenty five days...

12. If Mr. McLeod has time he will pay a visit to Fort Langley merely on account of the impression such a party of our people will make on the minds of the Natives, as it is certain they had planned last Spring to surprise Fort Langley & were only deterred from making the attempt by seeing our people constantly on their Guard.

13. In case of our being at any future time in the same disagreeable situation we are this year, it would be of advantage to us to be at liberty to employ the Vessel coming here in visiting such places on the Coast as may have committed or attempted violence on our people - It is not that the Vessel (or even a land party) can do them any personal injury if they choose to run, but even making them run would have a good effect, as it would inspire a dread of doing us an injury - I am certain a Vessel of the size of the Eagle or William & Anne merely paying a visit to Fort Langley would tend very much to the security of that place. If ever it is molested by the Natives, it will be by those of the Gulf of Georgia, Vancouvers Island or Pugets Sound, & as they reside in Villages on the Shores of the Ocean the dread of the Vessel paying them a hostile visit & destroying their habitations would make them more peaceable in their conduct....

I am
Honble. Sirs
Your Obt. Humble Sert
.John McLoughlin

To the Govr. Deputy Govr. & Committee   [undated]
Honble. Hudsons Bay Co.

Honble. Sirs

In my Letter of the 10th June I informed your Honors of the departure of Mr. Chief Trader Alexr. Rodk. McLeod accompanied by four Clerks & fifty nine Servants & Freemen on an expedition to punish the murderers of the late Mr. McKenzie & Party & I have now the pleasure of informing you that on the 15th Ult. he returned after having accomplished the object of his voyage & recovered

the woman who was with our people when they were murdered (whom the murderers detained in slavery) & without one of our party receiving the least wound or injury. The Murderers hearingour people were on their way expected they would come by Hoods Canal & collected their forces at their village at Port Townsend, but our people went round by Pugets Sound as predetermined to join the Cadboro' at the entrance of Admiralty Inlet & on their route fell in with a Party of the tribe of the murderers of whom they killed eight: the account of this reaching the main body & the Cadboro' appearing at the same time made them retreat to another village of their countrymen at New Dungeness & putting themselves in as strong a position as they could waited to give our people battle, but our people afraid the woman the murderers detained as a Slave might be killed refrained attacking them & entered into a Parley to recover her, to which they agreed & promised she would be brought on the morrow. The morrow came but the woman was not brought & kept putting off our people during five days & during this time pressed Mr. McLeod to allow our Linguist & the Indians he had with him as Interpreters (none of our people speak the language of the murderers) to go on shore to hold a Council with them, of course none of our people could be trusted among such a band of murderers. On the fifth day a Chief of a neighbouring tribe paid our people a Visit & Mr. McLeod explained to him the line of conduct we intended to adopt towards the tribe of the murderers, that we did not wish to injure the innocent, but only to punish the murderers of our people, which if they would give up we would refrain doing any injury to the rest & that they must also give up the Woman. Well says the Chief I will go & tell them what you say & let you know their answer. During the absence of this Chief the messingers from the Murderers again paid a visit to our people urging that our Linguist & the ten Indians went on shore with them to hold a Council & then that the woman would be given up, but Mr. McLeod told them to wait for an answer till the Chief he had sent to their relations was returned: to this they reluctantly agreed & when they saw the Chief return they leaped in their Canoes and paddled off. Our people suspecting they had been guilty of some act of treachery towards us called on them to stop or else they would fire, on hearing this they stopt for a few seconds & then in spite of the calls of our people to stop, paddled off as fast as they could; being aware their flight must proceed from some designed treachery which they knew would now be discovered & seeing they could not come up with them our people fired, killed one & wounded the other.

On our Messinger (sic) coming on board he informed Mr. McLeod that these two Men had come to him with a view of inducing him to send some of our people to hold a Council with them in which they were to have been murdered.   Mr. McLeod finding no good to result from forbearance requested Lieut. Simpson to fire a few Cannon Shot on the Village & Mr.

McLeod & Party landed under cover of the Cannon, burnt the Village with all their property & forty six Canoes, the third day after this the Natives gave up the Woman & we gave up the wounded Indian.

Having already exceeded the time allotted & further delay being extremely injurious to our business on this side of the Mountains, our people gave over the pursuit of the murderers & on their return burnt the Village at Port Townsend, this Village was two hundred paces in length, the Houses as on the Coast made of boards & built contigious (sic) to each other.

. . . though the loss the murderers have suffered may appear great & ought to deter them & their countrymen from committing any acts of violence towards us, still I doubt if it is sufficient for that object, as though the report that twenty one of their people were killed by us, & two of the murderers by their relations of those killed, yet they are so devoid of feeling that this does not effect [sic] them so much as the burning of their Village & property & destruction of their Canoes.

I am
Honble. Sirs
Your Obt. Humble Sert.
John McLoughlin

A FIERCE LOYALTY

Commentary

Mystery Solved is an account by Mary Ann Lambert which purports to give the background to the "Cadboro incident" from the Klallam point of view.

Throughout this collection I introduce various writings by Mary Ann Lambert to provide the Klallam viewpoint in a historical record that otherwise represents an exclusively white perspective.

Born November 1878, the daughter of a Swedish merchant sailor and a Klallam Indian woman of distinguished ancestry, Mary Ann showed a fierce loyalty to her Indian heritage. She learned the Klallam language at the age of seven and spoke it throughout her life. She would declare to her own children in later years that people who looked down on others because of their race were stupid. "Would you rather be Indian or stupid?" she would ask them.

In view of how her work helps bridge the distance between the Indian and white cultures even today, it is all the more interesting to discover that her ancestry is linked to a shipwrecked white woman who married a Klallam chief.

Born in Port Townsend, she attended school there and in Kansas, then went to work as a matron at Indian schools in Washington and Arizona. She worked as a nurse in New York and Connecticut where she met and married Thomas Maher, a travelling actor, and had four children by him.

By 1916, she had left the east coast, and her husband, and returned with her children to their ancestral lands on the Olympic Peninsula. Present at a critical time and able to communicate with storytellers of the Klallam people in their own tongue, she was able to capture, translate, and put into writing some of the oral history and legends of their rapidly disappearing traditional culture. She worked at this task until her death in 1966, collecting some 65 legends and publishing two books.

The five stories reprinted in this collection are from *The Dungeness Massacre and Other Regional Tales*, and were written to present the Klallam version of the often tragic encounters between natives and whites.

MYSTERY SOLVED

Mary Ann Lambert

In the year 1827, so the story goes as repeated and handed down by word of mouth to Old Quyats, the historian, then to the narrator of this story, we find the following to have happened.

Four men, equipped with packs on their backs, arrived at the Indian village of *Nuf-kay'it* (Port Gamble), making known by sign and Chinook language their desire to be conveyed across the Strait of Juan de Fuca to Fort Langley on the British side.   The men came from the direction of Skokomish and wished to hire some able paddler to take the job of ferrying them across.

"I pay *chikamin pe nesika killapie*", (I'll pay you money when we return) said the man who seemed to be in charge of the party.   The chief, always ready to pick up a few bits, complied at once.

Since *Towie-asum* and his friend, *Na-moy'elth*, were the most dependable young men of the village, they were detailed by the chief to convey the Boston men across the water to the British side.   The Boston men were anxious to get started but the father of Towie-asum replied in Chinook, "*Wake kata nika tenas klatawa okoe sun.   Ikt pola-klie klatawa pe hyas klosh.*" (It's not wise for my son to make the trip at this time.   One night shall pass before it's good to go.)

"Just as you say, Chief", responded the leader.   Then he asked, "*Mika iskum muck-amuck nasika delate hyas olo; nysika muck- muck comux.*" (Do you have any grub?   We are so hungry we could eat a dog.)

The words were no more than spoken by the white man when a passing dog stopped to investigate the newcomers.

"There's one now. I'll bargain for him."   Turning to the chief, the white man spoke, "*Nisika tiky mokook ookuk komux-kunsih dolla mika ticky koopa yaka.*" (We would like to buy this dog. How much do you want for him?)

"*Sitkum dolla, Boston man, sitkum dolla*", (half a dollar) answered the chief with a faint smile, thinking the whole thing a huge joke.

"All right, fellows!" commanded the leader, and in no time the dog was caught, killed, dressed and hung on a nearby tree limb, apparently all prepared for cooking and eating.

The Indians stood around and watched the proceedings. Turning to the man who seemed to be in charge, the chief said, "*All-a-same mowitch.*" (Looks like venison.)

Just what the Boston's idea was could never be explained by the Indians since the next day when the white men departed, the carcass was left dangling from the limb, untouched.

Whether this was meant to intimidate the Indians or was just a crude joke was never ascertained. The Klallams of course never understand why the Boston men killed the dog just to let it hang uneaten on the tree.

Before dawn the next morning, preparations were begun for the journey to the other side of the Long Waters. A large touring canoe (*oo-okwst*) was used because it was a staunch craft capable of weathering any storm if such were encountered in crossing the strait.

All went well until the travelers reached Eennis (Port Angeles) the first camping place, where they were to spend the night, hoping to get an early start at dawn for the crossing before the wind arose.

Because Towie-asum and his companion were not always prompt in complying with demands from the Boston men - nor did the Indian youths always understand what was wanted of them - the white men handled the Indian boys roughly. They were frequently cuffed about and on one occasion Towie-asum was kicked in the stern, resulting in black and blue marks and injury to the lower spine. The Indian boys took this ill treatment without a word, which caused one of the men to object, or so it seemed to the Indian boys as they listened to a heated argument that ensued between the white men. In spite of their humiliation at the hands of the Bostons, the Indian boys did their duties as best they knew how, and completed the first lap of their journey safely late the next afternoon, arriving on the British side.

The white men proceeded on foot to their objective, leaving the Indian boys at camp until their return. A week later the Boston men returned to camp. They brought along with them an Indian woman as an additional passenger. Why she was with them the Indian boys did not know. However, they recognized the woman to be of the slave people - the Kioquot tribe - so had scruples against carrying an enemy slave in their canoe back to their homeland, but said nothing about it to the Bostons.

Eventually, the village of *Nuf-kay'it* (Port Gamble) was reached safely. It was natural, therefore, that Towie-asum's father, the chief, should ask for the chick-a-mon promised the two young men.

In answer to the chief's demand for payment the leader of the Bostons, who stood directing his companions about the arrangements of their packs preparatory to departure, looked at the chief and said, "*Helo mika potlatch chickamon kupo ookuk tanass man. Thasky halo kumtax ikta.*" (I don't intend to pay the young men. They are worthless. They know nothing.)

Then without further argument the Boston men threw their packs on their backs and started out in the same direction from which they had come,

taking the Kioquot woman along. The Indians stood a long while without speaking a word as though slapped in the face. Had the mystery men turned for a last look at the crowd they would have seen hatred and swift revenge pictured in the eyes of their victims.

Not until the white men disappeared into the distance did the Indian village become alert. Indignation and anger at the unreliability, deceit and insult of the white men ran high. A few hours after the departure of the mystery men, a council of war was assembled. The two boys, Towie-asum and his companion Na-moy-elth were called. Many questions were asked of them.

"How were you treated by the Bostons on the trip across the Long Waters and back?" asked the chief.

"We weren't treated very well, at times badly, because we didn't always understand what they wanted and expected of us; especially by the leader of the Bostons. They even pushed us around and kicked us," answered one of the young men.

Then a visiting chief spoke, "What has happened to these our kinsmen you can see with your own eyes. These wounds, bruises of the flesh, can be healed and cured; but a promise broken, humiliation and lies cannot be healed. What, therefore, is your word, my kinsmen?"

Then to his son, Towie-asum, the chief spoke, "My son, you have heard what has just been spoken. Have you anything to say?" "My father, already you have heard our story. I have nothing more to say."

Friends, "spoke the chief, "you have heard what has taken place. What is your word? Shall we let an offense like this pass? Are we women? What would the Bostons do if we had done this thing to them? Answer in all fairness, friends, yes, answer."

"The Bostons would pay back," spoke an old man. "They would not let an act like this pass."

"Yes, pay back, pay back!" responded several men standing within the council circle. "Let it be this way then."

"Aye, aye! That is true," spoke a bystander. "We too, will pay back. We too will punish. Yes, let it be this way!"

Soo-yanitch, the wise one, spoke like this: "My friends, kinsmen, be not too hasty. Let several nights pass over your heads before making this decision. Our grandfathers often told us, 'Anything done in anger and haste is not good for a people.' Therefore, my friends, consider this action well. Yes, tribesmen, consider, consider."

"Your words, O Soo-yanitch, are wise words, but words will not prevent another such disgrace as we have had thrust upon us by the Bostons", spoke Squil-aqualem. "I can no more than advise you. Therefore do as you see fit," answered the peacemaker, Soo-yanitch.

Then Squil-aqualem, the aggressive one, arose and spoke in a loud voice so that all might hear and understand. "We will follow the Boston men tonight. We will exterminate him."

This was all the heated crowd needed. The council broke up. Preparations began at once. By the time dark descended six canoes, each bearing six men, shoved from the shore of Port Gamble. Led by Squil-aqualem, the trouble-maker, they followed in the direction the white men had taken. Swiftly and cautiously the naked and blackened Klallams paddled along the east shore line of Hood Canal until they reached the first long spit, which gave them a view of the beaches to the next spit. Beyond this spit was a spring, at which place the Indians were reasonably sure the Bostons would camp that night.

After reaching the second spit the warriors beached their canoes to wait for the return of the scout who had gone around the spit to make observations. It wasn't long before he returned, reporting he had seen a dim fire burning near the spring. No one spoke. Strong hearts must be theirs until their mission was accomplished. Squil-aqualem gave the sign to proceed.

Then these savages - for such they had become for the time Being - rounded the spit, and beaching their canoes they crept along the edge of the dark woods until they were a short distance from the Bostons. They noticed one man reclining against a long log beside which was a fire. The others had bedded down for the night and apparently were sleeping. Squil-aqualem, who was in the lead, waved back. The Klallams fell flat, waiting until the more wakeful Boston finally adjusted himself for the night. The fire gradually died down. The Klallams crept closer. Squil-aqualem gave the sign to advance cautiously.

At that moment a flock of ducks, alarmed by what they heard or sensed in the dark, arose from the water and flew over the nose of the spit into the distance. The sound of rapidly flapping wings and the night-cry of the ducksstartled the man who was last to bed down. Suddenly he sat up right. Calling to the others in a low voice, he spoke alarmed. "Fellows, I believe those damned Siwashes are following us. Those ducks didn't fly away for no reason. Besides, I'm sure I heard a noise close by."

The man sleeping next to him said, "Bed down. You've got the jitters for no good reason. Those Klallams haven't the sense or the nerve to follow us. "

Assured by the remarks of his companion, the fellow lay down, and soon all were sleeping soundly.

The Klallams crept closer and closer to the sleeping Bostons. Now was the moment. Squil-aqualem gave the signal. The Klallams pounced upon the men, clubbing them to death except the slave woman and her man, who escaped to the edge of the dark woods. The couple were soon overtaken by the pursuing Squil-aqualem and the white man was clubbed to death. The woman was taken prisoner.

In the dark, Squil-aqualem, the trouble maker, searched the pockets of the dead men. He found and confiscated articles such as pocket knives, watches, and other odds and ends. Before returning to the waiting tribesmen, Squil-aqualem hid in his loin-string a packet of letters taken from a dead man's large vest pocket.

Soon the warriors - for such they called themselves - were on their way back to the village of Port Gamble, satisfied that the debt had been paid, not realizing that in six month's time a like disaster awaited them.

Elements of the above story - the Klallam version - always remained a mystery. Who were the white men the Klallams murdered on Hood Canal on what later became known as Dead Man's Spit? Why were they there?

An explanation was offered when "The Letters of John McLoughlin," was published with an account similar to the story related by the old Klallams.

Alexander McKenzie and his four servants were murdered by the Indians on Dead Man's Spit on Hood Canal in 1828. According to the book's account the Indians were motivated by robbery. A subsequent punitive expedition was ordered by Lieut. Simpson and led by Alexander McLeod.

From the letters of John McLoughlin:
"Alexander McKenzie and four servants of the Hudson Bay Company, on December 1827 left Fort Vancouver to carry dispatches to the newly established post at Fort Langley on the Frazier River, where they arrived on December 29.

"He left on his return voyage Jan. 3, 1828. He and his four companions were murdered by the Klallam Indians on Hood Canal in Washington.

"The Klallam Indians took possession of the slave woman who was with McKenzie and his men.

"A punitive expedition against the Indians was led by Chief Trader Alexander McLeod in the summer of 1828. He killed 27 Indians and burned their village with the artillery of the "Cadboro". The action was criticized and Alexander was not made chief factor as he wished.

"The Indian woman referred to was Princess of Wales, Alexander McKenzy's woman. The woman was recaptured by McLeod on the punitive party and returned to Vancouver, B.C."

The packet of letters confiscated by Squil-aqualem was kept in the Klallams' possession and handed down until about 1866 when Judge Swan, who was a friend to all Indians, was approached one day by a decrepit Klallam who handed him the letters, asking in Chinook, "Ikla okok pepa wa-wa?" (What does this paper or letter say?)

Judge Swan took the letters, and while still holding them asked the Indian, "*Kah mika iskum okok pepa?*" (Where did you get these letters?) The old Indian became suspicious. Without answering he grabbed the letters out of Judge Swan's hands and walked away. Judge Swan, surprised by the Indian's actions, stood and watched him walk away and disappear around Point Hudson. The contents of the letters never became known. Supposedly they were the Federal Government documents which never reached their destination.

II

Point No Point
Treaty

PIONEER EXISTENCE

Until 1846, Great Britain and the United States jointly occupied the territory known as the Oregon country. By the 1840s American settlement in the region led to the creation of a provisional American government. By the time Polk became president, an expansionist mood fueled by a widespread belief in American "Manifest Destiny," allowed him to declare in his inaugural address in 1845, that American title to Oregon was "clear and unquestionable."

By 1846, Britain and the United States agreed to divide the Oregon country along the 49th parallel from the crest of the Rocky Mountains to the Puget Sound region. There the line dipped south and west through the Strait of Juan de Fuca, leaving Vancouver Island in British territory.

By 1848, Congress created the Oregon Territory to include all those lands north of California, south of the 49th parallel and west from the continental divide to the Pacific.

In 1853, Washington Territory was carved from this huge area to include everything north of the Columbia and west from the continental divide to the Pacific Ocean. Isaac Stevens was appointed Governor and Superintendent of Indian Affairs for this new territory, and also was chosen to lead a survey party to explore a northern route for a transcontinental railroad from St. Paul to Puget Sound.

If any date could be said to separate the period of fur traders from that of settlers it would be 1858. That year marks the sudden growth of Victoria, British Columbia, the staging area for gold seekers bound for the Fraser River where gold was discovered the previous year; but the earliest settlers came to the Olympic Peninsula in the 1850s when it was still Oregon Territory.

The Donation Land Act of 1850 rearranged the political landscape of the Northwest and superimposed a racial and political geographic pattern that persists to the present. The measure established a system for white settlers to acquire land while excluding blacks and Hawaiians (who made up part of the early Northwestern work force), and appropriated land from the native American inhabitants before treaties were made to legalize this process.

According to this act, any white male citizen 18 years or older was entitled to 320 acres if single and, if married, his wife could hold an additional 320 acres in her own right. A person had only to reside on the land and cultivate it for four years.

In the first five years of the Donation Land Act's existence more than 7,000 claimants acquired in excess of 2.5 million acres. Furthermore, because claims were supposed to be square, the act superimposed a geographical pattern that shaped land ownerships until the present, creating arbitrary political boundaries that cut across natural and cultural areas that largely coincided under traditional native American occupation (Schwantes, 1989).

Port Townsend was named by Capt. George Vancouver "in honor of the noble Marquis of that name" (Meany, 1957) and in 1851, the names of the first 10 land claimants were registered in the surveyor general's office in Olympia, 100 miles by canoe (Gregory, 1966; Simpson & Hermanson, 1979).

The first claim in the official records for the Dungeness area is John Thornton's on June 14, 1852. Thornton first logged the heavily timbered land in that area, floating the logs down the Dungeness River and loading them at tideland for San Francisco.

In Thornton's time, about 1,000 Klallams lived on the flats in front of Dungeness. In 1853, the settlement of Dungeness was on Whiskey Flats at the mouth of the Dungeness River just west of the Klallam village on Cline's Spit. B.L Madison gave Whiskey Flats its name by selling contraband liquor to the Indians there. By 1862, there were only about 35 settlers in the area, one store, a saloon and a court house. Church and Sunday school services, marriages and christenings were conducted whenever a circuit riding minister journeyed by (Keeting, 1976).

In 1891, the Hon. Allen Weir delivered a paper before the Washington Pioneer Association describing the probably typical experience of his pioneering family in the Dungeness area.

The Weir family landed in Port Townsend, having made the trip from California in a steamer and from there went to Dungeness in a whaleboat, stopping to eat lunch at Protection Island. The family settled in a 12' x 26' log cabin close by the river, a mile from the waterfront and one-half mile from the nearest road. His description follows:

> The cabin had a split cedar door on wooden hinges and an old fashioned latch with a buckskin string hanging out, to be pulled by a person desiring to enter. It had a fireplace and chimney of clay and sticks built outside at one end. There was no window to the house. The roof of clapboards completed the picture. There was no clearing. So dense was the forest that we lived there all summer without knowing of the existence of a hill within 100 yards of the house. Father's old muzzle-loading rifle kept the table supplied with wild meat. When we had "jerked" elk meat, fresh venison, an occasional bear steak and potatoes or clams to match, we thought ourselves lucky... our family consisted of father, mother, John Weir and S.J. Weir and five children....The Indians were quite numerous in those days. Now and then a big potlatch would bring many more from British Columbia or other points....

> John Allen went to Victoria in 1861, and while away his squaw wife at Dungeness was killed. On his return, blaming the Indians for her death, Allen shot an Indian. The next day the Indians were arrayed in war paint on one side of the Dungeness River, and the white men of the settlement (a mere handful compared with the Indians) were gathered on the opposite bank prepared for the worst. Fortunately the affair was patched up without further bloodshed by John Allen paying the relatives of the dead Indian a sum of money....

> As an instance showing the usual mode of travel in those days, I may mention father's homestead filing, made in the summer of 1860. The land office of the district was in Olympia, over 100 miles distant by water. Father and three others went from Dungeness to Olympia and returned in a canoe. Four days were consumed, and it was considered an unusually quick trip....C.H. Mason, Secretary of the Territory, wrote from Olympia on the 25th of February to acknowledge prompt receipt of an official letter from Elisha Whittlesey, first Comptroller of the United States Treasury at Washington City, dated on the 18th of December preceding. Such was the then prevailing idea of rapid transit (Weir, 1900).

These early settlements of Washington Territory were surrounded by one of the densest populations of Indians in North America.

Besides the resident tribes of Puget Sound, the settlements were liable to incursions from the Haidas of Queen Charlotte Islands and even from the tribes of the coast as far north as Fort Simpson, these tribes being excellent seamen with large and strong war canoes in which they made long voyages to wreak havoc on both natives and settlers.

In November 1853, the new territorial Governor arrived in Olympia, a "clearing of tangled timber and tree stumps which contained a scattering of twenty or thirty rough-hewn cabins and an Indian village." In his welcoming speech he told the citizens of that frontier town "from your hands an imperial domain will descend to our children, and power accede to the country, and all too in the cause of humanity and freedom" (Richards, 1979). He promised that resolution of the "Indian question" (meaning extinguishing Indian land title) was foremost on his agenda, to be disposed of through the treaty-making process granted him by the Federal government.

Bloody clashes between Indians and whites occurred throughout the territory with increasing frequency. In his message to the opening legislature in Olympia on Dec. 4 Gov. Stevens pledged to arrange "on a permanent basis the future of the Indians in the territory."

The first vessel to come into the harbor of New Dungeness for a cargo was the "John Adams" in the spring of 1853. Jewell, the master, started with his steward to go to Port Townsend in a small boat when both were killed by the Klallams at Dungeness, which led to an early military encounter between Indians and whites.

No Indian agents as yet having been commissioned for Washington, Gov. Stevens appointed M. T. Simmons special agent for the Puget Sound district. "Simmons entered upon his duties by publishing a request to all good citizens to aid in the suppression of liquor-selling to Indians, by informing him of every such infraction of the law...by advising persons employing Indians to have a written contract witnessed by a white man; and by refraining from punishing suspected Indian criminals except upon certain proofs of their crimes" (Bancroft, 1890).

By Dec. 26, at Medicine Creek, Gov. Stevens concluded the first of the Puget Sound treaties with the Nisqually and Puyallup bands at the head of the Sound. Moving north he convened the Point Elliott Council Jan. 22 with the Duwamish, Snoqualmie, Skagit and Lummi tribes.   On Jan. 24 the commissioners made the short sail across the Sound and the next day began the Point No Point proceedings.

A few points need to be made about the treaty-making process: Chinook Jargon, a trade language consisting of a few hundred words useful for limited kinds of communication, was an inadequate language for treaty-making; Indians frequently did not understand the provisions of the treaty in the same way as the whites who negotiated it.   Owen Bush, who was present at the Medicine Creek negotiations with the Nisqually tribe, is quoted by Ezra Meeker (1905): "I could talk the Indian languages, but Stevens did not seem to want anyone to interpret in their own tongue, and had that done in Chinook. Of course, it was utterly impossible to explain the treaties to them in Chinook." Cultural differences (for example the very different concepts of ownership rights) compounded communication problems. The political structure, tribal divisions, and appointed "chiefs" were imposed on natives by a foreign government seeking to transfer title to Indian lands according to their legal customs.   Altogether, the Klallam people ceded away 438,430 acres at Point No Point.   Population pressure from settlers rendered the treaty out of date before it was ratified by the Senate four years later. Annuity goods for the Indians under their treaty of January 1855 were distributed for the first time in 1861.

This brings us to the readings on the Point No Point Treaty.   Here I have reprinted the actual text of the treaty, a document which resonates to the present with the Puget Sound salmon wars of the 1960s and the notorious Boldt decision based on key phrases in that treaty (see Art. IV, Treaty of Hahd-Skus, p.47).   This is followed by an eyewitness account of the treaty proceedings by the lawyer-ethnographer George Gibbs; some comments on the treaty proceedings by two anthropologists, and an excerpt from Kent Richards' biography of Stevens which provides an excellent historical background for considering the treaty. Following this is an excerpt from the biography of his father by Hazard Stevens, which generally attempts a justification of Stevens' treaty-making.   Finally, I have included another piece by Mary Ann Lambert, and a succinct but very telling conversation between See-hem-itza, widow of the Klallam chief Chet-ze-moka, and a government agent; both pieces convey something of the Klallam view of the Point No Point Treaty.

THE RECORDS OF THE STEVENS TREATY COMMISSION IN WESTERN WASHINGTON

Barbara Lane, Phd

On December 7, 1854, [Territorial Governor] Isaac I. Stevens organized a commission to make treaties with the Indians in Washington Territory...[The official record of that treaty commission] provides background information as to how the treaties were made, who made them, how the treaty councils were organized, and what was discussed at the treaty grounds. It also includes the original treaties. The part of the record included here covers the...Treaty of Point No Point.

The entire record reproduced here was written by George Gibbs, a lawyer who served as a member of the Stevens' treaty commission in western Washington. Gibbs had experience with previous treaty commissions in Oregon and California. He served on the Stevens' commission in several capacities: legal advisor, ethnographer, surveyor and secretary.

While the entire record reproduced here appears to have been written by Gibbs, he was not the Secretary of the Commission at the outset. There is less information in the earlier part of the record covering the period before Gibbs became secretary.

Originally, Stevens appointed James Doty as Secretary of the Commission and Doty signed the Treaty of Medicine Creek in that capacity. Immediately afterward, Doty was sent east of the mountains to prepare the Indians there for future negotiations.

On December 27, Gibbs was appointed acting secretary. When Stevens arrived at the Point Elliott treaty ground on January 21, 1855, he formally appointed Gibbs as Secretary of the Western Commission.

One important difference between Doty's work as Secretary and that of Gibbs is that Doty apparently made no record of the Indian discussions at the Treaty of Medicine Creek. The official report of Indian reaction and participation at that treaty is notable for its brevity

The official record of the proceedings at Medicine Creek disposes of Indian reaction in two sentences.

The Indians had some discussion, and Gov. Stevens then put the question. Are you ready, if so I will sign it? There were no objections, and the Treaty was then signed by Gov. I. I. Stevens and the Chiefs, Delegates & Head men on the part of the Indians and duly witnessed by the Secretary, Special Agent, and Seventeen Citizens present.

It is safe to assume that Indian views and reactions as well as Indian participation at the treaty councils are not fully recorded.

Nevertheless the record is important for what it tells about the speeches made by Stevens and what it tells about the movements and activities of other members of the Commission.

The record is interesting not only for what it contains, but also for what it does not contain. It does not contain a translation of any of the treaties or any clause of any of the treaties into Chinook Jargon.

Only one text in Chinook Jargon appears in the proceedings for any of the councils in western Washington. This is a speech given at the Point Elliott treaty ground by Michael T. Simmons, Indian Agent for the Puget Sound District.

The speech has little to do with the substance of the treaty. Simmons speaks of his concern for the welfare of the Indians and tells them that rum is their downfall. He advises them to trust the Great Father in the American country.

It is striking that Gibbs should have recorded the speech by Simmons in Chinook Jargon but has not recorded any translation of the treaty clauses into Chinook Jargon.

Besides Governor Stevens, Gibbs, and Simmons there was one other active member of the Commission. This man was Benjamin Franklin Shaw, who held the post of interpreter. Shaw is reported to have translated the treaties and the English speeches into Chinook Jargon at each of the treaty councils.

Shaw's Chinook Jargon was then translated by Indians who knew the jargon into the several Indian languages for the benefit of those people who did not understand the Jargon.

Gibbs wrote that the treaties were read to the Indians clause by clause and thoroughly explained to them. If that is so, it seems odd that no record was made of the way in which the treaty clauses were rendered in the jargon. As a lawyer, Gibbs might have been expected to provide such documentation.

The official record does not provide an opportunity to assess the adequacy of the Chinook Jargon translation by which the treaty was explained.

The record of the treaty council at Point No Point provides the first inkling in the official record that there was Indian resistance to selling the land or any attempt on the part of the Indians to negotiate the terms of the treaties.

One of the Skokomish speakers at the Point No Point council is quoted as saying:

I am not pleased with the idea of selling at all. I want you to hear what I have to say. All the Indians have been afraid to talk, but I wish to speak and be listened to. I don't want to leave my land. It makes me sick to leave it. I don't want to go from where I was born. I am afraid of becoming destitute.

In order to understand why the Indians at the Point No Point council may have been afraid to speak, it is relevant to know that one of the Klallam villages had been shelled by a ship shortly before as a punitive measure.

Much of the material in the record of the treaty proceedings is understandable by itself, but much requires additional information not contained within the record.

The record of the proceedings provides valuable clues as to what happened during the treaty-making process in western Washington. Equally important pieces of the picture have to be taken from other documents. The unofficial diaries, correspondence, and views of the men who participated in the Commission as well as other contemporary observers provide other views and perspectives.

TREATY OF HAHD-SKUS
or POINT NO POINT

George Gibbs

WEDNESDAY, JANUARY 24TH.   Reached "Point No Point," and the steamer (leaving the schooner at anchor and the men on shore to form camp) ran down to Port Gamble to bring up additional provisions and returned in the afternoon. The Indians began to arrive at the ground.

THURSDAY, JANUARY 25TH. The weather was very stormy, but the Indians having all assembled during the night, it was decided to go on with the Treaty. The Tribes consisted of the Clallams or Sklallums, Chemakums, and Sko-komish or Too-an-hooch, and on a careful enumeration they were found not essentially to vary in number from 1200.

The Indians having arranged themselves in a circle under their principal chiefs the Duke of York, or Chits-a-mah-han of the S'Klallums, Nah-whil-luk of the Skokomish and Kul-kah-han or Gen. Pierce of the Chemakums, Gov. Stevens addressed them as follows:

"My children. You call me your father, I too have a father, who is your great father. That Great Father has sent me here today to pay you for your lands, to provide for your children, to see that you are fed and that you are cared for. The Great Father wishes you to be happy, to be friends to each other. The Great Father wants you and the Whites to be friends, he wants you to have a home of your own, to have a school where your little children can learn. He wants you to learn to farm, to learn to use tools, and also to have a Doctor. Now, all these things shall be written down in a paper. That paper shall be read to you. If the paper is good you will sign it, and I will sign it. I will then send the paper to the Great Father. If the Great Father finds that paper good he will send me word, and I will let you know. If the Great Father does not find the paper good he will send it back to me, and say what alterations he wants in it. If you then agree to the changes, the paper is a bargain and will be carried out. The Great Father lives a great way off and some time will be required to hear from him. I want you to wait patiently till you hear from him. In the meantime the Great Father has sent to you some presents simply as a free gift. Some of these presents I will give you today; but I shall give you more in the course of the summer. Your agent Mr. Simmons will give you notice of these presents. But besides these presents, you will have to take care of you, your Agent Mr. Simmons. You will also have a man you know, Gov. Mason, to take care of you. This you will have all the time and when the paper comes from the Great Father then you will have your own houses and homes and your schools. Now what have you to say - if good give your assent - if not say so. (Cheers of approbation.) Now sit quiet a moment and the paper will be read."

The treaty was then read and interpreted to the Skokomish by Hool-hole-tan or Jim, the first sub-chief and to the S'Klallams and Chemakums by Yaht-le-min or Gen Taylor. The reading being concluded Gov. Stevens asked if they had anything to say.

Che-lan-teh-tat, an old Skokomish Indian then rose and said, "I wish to speak my mind as to selling the land. Great Chief! What shall we eat if we do so? I don't want to sign away all my land, take half of it, and let us keep the rest. I am afraid that I shall become destitute and perish for want of food. I don't like the place you have chosen for us to live on. I am not ready to sign the paper."

Shau-at-seha-uk, a To-an-hooch next spoke. "I do not want to leave the mouth of the River. I do not want to leave my old home, and my burying ground. I am afraid I shall die if I do."

Mr. F. Shaw, the Interpreter, explained to them that they were not called upon to give up their old modes of living and places of seeking food, but only to confine their houses to one spot.

Nah-whil-uk, the Skokomish head chief, an old man rose and said, "I do not want to sell my land because it is valuable. The Whites pay a great deal for a small piece and they get money by selling the sticks. Formerly the Indians slept but the whites came among them and woke them up and we now know that the lands are worth much."

It was explained that it was only by the labor laid out upon the land that it became valuable and that his country was poor at best.

Hool-hol-tan, or Jim. "I want to speak. I do not like the offers you make in the Treaty to us. You say you will give us land but why should you give us the mouth of the river? I don't like to go on a reserve with the Klallam and in case of trouble there are more of them than of us and they will charge us with it. Before the whites came among us we had no idea who made the land, but some time ago the Priests told us that the Great Chief Above made it, and also made the Indians. Since then the Americans have told us that the Great Father always bought the land and that it was not right to take it for nothing. They waked the Indians up by this, and they now know their land was worth much. I don't want to sign away my right to the land. If it was myself alone that I signed for I would do it, but we have women and children. Let us keep half of it and take the rest. Why should we sell all? We may become destitute. Why not let us live together with you."

Mr. Simmons, the Agent explained that if they kept half their Country, they would have to live on it and would not be allowed to go anywhere else they pleased. That when a small tract alone was left the privilege was given of going wherever else they pleased to fish and work for the whites. "If you can cultivate more land than this, you can have it."

Jim resumed "I am not pleased with the idea of selling at all. I want you to hear what I have to say. All the Indians here have been afraid to talk, but I wish to speak and be listened to. I don't want to go from where I was born. I am afraid of becoming destitute.

Chits-a-mah-han, or the Duke of York, (The Duke stutters somewhat and dictated to Soo-ich one of his Tribe.) "My heart is good (I am happy) since I have heard the paper read, and since I have understood Gov. Stevens, particularly since I have been told that I could look for food where I pleased and not in one place only. I will always be the same. My heart has lately become better. Formerly the Indians were bad towards each other, but Governor Stevens has made them agree to be friends, and I am willing he should act as he pleases. I think the more I know of him the better I shall be satisfied. Before the Whites came we were always poor. Since then we have earned money and got blankets and clothing. I hope the Governor will tell the Whites not to abuse the Indians as many are in the habit of doing, ordering them to go away and knocking them down. We are willing to go up the Canal since we know we can fish elsewhere. We shall only leave there to get salmon, and when done fishing will return to our houses. I am glad to acknowledge you and the Great Father as our Fathers." (Cheers.)

Governor Stevens. "What are you now? What were you formerly? Have you not already been driven from your burial grounds? The Great Father wants to put you where you cannot be driven away. The Great Father besides giving you a home will give you a school, protect you in taking fish, break up your land, give you clothes and seeds. Was this good or not? I want an answer."

Che-lan-teh-teel again spoke. "What I want to say is to thank you. I have changed my mind. What you have said is good. I see that you mean well towards us. I look upon you as our father."

Spote-keh a Klallam. "I have become satisfied since I have heard you. I know now that you are our father. I shall always be the same. I was once poor but am now better off and shall always look to you for aid."

Kahts-ass-mehtl, or Gov. Stevens, a subchief of the Klallams. "Why should my heart be bad. I will be the last to become bad. I feel that you should do as you think best. I am willing to submit. Such is my mind now and I don't think I shall change it." (Cheers.)

Governor Stevens then asked them what they wished to do about the signing of the paper.   The Skokomish Chief said they would rather wait till tomorrow.   They would talk it over and understand it thoroughly. Accordingly the Council was adjourned till the next morning.

FRIDAY, JANUARY 26TH.   The Indians came up bearing white flags. Governor Stevens proceeded to address them as follows.

"We meet here this morning, having a pleasant day, one sent by the Sokali Tyee to accomplish a great work. I trust that from today we shall be good friends, and you prosperous and happy. The Treaty was read to you last night, you have talked it over, we will now consider it. I think the paper is good and that the Great Father will think so. Are you not my children and also children of the Great Father? What will I not do for my children and what will you not for yours? Would you not die for them? This paper is such as a man would give to his children and I will tell you why. This paper gives you a home. Does not a father give his children a home? This paper gives you a school. Does not a father send his children to school. It gives you mechanics and a doctor to teach and cure you. Is not that fatherly? This paper secures your fish? Does not a father give food to his children?

Besides fish, you can hunt, gather roots and berries. Besides it says you shall not drink whiskey and does not a father prevent his children from drinking the fire water. Besides all this, the paper says you shall be paid for your lands as has been explained to you. In making this paper I knew the Great Father was good to his children, and did not wish to steal their lands. I think the Treaty is good, and your friend here whom you have long known thinks so. Ask him! Is it good and are you ready for me to sign, and for yourselves. I think so. It is for you to say what you think right. If you have anything to say, say it now. I have done."

Duke of York. Wanted to speak. "His heart was white, so were those of his people and he will never stain it with blood or blacken it. It is the same as the Governor's. He has talked all. He never talks much. Presents a white flag to Gov. Stevens who addressed him. His heart grew big to him, at receiving this flag, and towards his people."

Nah-kwil-luk. The Skokomish Chief. "His heart too had become white and he gave it to the Chief. He put away all his bad feelings. He would be as a good man, not stealing or shedding blood. He sent this word to the Great Father. About what should we talk today. We have thrown away the feelings of yesterday, and are now satisfied. We want you to say to him." He gives a flag to Gov. Stevens who says on receiving it, "I call you my son, but when I see your grey head, I should rather call you, Father. I thank you for the expression of your heart. I am sure you will keep this feeling towards the Agent, and those who succeed us. These children are my children. I hope you will always preserve them, and look with satisfaction to this day."

Chim-a-kum Chief Hul-kah-had or Gen. Pierce. "We talk to you, but what should we say? We can say nothing but what this flag tells. We give our hearts to you with it, in return for what you do for us. We were once wretched, but since you come you have made us right. When the Americans come to my country they shall find my heart like this. Formerly other Indians did wrong to us. Since the Whites had come, we are free and have not been killed." Gave a flag, and Governor Stevens addressed him. "You are young. I hope your heart will always be white as your flag, and that you will be a father to your people. I too will take care of them and we will keep the record of the people on that flag, and trust it will always be good."

Gov. Stevens once more asked them if they were satisfied to sign the Treaty. They all declared themselves so. It was accordingly signed, and a salute fired from the Steamer as a signal.

Some hostile feeling having previously existed on the part of the Chemakums toward the Klallams and Skokomish, Gov. Stevens now desired that they should stop it forever, and that their hearts towards each other should be good as well as toward the whites. The three chiefs then on behalf of their people shook hands. The presents were then distributed to them as in the other cases, and in the afternoon the party reembarked, Mr. Mason returning to Olympia in the steamer and Governor Stevens with the rest proceeding to Port Townsend in the schooner, on his way to Cape Flattery the next point of meeting.

George Gibbs
Secretary

THE POINT NO POINT TREATY

Isaac I. Stevens

Articles of Agreement and Convention made and concluded at Hahd-skus or Point No Point, Suquamish Head in the Territory of Washington, this twenty sixth day of January, Eighteen hundred and fifty five, by Isaac I. Stevens Governor and Superintendent of Indian Affairs for the said Territory on the part of the United States and the undersigned Chiefs, headmen and delegates of the different villages of the S'Klallams, viz: Kah-tai, Squah-quaih'tl, Tch-queen, Ste-teht-lum, Tsokw, Yennis, Elh-hwah, Pishtst, Hun-nint, Klat-la-wash and Oke-ho, and also of the Skos-ko-mish, To-an-ooch and Chem-a-kum tribes, occupying certain lands on the Straits of Fuca, and Hoods Canal in the Territory of Washington on behalf of said tribes and duly authorized by them.

ART. I. The said Tribes and bands of Indians hereby cede, relinquish and convey to the United States all their right, title and interest in and to the lands and country occupied by them, bounded and described as follows: viz, Commencing at the mouth of the Oke-ho river on the Straits of Fuca, thence South Eastwardly along the westerly line of Territory claimed by the Makah tribe of Indians to the summit of the Cascade Range, thence still South Eastwardly and Southerly along said summit to the head of the west branch of the Satsop river, down that branch to the main fork, thence Eastwardly and following the line of lands heretofore ceded to the United States by the Nisqually and other tribes and bands of Indians to the summit of the Black Hills, and North Eastwardly to the Portage known as Wilkes' Portage, thence North Eastwardly and following the line of lands heretofore ceded to the United States by the Duwamish, Suquamish and other Tribes and Bands of Indians to Suquamish head, thence Northerly through Admiralty Inlet to the Straits of Fuca, thence Westerly through the said Straits to the place of beginning. Including all the right, title and Interest of said tribes and bands to any land in the Territory of Washington.

ART. II. There is however reserved for the present use and occupation of the said tribes and bands, the following tract of land, viz: the amount of six sections or three thousand eight hundred and forty acres, situated at the head of Hood's Canal to be hereafter set apart and so far as necessary surveyed and marked out for their exclusive use: nor shall any white man be permitted to reside upon the same without permission of the said tribes and

bands and of the Superintendent or Agent; but if necessary for the public convenience roads may be run through the said reservation, the Indians being compensated for any damage thereby done them.   It is however understood that should the President of the United States hereafter see fit to place upon the said reservation any other friendly tribe or band, to occupy the same in common with those above mentioned, he shall be at liberty to do so.

ART. III. The said tribes and bands agree to remove to and settle upon the said reservation within one year after the ratification of this Treaty, or sooner if the means are furnished them.   In the meantime it shall be lawful for them to reside upon any lands not in the actual claim or occupation of citizens of the United States, and upon any lands claimed or occupied if with the permission of the owner.

ART. IV. The right of taking fish at usual and accustomed grounds and stations is further secured to said Indians in common with all citizens of the United States, and of erecting temporary houses for the purpose of curing; together with the privilege of hunting and gathering roots and berries on open and unclaimed lands: provided however that they shall not take shell fish from any beds staked or cultivated by citizens.

ART. V. In consideration of the above cession the United States agree to pay to the said Tribes and Bands the sum of Sixty Thousand Dollars in the following manner, that is to say: During the first year after the ratification hereof Six Thousand Dollars: For the next two years, five thousand dollars each year: for the next three years, four thousand Dollars each year: For the next four years, three thousand Dollars each year: and for the next five years, two thousand four hundred dollars each year: and for the next five years, one thousand six hundred dollars each year.   All which said sums of money shall be applied to the use and benefit of the said Indians under the direction of the President of the United States who may from time to time determine at his discretion upon what beneficial objects to expend the same. And he Superintendent of Indian Affairs or other proper officer shall each year inform the President of the wishes of said Indians in respect thereto.

ART. VI. To enable said Indians to remove to and settle upon their aforesaid reservation and to clear, fence and break up a sufficient quantity of land for cultivating, the United States further agree to pay the sum of Six Thousand Dollars to be laid out and expended under the direction of the President, and in such manner as he shall approve.

ART. VII. The President may hereafter when in his opinion the interest of the Territory shall require and the welfare of said Indians be promoted, remove them from said reservation to such other suitable place or places within said Territory as he may deem fit on remunerating them for their improvements and the expenses of their removal, or may consolidate them with other friendly tribes or bands. And he may further at his discretion cause the whole or any portion of the lands hereby reserved or of such other lands as may be selected in lieu thereof, to be surveyed into lots and assign the same to such individuals or families as are willing to avail themselves of the privilege and will locate thereon as a permanent home, on the same terms and subject to the same regulations as are provided in the Sixth Article of the Treaty with the Omahas, so far as the same may be applicable. Any substantial improvements heretofore made by any Indian and which he shall be compelled to abandon in consequence of this Treaty shall be valued under the direction of the President and payment made therefore accordingly.

ART. VIII. The annuities of the aforesaid Tribes and bands shall not be taken to pay the debts of individuals.

ART. IX. The said Tribes and Bands acknowledge their dependence on the Government of the United States, and promise to be friendly with all citizens thereof, and they pledge themselves to commit no depredations on the property of such citizens. And should any one or more of them violate this pledge and the fact be satisfactorily proven before the Agent, the property taken shall be returned or in default thereof, or if injured or destroyed, compensation may be made by the Government out of their annuities. Nor will they make war on any other tribe except in self defense, but will submit all matters of difference between them and other Indians to the Government of the United States or its Agent for decision and abide thereby. And if any of the said Indians commit any depredations on any other Indians within the Territory the same rule shall prevail as that prescribed in this Article in cases of depredations against citizens. And the said Tribes agree not to shelter or conceal offenders against the United Sates, but to deliver them up for trial by the authorities.

ART. X. The above tribes and bands are desirous to exclude from their reservation the use of ardent spirits, and to prevent their people from drinking the same, and therefore it is provided that any Indian belonging thereto, who shall be guilty of bringing liquor into said reservation, or who drinks liquor, may have his or her proportion of the annuities withheld from him or her for such time as the President may determine.

ART. XI. The United States further agree to establish at the General Agency for the District of Puget's Sound, within one year from the ratification hereof, and to support for the period of twenty years, an Agricultural and Industrial School, to be free to children of the said Tribes and bands in common with those of the other tribes of said District, and to provide a Smithy and Carpenter's Shop, and to furnish them with the necessary tools and employ a blacksmith, carpenter and farmer for the term of twenty years, to instruct the Indians in their respective occupations. And the United States further agree to employ a Physician to reside at the said Central Agency who shall furnish medicine and advice to the sick and shall vaccinate them: the expenses of the said school, shops, persons employed and medical attendance to be defrayed by the United States and not deducted from the annuities.

ART. XII. The said tribes and bands agree to free all slaves now held by them and not to purchase or acquire others hereafter.

ART. XIII. The said tribes and bands finally agree not to trade at Vancouver's Island or elsewhere out of the Dominions of the United States, nor shall foreign Indians be permitted to reside in their reservations without consent of the Superintendent or Agent.

ART. XIV. This Treaty shall be obligatory on the contracting parties as soon as the same shall be ratified by the President of the United States.   In Testimony Whereof, the said Isaac I. Stevens, Governor and Superintendent of Indian Affairs, and the Undersigned, Chiefs, headmen, and Delegates of the Aforesaid tribes and Bands of Indians have hereunto set their hands and seals at the place on the day and year hereinbefore written.

THE GREAT WHITE FATHER

Kent D. Richards

As superintendent of Indian affairs, [Washington Territorial Governor Isaac I.] Stevens soon became a key figure in the new reservation policy that federal officials had proposed as the latest in a long series of attempted solutions to the perplexing problem of dealing with the native inhabitants. Stevens' views on Indians had been shaped by the prevailing assumptions of his fellow Americans during the Jacksonian era. Their attitudes fell into two broad categories: one group believed that the natives were savages who, for their own protection as well as that of white society, needed to be isolated beyond a permanent Indian frontier. The other group argued that the Indians should be assimilated into white culture - taking the best from Indian and white civilizations. Common to both points of view was the assumption that all Indians were essentially the same - an assumption which lumped vastly diverse cultures under one label.

Historically, conflicting viewpoints, abetted by the realities of an advancing frontier, resulted in a vacillating Indian policy which had begun with the British government's Proclamation of 1763. This pragmatic decision to create a barrier to "Indian country" beyond the Appalachians was based on the experience of more than a century of bitter and bloody conflict-warfare in which Isaac Stevens' ancestors had often been participants. The new nation continued this policy, but it broke down under the pressures of white settlement, and, during the latter years of the 18th century, the government began moving in new directions. Under the Northwest Ordinance of 1787, the federal government reserved the right to extinguish Indian land title, and, with the Treaty of Greenville in 1795, there began a systematic process of treaty negotiations. Once the lands were purchased, the Indians became the responsibility of the government, and, at least in theory, they were to be instructed in farming and given the benefits of a common school education. In this way there would be assimilation. Some confidently predicted the process would take only a generation or less.

The assimilation policy often met with Indian resistance, the failure of agents to provide promised services, and the reluctance of Congress to appropriate funds. Even when the policy bore fruit, as with the Cherokees of

Georgia, white greed placed enormous pressure upon the government to force the tribes from the rich land they occupied. President Andrew Jackson, who called for removal of all Indians west of the Mississippi River, argued that, even in the case of the Cherokees, "All previous experiments for the improvement of the Indians have failed. It seems now to be an established fact that they cannot live in contact with a civilized community and prosper."

The removal of the "Five Civilized Tribes" led to the establishment of a new permanent Indian boundary running from northern Wisconsin across Iowa and following the present western borders of Missouri and Arkansas. Opinion differed in the 1830s as to the eventual fate of tribes sent to the West. Washington Irving predicted that a new, mongrel race would develop as "the amalgamation of the debris and abrasions of former races, civilized and savage; the remains of broken and almost extinguished tribes; the descendants of wandering hunters and trappers." It was visitor Alexis de Tocqueville who most accurately foresaw the future. He described how the Americans would take the Indians "by the hand and transport them to a grave far from the lands of their fathers," and he noted that it would be accomplished "with a singular felicity; tranquilly, legally, philanthropically." De Tocqueville predicted they would remain undisturbed in their new homes only until the whites needed the land. He erred only in placing that need at a point in the distant future. In the early 1840 settlement pushed west from Missouri, following the river valleys and trails cut across the continent to California and Oregon. By 1850 it was impossible to draw a straight line that would separate Indian and white settlements even if the government had wished to.

Before 1853, Isaac Stevens' direct contact with Indians was limited to viewing the survivors of tribes in Maine, but he was well aware of frontier conflicts such as the Seminole War. To the extent that Stevens had a philosophy of Indian-white relations, he assumed the superiority of European civilization and the necessity of removing the Indian from its path. He hoped the removal could be accomplished peacefully and that, during a period of benevolent care, the Indians could be educated to cultivate the soil and become productive, valued members of white society.

One anomaly of American Indian policy was the treaty system, which assumed an equality between the contracting parties that did not exist. It was suggested to President James Madison in 1811, as it was often suggested to other political leaders, that the treaty process was a farce and that it would be more equitable for the United States to dictate benevolent terms without negotiation. Madison and other presidents hesitated - partially because they did not wish to leave the nation open to charges of aggression or nondemocratic procedures. The fiction of negotiations between equal, consenting parties continued and Superintendent Stevens was obliged to work within this well established treaty framework. The movement of settlers to the Pacific Coast had ended any real possibility of a permanent Indian frontier, and beginning with the Treaty of Fort Laramie in 1851, the federal government moved toward the reservation system as an alternative to the frontier line. In 1854 Stevens was charged with the responsibility of extinguishing Indian title in Washington Territory under the basic policy then in operation: placement of the Indians on reservations under the treaty process.

The Pacific Northwest differed from the typical American frontier in that extensive Indian-white contacts existed for many years prior to widespread agrarian settlement. Under the aegis of the Hudson's Bay Company, a pattern of Indian - white relationship began in the 1820s. Sir George Simpson and John McLoughlin, who disagreed on many matters, at least agreed that the Indians should receive fair treatment from the Company. This meant consistent policies, fixed prices for furs, and an end to the liquor traffic. The relationship benefited both sides: the Company provided goods, which raised the Indians' standard of living, and the Indians provided the Company with furs. Employees of the Company, including leaders like McLoughlin, tended to take Indian wives, and this brought the two races closer as time passed. During his long tenure in the Northwest, John McLoughlin became a larger-than-life figure respected by whites and Indians alike; he ruled with a firm hand, but he did not interfere much with the Indian way of life. For most tribes the arrival of the Hudson's Bay Company was a positive factor as it brought stability and economic progress. The major negative factor was the appearance of influenza, smallpox, measles, and syphilis, which took a heavy toll.

The first American missionaries, who came to Oregon, in 1834, did not disrupt the pattern. Jason Lee, for example, was steered to the Willamette Valley by McLoughlin, and Indians who wished contact with the Americans had to visit the mission posts. The American community grew for a few years without having a serious negative impact on the Indians, and efforts to bring cattle up from California proved to be beneficial. Significantly, the first American settlement of consequence in Indian country - that of Marcus Whitman - led to the first major conflict in the Northwest. Many American settlers believed that the Hudson's Bay Company encouraged the Indians to oppose the "Bostons." The charge was false. McLoughlin had warned Whitman that he was in danger; and, in any open conflict, the company always sided with the Americans. But the contrast between the company's impact on the region and the effect of American settlement was readily apparent. The Whitman mission was a permanent agricultural settlement, and the many settlers who stopped there indicated to the Indians that it was only the first of many settlements. In addition, the missionaries frankly admitted that they wished to destroy the Indians' traditional way of life and replace it with white culture. The outbreak of disease was only the last straw leading to the massacre and, subsequently, the Cayuse War.

By the 1850s the future of Indian-white relations in the Northwest was clear to experienced observers and incidents began to occur with increasing frequency. According to one government estimate, 16 whites in Oregon were killed by Indians during the 1847-48 Cayuse War. In the next two years no deaths were reported, but in 1851 and 1852 there were six fatalities each year, and in 1853, the number ballooned to 47. Most of the deaths resulted from squabbles and misunderstandings between individuals, and more often than not, one or both parties were under the influence of alcohol - another exacerbating influence contributed by the Americans. Indians reacted to physical abuse from whites, and the settlers often objected to Indian thievery. The Indians quickly discovered that, unlike McLoughlin, the Americans would seldom if ever punish a white for harming an Indian. In addition, many "Bostons" made it clear that they were determined to remove the Indians from their neighborhood, if not from the face of the earth. One outspoken but not atypical Oregon settler called for an end to the "sickly sentimentality," of "pseudo-philanthropists who seek to disguise the real Oregon Indian by representing him as possessing such ennobling traits of character as are seldom found within the realms of civilization." This Oregonian suggested that it was time for vigorous action: "'Lo! the poor Indian' is the exclamation of... love sick novel writers. 'Lo! the defenseless men, women and children, who have fallen victims and suffered more than death itself at their hands' is the immediate response of the surviving witnesses of the inhuman butcheries perpetrated by this God-accursed race."

The problem of Indian-white relations was further complicated in 1850 with the passage of the Oregon Donation Land Act which allowed new families to claim as much as 320 acres of land. The act did not state specifically that these claims could be taken before extinguishment of Indian title or completion of land surveys, but it implied immediate settlement. The new settlement brought greater pressures, and in 1851, the Rogue Indians of southern Oregon lashed out against miners and settlers. At the same time the Snake Indians (along the Oregon Trail) were becoming increasingly hostile to emigrants. After 1851, military officers and Catholic priests in the Northwest frequently warned their superiors, government officials, and settlers that Indian outbreaks were not only possible but probable. A typical alarm was sounded by Maj. Gabriel Rains, who wrote from Fort Dalles to the headquarters of the Department of the Pacific, "The time has arrived when it becomes necessary to determine the question of peace or war between the citizens of the United States and Indian tribes on this frontier." Rains reviewed Indian complaints, noted the presence of an extensive liquor traffic, protested that Indians had no rights in the courts, and concluded that it would be best if the area east of the Cascade Mountains remained Indian country. But even as the major warned, "prompt action is required...to prevent an Indian war," Wasco County, south of Fort Dalles and east of the Cascade Mountains, was in the process of organization.

Gov. Stevens was aware of all the above factors, but he tended to play down the danger signals for a variety of reasons. Above all, he had great confidence in his own ability to handle the Indians. This cocksureness had developed as he came west with the railroad survey; he had expected the worst, particularly from the Blackfeet, but the survey party had come through with no serious incidents. Stevens did not recognize that their good fortune resulted in large measure from the excellent liaison work of Alexander Culbertson. Stevens exaggerated his own role and assumed that other whites either had not known how to handle the Indians successfully, or had overestimated the danger. He became even more sanguine upon arrival west of the Cascade Mountains. Before coming west he had read George Simpson's Narrative of a Journey Around the World, in which the Puget Sound Indians were described as "quiet, inoffensive, and industrious people" who did well as agricultural helpers. When Stevens reached Olympia it appeared that Simpson's assessment was correct for he found the various tribes trading with the whites, acting as guides, and working as servants. The Nisqually Indians, who camped in and near Olympia, seemed anything but a threat to the settlers. Meg [Stevens' wife] echoed her husband's view that the Indians could be easily controlled when she declared that they "think so much of the whites that a child can govern them." She boasted, "Mr. Stevens has them right under his thumb – they are afraid to death of him and do just as he tells them." On one occasion, as Meg told it, when their night-long singing and chanting, which she likened to the howling of a band of wolves, kept the governor's family awake, he took a club, walked into the center of the group, and threatened to knock down the first one who opened his mouth. The singing ended, Meg said, at least for the night.

Soon after arriving in the territory, Stevens outlined his plans for the Commissioner of Indian Affairs, George Manypenny. He noted the conflict that apparently existed between the Donation Act and laws governing Indian affairs and urged speed in defining Indian lands before settlers spread over the whole territory and further complicated the situation. Stevens knew that most tribes would not wish to move very far from their existing locations, but he also knew that the federal government still tended to think in terms of an Indian-white frontier as clearly defined as possible. (Treaties made by Anson Dart in Oregon in 1851-52 were disallowed because they provided for numerous reservations located near settlements in the western part of the territory). Stevens cautiously suggested that it would be impractical to move the Puget Sound tribes east of the Cascade Mountains and argued that it would be more humane and less expensive to locate them on the sound where they could catch fish, dig roots, and pick berries. Although confident of his ability to resolve the Indian question, Stevens constantly urged the government to act quickly because delay would only complicate a solution equitable to both whites and Indians.

Events in 1854 confirmed the truth of Stevens' position. Conditions on the Oregon Trail worsened as Shoshone Indians attacked the "Ward Party" on the Boise River and killed 17 in a particularly shocking massacre. The rescue party reported that many victims showed signs of the "most brutal violence." Violence occurred periodically near Seattle and at Bellingham Bay, where several whites lost their lives in 1853-54. In most instances the white settlers retaliated against the Indians they assumed to be guilty of the crimes. For example, in July 1853, three white men hanged an Indian near Seattle. The hangmen were brought to trial: one man was acquitted and charges against the other two were dismissed.

Stevens became involved in one incident when a party of men from Seattle arrived in Olympia in March 1854, with the news that a man named Young had been murdered and a second, Dr. Cherry, had died during a subsequent skirmish at Holmes Harbor. The governor, with George Gibbs, Michael Simmons, and a squad of soldiers under the command of Lt. William Slaughter, sailed north down the sound. Stevens met with Chiefs Seattle and Patkanim of the Duwamish and Snoqualmie bands. The chiefs told him that

Young, a new settler headed for Whidbey Island, and two hired Indians had become drunk and had quarreled. Young killed one Indian with his sword and wounded the other. The son of the dead man later killed Young for revenge. The young Indian was seized, and the fight at Holmes Harbor resulted when friends came to his rescue. In the ensuing battle, Cherry and an Indian with the white party were killed. Testimony from whites made it clear that they feared a general uprising, and they pleaded with the governor to take strong measures to prevent further deaths. Stevens judiciously declared both sides at fault and promised justice would be meted out to all. Chiefs Seattle and Patkanim named the Indians involved in the Holmes Harbor affair but claimed they had disappeared into the woods. The governor then took his party to Holmes Harbor, where a number of Snohomish Indians were encamped, and demanded they give up the guilty parties. When they refused Stevens ordered their canoes burned and returned to Olympia empty handed. Stevens reported that his action had a salutary effect, which may have been true, but the Indians must have wondered why only they received punishment as a result of the incident.

Federal officials reacted positively when confronted with the urgent demands of Governor Stevens, Oregon officials, army officers, and a number of private citizens. Commissioner Manypenny, with masterly bureaucratic prose, informed Congress,

> An enlightened forecast indicates that the present is a favorable time to institute and establish definite relations of amity with the wild tribes of Indians....With many of the tribes in Oregon and Washington territories, it appears to be absolutely necessary to speedily conclude treaties for the extinguishment of their claims to the lands now or recently occupied by them.

Manypenny reminded Congress that it had promoted settlement in the Northwest, "Yet the Indian tribes still claim title to the lands on which the whites have located, and which they are now cultivating." This, the commissioner reported, led to hostilities and resulted in "the murder of white settlers, and in hindering the general growth and prosperity of the civil communities of these territories."

After returning to Olympia in December 1854, Stevens set to work on his program to conduct treaty negotiations. He planned to negotiate with the tribes on the Sound during the winter and then to move east of the Cascade Mountains in the spring and work his way to the Blackfoot council. The governor and his associates had attempted to prepare the tribes for the treaties during 1853-54 when they advised all to keep the peace, promising that treaties would soon be made to provide justice for all. Most Indians in the territory had forewarning of the treaty councils, although in some instances this increased rather than lessened fears. The first council took place at the mouth of Medicine Creek (on the Nisqually Flats between Olympia and Fort Steilacoom). While men rode out to escort the Indians to the councils, set up the council grounds, and procured the necessary supplies, the governor gathered his negotiating team in Olympia. In addition to Michael Simmons (who had been named Indian agent for Puget Sound), the group included James Doty as secretary, Benjamin F. Shaw as interpreter, George Gibbs as surveyor, and Hugh A. Goldsborough as commissary. Simmons and Shaw were veteran frontiersmen and early settlers on the sound. (Shaw was alleged to be the only man in the territory who could translate from English into the Chinook tongue while a man talked at normal speed.) Gibbs was rapidly becoming the most apt student of Indian language and customs in the Northwest, and Doty had just arrived on the Sound after his year's residence among the Blackfoot Indians. Goldsborough, an eastern lawyer who had been in the territory for several years, was the only member of the commission who lacked previous experience in Indian relations.

Several of these men later concluded that the policy of treaty councils was a mistake. Benjamin Shaw argued that the United States in fact had the land and erred in letting the Indians think they were equal parties in decisions relating to land disposal. Stevens' thoughts on this question in December 1854 are not known, but his earlier statements would indicate that given a choice, he would have dictated a policy that would speed settlement yet offer protection for the Indian. This hypothetical policy could not have brought worse results than the treaties; whether it would have produced a more favorable climate for Indian-white relationships is open to conjecture. A consistent policy largely under the supervision of one man (McLoughlin)

had earlier produced an environment acceptable to whites and Indians, but although there were similarities between Stevens and McLoughlin, the territorial system was not the Hudson's Bay Company's style, the American settlers were not Company employees, and 1855 was not 1825. In any event, there was no alternative to the treaty process. It was fixed government policy, and Stevens realized that he would have to work within its frame-work. There was no question as to if or when the Indians would be brought under treaties; the only issue open to discussion was how.

Drawing on their knowledge of the Puget Sound region, its tribes, and previous treaties, the [treaty] commissioners adopted nine principles as guidelines: to concentrate the tribes as much as practicable; to encourage soil cultivation and other civilized habits; to pay for the land with annuities consisting of useful goods rather than cash; to furnish teachers, doctors, farmers, blacksmiths and carpenters; to prohibit war between the tribes; to end slavery; to halt the liquor trade; to allow the Indians to hunt, fish and gather berries until the civilizing process was complete; and, in time to allow division of the reservation lands in severalty. It was an enlightened policy in that it allowed for a transition period and a process of gradual assimilation. The policy was, however, based on several assumptions that the commissioners erroneously accepted as truisms: that it was best for the Indians to be converted to the European way of life; that this transition could be accomplished by an economic shift from hunting and fishing to farming; that the federal government and its agents would faithfully provide the goods and services stipulated in the treaties; and that the Indian could be persuaded that all of the above were in his best interests.

To Governor Stevens the signed treaties became legal agreements binding both parties. In conducting the treaty sessions, he did not think it necessary to pay much heed to Indian complaints that traditional customs, habits, superstitions or religious mores would be violated by the treaties. After all, the long-term consequence of the treaties, in Stevens' view, was to replace the traditional pattern of Indian life with the superior white civilization. There was no doubt in his mind that the Indians would have to sign and that it was in their best interest to sign. The treaties offered certain guarantees and protections - without the treaties they would be swallowed up by white settlement and would receive nothing in return. Stevens ran the treaty sessions as if he were a judge in a court of law. Though all had the opportunity to speak, to ask questions, and to demand explanations, and though there was room for minor modifications of the treaty drafts, the end result of the councils was inevitable.

In certain respects Stevens was a good choice as superintendent of Indian affairs: he was an efficient, hardworking, honest administrator. In his own words, he was a stern but just "father" to the Indians. However, despite Stevens' constant assertions to the contrary, the Indians were not his children, and he did not always understand (or try to appreciate) their desires - or their best interests. He was a father who interpreted his "children's" welfare as corresponding to his own. In many parental relationships this can be a serious flaw; for Stevens and the Indians of Washington Territory it was fatal.

Most white citizens on the Sound approved of the whirlwind treaty negotiations. They remarked on the energy with which the treaties were pushed and observed that extinguishment of Indian title was "a consummation devoutly to be wished." The Pioneer and Democrat published a list of reservations that had been surveyed or were "defined by natural boundaries," and declared, "Information is given to the public that settlers may take action accordingly in locating claims." Subsequent settlement caused de facto ratification of treaty boundaries even though Congressional approval of all but the Medicine Creek Treaty was delayed until 1859.

INDIAN POLICY-
TREATIES ON PUGET SOUND

Hazard Stevens

Gov. Stevens regarded his Indian treaties and Indian policy, and his management of the Indians of the Northwest, as among the most important, beneficial and successful services he rendered the country. With ten treaties and many councils and talks, he extinguished the Indian title to a domain larger than New England; and with the Blackfoot council and treaty he made peace among those fierce savages and the whites and all the surrounding tribes, and permanently pacified a region embracing the greater part of Montana and northern Idaho. During the years 1853-56, he treated and dealt with over 30,000 Indians, of numerous and independent tribes and bands, and occupying the vast region from the Pacific to and including the plains of the upper Missouri and now comprising the state of Washington, part of Oregon, northern Idaho and the greater part of Montana. Moreover, by gaining the unwavering friendship and fidelity of doubtful tribes, and even many members of the disaffected, he frustrated the well-planned efforts of the hostile Indians to bring about a universal outbreak of violence and saved the infant settlements from complete annihilation at the hands of the treacherous savages.

His Indian policy was one of great beneficence to the Indians, jealously protected their interests, and provided for their improvement and eventual civilization, while at the same time it opened the country for settlement by the whites. The wisdom with which it was planned, and the ability and energy with which it was carried out, during this brief period, are attested to by the remarkable success which attended it, and by the fact that many of these tribes are today living under those very treaties and have made substantial progress towards civilized habits. It is believed that in their extent and magnitude, in their difficulties and dangers, and in the permanence and beneficence of their results, these operations are without parallel in the history of the country.

Yet for several years Gov. Stevens' Indian treaties were bitterly assailed and misrepresented both by hostile Indians and by officers in authority; their confirmation was refused by the United States Senate, and Stevens himself was made the target for virulent abuse. It was his intention to write the history of these operations, an intention unfulfilled because of the pressure of public duties during the few remaining years of his life, and his early death.

In his final report on the Northern route he remarks, in words of manly fortitude and confidence:

> I trust the time will come when my treaty operations of 1855, the most extensive operations ever undertaken and carried out in these latter days of our history, I repeat, I trust the time will come when I shall be able to vindicate them, and show that they were wise and proper, and that they accomplished a great end. They have been very much criticized and very much abused; but I have always felt that history will do those operations justice. I have not been impatient as to time, but have been willing that my vindication should come at the end of a term of years. Let short-minded men denounce and criticize ignorantly and injuriously, and let time show that the government made no mistake in the man whom it placed in the great field of duty as its commissioner to make treaties with the Indian tribes.

Immediately on his return to Olympia the governor sent out the agents and messengers to assemble the Puget Sound Indians at designated points for council and treaty making and early in January dispatched Mr. Doty with a small party east of the Cascades to make the preliminary arrangements for bringing together in council the Indians of that region.

On December 7, only two days after delivering his message to the legislature, Gov. Stevens organized his treaty-making force by appointing James Doty secretary, George Gibbs surveyor, H.A. Goldsborough commissary, and B.F. Shaw interpreter, Colonel M. T. Simmons having already been appointed agent. The governor assembled these gentlemen to confer upon the projected treaties. After giving his views, and showing the necessity of speedily treating with the Indians and placing them on reservations, he had Mr. Doty read certain treaties with the Missouri and Omaha tribes, which contained provisions he deemed worthy of adoption, and invited a general and thorough discussion of the whole subject. So many points were settled by this frank and free interchange of views that Mr. Gibbs was directed to draw up a programme, or outline of a treaty which on the next meeting on the 10th, after discussion and some changes, was adopted as the basis of the treaties to be made with the tribes on the sound, coast, and lower Columbia.

No better advisers could have been found than the men with whom he thus took counsel; and one is struck by the clever and considerate way in which he secured the best fruits of their knowledge and experience, and enlisted their best efforts in carrying out the work.   Simmons and Shaw were old frontiersmen, among the earliest settlers, and had dealt with and thoroughly understood the Indians, and were respected and trusted by them.   Simmons had been justly termed the Daniel Boone of Washington Territory.   Shaw was said to be the only man who could make or translate a speech in Chinook jargon offhand, as fast as a man could talk in his own vernacular. The Chinook jargon was a mongrel lingo, made up for trading purposes by the fur-traders from English, French and Indian words, and had become the common speech between whites and Indians, and between Indians of different tribes and tongues.   He greatly distinguished himself afterwards in the Indian war as Lieutenant-Colonel of volunteers.   Gibbs and Goldsborough were men of education, and had lived in the country long enough to know the general situation and conditions, and to learn much about the Indians.   Gibbs, indeed, made a study of the different tribes, and rendered an able report upon them as part of the Northern Pacific Railroad exploration.   Doty, a son of ex-Governor Doty, of Wisconsin, was a young man of uncommon ability and energy, who had spent the preceding winter at Fort Benton, and had studied and made a census of the Blackfeet.

The schooner "R. B. Potter," Captain E.S. Fowler, was chartered at $700 per month, manned and victualed by the owner, to transport the personnel and treaty goods from point to point on the sound. Orrington Cushman, Sidney S. Ford, Jr., and Henry D. Cock, with several assistants, were employed as quartermasters, to prepare camps and council grounds, make surveys, etc.

In all his councils Gov. Stevens took the greatest pains to make the Indians understand what was said to them.   To ensure this he always had several interpreters to check each other and prevent mistakes in translation and was accustomed to consult the chiefs as to whom they wanted as interpreters.

"It was my invariable custom," he states in the introduction to his final railroad report, "whenever I assembled a tribe in council, to procure from them their own rude sketches of the country, and a map was invariably prepared on a large scale and shown to them, exhibiting not only the region occupied by them, but the reservations that were proposed to be secured to them...to give them absolute and entire confidence in the government."

He always urged and encouraged the Indians to make known their views, wishes and objections, and gave them time to talk matters over among themselves and make up their minds. Between the sessions of the council he would have the agents and interpreters explain the terms and point out the benefits of the proposed treaty, and would frequently summon the chiefs to his tent, and personally explain matters to them and draw out their ideas. He also frequently invited public officers and citizens of standing to attend the councils, and would make use of them also to talk with and satisfy the Indians.

All the proceedings of these councils, the deliberations and speeches as well as the treaties, were every word carefully taken down in writing, and transmitted to the Indian Bureau in Washington, where they are now on file. No one can read these records without being impressed with Gov. Stevens' great benevolence towards the Indians, and the absolute fairness, candor and patience, as well as the judgment and tact he manifested in dealing with them.   One is also likely to be enlightened as to the native intelligence, ability and shrewdness of the Indians themselves.

The next council was held at Point-No-Point, on the west side of the Sound, opposite the southern end of Whitby [sic] Island.   The weather was very stormy on December 24th and 25th, but 1,200 Indians assembled here, comprising the S'Klallams or Clallams, who occupied the shores from half way down the Strait of Fuca to the Council ground; the Chim-a-kums, of Port Townsend Bay and the lower end of Hood's Canal; and the Skokomish or Too-an-hooch, from Hood's Canal and the country about its southern extremity. The "Major Tompkins" reached Point-No-Point on the 24th, and, leaving the schooner at anchor, and the men on shore to form camp, ran down to Port Townsend to bring up additional provisions, and returned in the afternoon.   On the 25th, notwithstanding the storm, the Indians gathered at the council ground and, having seated themselves in a circular row under their chiefs, Gov. Stevens addressed them....

It will be observed that this treaty encountered considerable opposition on the part of the Skokomish, who were, however, the most benefited by it, as the reservation was located in their country.   They were largely influenced by the example of the other tribes, and after much discussion among themselves, and talks between sessions with the governor and his assistants, concluded to accept it.

The next morning was a fine, pleasant one, and the Indians came to the council bearing white flags. The governor addressed them, pointing out that the treaty gave them all those things that a father would give his children, as homes, schools, mechanics and a doctor; the right to fish, hunt and gather roots and berries. Besides, it prohibited fire-water, and does not a father prevent his children from drinking fire-water? The Great Father was good to his children, and did not wish to steal their lands. It was for them to say what they thought right. If they had anything to say, say it now....

Then all signed the treaty, and at a signal a salute was fired from the steamer in honor of the event. Some hostile feelings having previously existed between the tribes, Gov. Stevens now declared that they must drop them forever and that their hearts towards each other as well as towards the whites should be good. Accordingly the three head chiefs, on behalf of their people, then shook hands. Then the presents were distributed to them. In the afternoon the party embarked, [territorial secretary Charles M.] Mason returning to Olympia on the steamer, and Gov. Stevens with the remainder proceeding to Port Townsend in the schooner, on his way to Cape Flattery, the next point of meeting....

A 3,480 acre reservation was set off at the mouth of the Skokomish River. The usual annuities amounting to $60,000, and $6,000 for the improvement of the reservation, were provided, and the other provisions were the same as in the Tulalip and She-nah- nam Creek treaties. This treaty was witnessed by the same gentlemen who witnessed the preceding....

This brief campaign was Napoleonic in rapidity and success. In six weeks Gov. Stevens met and treated with 5,000 Indians, of numerous independent and jealous tribes and bands, and in four separate councils carefully and indefatigably made clear to them the new policy, convinced them of its benefits to them, and concluded with them four separate treaties, by which the Indian title to the whole Puget Sound basin was extinguished forever, and the great source and danger of collision between the races was removed.

For the 8,500 Indians hitherto ignored by Congress and treated by the settlers as mere vagrants, to be shoved aside at the whim or self-interest of any white man, he established nine reservations, containing over 60,000 acres, for their permanent homes and exclusive possession; provided annuities of clothing, goods, and useful articles for 20 years, aggregating $300,000, abolished slavery and war among them; excluded liquor from the reservations; extended over them the protection of the government, with agents, schools, teachers, farmers, and mechanics to instruct them; and, in a word, set their feet fairly on "the white man's road." To accomplish this astonishing work in such brief time, he traveled 800 miles upon the sound and strait in the most inclement season of the year, half the distance, and that the most dangerous, in a small sailing craft. He disregarded the storms and rains of that inclement season and spared neither himself nor his assistants. It is not easy to say who had the hardest task, the agents and messengers who traveled all over the sound in canoes in the tempestuous rainy season to call the scattered bands together, or the unfortunate secretary, who had to catch and set down on paper the jaw-breaking native names.

The success and rapidity with which he carried through these treaties were due to the careful and thorough manner in which he planned them, and prepared the minds of the Indians by his tour among and talks to them a year previous, and by the messages and agents he had sent among them. Besides, the Indians realized their own feebleness and uncertain future, divided into so many bands, exposed to the depredations of the northern Indians, and dreading the advent and encroachments of the whites. Their minds consequently were well attuned for negotiating; and when they understood the wise and beneficent policy and liberal terms offered by the governor, they gladly accepted them, and put their trust in him as their friend and protector, a trust never withdrawn and never forsaken.

The Indian war which occurred soon after, and the delay in the ratification of the treaties, seriously militated against carrying out the beneficent policy so well inaugurated, and later the occasional appointment of inefficient and dishonest agents has proved even more detrimental; but notwithstanding all these drawbacks the Indians have made substantial advances in civilization, and it is interesting to compare their present condition, as given in the last reports of the Commissioner of Indian Affairs, and from local sources. Their numbers have diminished only about one half. No one seeing their debased condition in 1850 to 1860 (except the Makahs) would have deemed it possible for them to hold their own so well....

All now wear civilized dress, and live in houses. Many can read and write and many of their children attend the reservation schools....

All the reservations on the sound have now been allotted, and the Indians are living on their respective allotments. A considerable number have taken up farms under the homestead laws, or purchased lands from the whites, and are farming successfully.   Such Indians are frequently seen driving into the towns with good wagons and teams, as well dressed as the average white rancher, and accompanied oft times by their wives and children....

During the fall hundreds of them congregate on the hop fields, where they supply the most reliable hop-pickers, whole families - men, women and children - diligently working together. After this harvest crowds of them flock into the towns, and lay in stores of clothing and provisions for the winter before returning home.

POINT NO POINT TREATY

Mary Ann Lambert

According to the Indian version of history, the terms of Isaac Stevens' Point No Point Treaty of 1855 have never been fulfilled.

The Indians' version of subsequent events indicates that the white man never lived up to his part of the bargain - as understood by the Indians. As of this writing in 1961, the Klallam Indians had not received any benefits from the treaty, even the fishing rights in Article IV being denied them.   Instead, ironically enough, some years after the treaty was signed the Klallam village at Port Townsend was burned to the ground by a contingent of soldiers from Fort Townsend near Station Prairie. Presumably this order came from a government official in Washington, D. C. The act was obviously to force the Klallams to remove to Skokomish Reservation.

Research brings only the following to light from the historical recorded:

The only mention of destruction by fire was found in the annual report of Edwin Eells, Indian Agent for the Skokomish Reservation, dated Aug. 31, 1871, stating that during the summer a destructive fire accidentally started in the Indian village, destroying the tenements of 45 families. The report did not indicate in which Indian village the fire occurred.

The Klallams' story of the burning of their small village in Port Townsend, which stood near the present intersection of Water and Jackson streets, is as follows:

Orders had come to Chet-ze-moka (the Duke of York) that all Klallams living in Port Townsend would have to vacate their homes and relinquish their aboriginal domain to Uncle Sam by permanently transferring to the Skokomish Reservation. This was a command, and the Indians had learned by that time that a command from the white man was not to be disregarded.

The day soon arrived for the Indians to load their personal belongings into canoes and leave their beloved "Kah Tai" forever. The side-wheeler "North Pacific" waited, anchored in the bay, for the 20 or more canoes she was to tow to the head of the Hood Canal.

Only one Klallam remained behind, refusing to leave. "My parents and grandparents were born here on this very soil upon which I now stand," he said. "I was born a Klallam, not Skokomish. I will die here, a Klallam." He stood alone on the beach and watched as the others paddled slowly toward the waiting ship.

When the canoes reached the "North Pacific," they were tied to her stern, one canoe behind the other, and the ship departed. As the side-wheeler was about to round Marrowstone Point, the canoes' occupants, looking back at their ancestral homes, could see their village in flames, burning rapidly to the ground-by order of the Great White Father in Washington, D.C.

The waters bounding the Skokomish Reservation were finally reached and the canoes were cut loose from the stern of the "North Pacific." Sadly the Klallams paddled towards the beach, then sat dejectedly in their canoes, staring unhappily at the shore, very much resembling the "Wooden Indian" description often used in ridicule by the whites.

In fewer than five days, however, every Klallam stealthily, by cover of night, returned to the heap of ashes which was their Port Townsend village.

Chetzemoka went to Olympia to appeal for help. After a few days he triumphantly returned, bringing a written promise assuring his tribesmen that the

Great White Father would rectify the wrong done them by compensating the Klallams for the burning of their homes.

The note, yellowed with age, was carried by Queen Victoria (wife of Chief Chetzemoka) until her death-fastened to her chemise with an old brass safety pin.

The note's promises were never fulfilled. Said one old tribesman after many weeks of waiting, "Meaningless words, broken promises. This, then, is what the Bostons (white men) stand for!" But still today there are those Klallams who say, "It will come; the Stevens Treaty of 1855 will be fulfilled." The year is now 1961. Still the Klallams wait.

In the meantime, the Chimacums and Colceans (Quilcenes) have vanished from the face of the earth and the end for the Klallams, a rapidly diminishing race, is not far off.

TESTIMONY OF SEE-HEM-ITZA REGARDING THE POINT NO POINT TREATY

A meeting was held at Jamestown Day School, Clallam County, Washington, Oct. 18, 1915, between Dr. Chas. E. McChestney, a special government inspector, and representatives of the Klallam Indians. This meeting was held for the purpose of ascertaining what claims the Klallam Indians had against the government relative their treaty made with the government at Point No Point dated Jan. 26, 1856.

A number of old Indians were present and gave their understanding of the treaty and one old Indian woman, known as the "Queen," and who was the wife of the leading Klallam Chief that signed the treaty, and who was present at the time of the meeting of the Indians and Gov. Stevens at Point No Point, was questioned as follows by Dr. McChestney: Wilson Johnson acted as interpreter, interpreting the question from English into Klallam and the answers in Klallam into English:

Q.   Was she at Point No Point at the time that Governor Stevens made the Treaty with the Indians?

A.   Yes, she was a young woman, and was there at that time.

Q.   Was she married?

A.   Yes, she was married to the Chief.

Q.   Where there many Klallam Indians there?

A.   Yes, there were a great many.

Q.   Were there many Skokomish Indians there?

A.   Yes, but not so many as Klallam.

Q.   Where did the Klallams think they were to receive land?

A.   Near where they lived at Dungeness.

Q.   How much money did Governor Stevens promise the Indians?

A.   That the old Indians would get a hat full of money, and that they would get canoes, nets, farming implements, and that the younger Indians would get a hat full, but not as much as the older Indians.

Q.   What did she receive from Governor Stevens?

A.   About three yards of calico, some beans, some molasses, but no money. That now they have to pay a thousand dollars for as much land as they got a rotten shirt for.

Q.   Why did not the Klallams go to Skokomish and get land?

A.   They wanted their own tribal lands, they wanted the land from Sequim Bay down to Port Angeles.

Q.   What language was used in making the treaty?

A.   Chinook, but some of the Indians knew a little English.

Q.   Did they understand that they were to move on a reservation with the Skokomish?

A.   She had no recollection about that. That the only thing she knew was that they were to be allowed to go there during the fishing season, that Dungeness was to be their home, and that they be allowed the right to fish on Hoods Canal as formerly.

Q.   When did they find out that they had lost their homes at Dungeness?

A.   They were driven first from the upland by Capt. McAlmond, then later from the beach. They used land on both sides of the river for planting potatoes. Lord Jim Balch found out that all their land was gone. They saw Dick Delanty and he agreed to sell the Jamestown land for $500. The tract was deeded to Lord Jim Balch, the Chief, forty years ago last July. By advice of Edwin Eells, Indian Agent at Puyallup, the land was divided in proportion to what each Indian had to put into the deal. After the Indians moved to Jamestown Mr. Eells sent four cross cut saws, four plows, four mattocks and some garden rakes.

Q.   When was the school first started?

A.   In about two, three, four or five years.

Q.   How many Klallams were there at the time of the treaty?

A.   A great many.

Q.   What caused the death of so many Indians?

A.   Whiskey. Whiskey had killed more than disease.

III
The
Post-Treaty
Years

Myron Eells was born into a missionary family. His father, Cushing Eells, was a Congregational missionary from New England who came to the Pacific Northwest in 1838 to aid the work begun by Marcus Whitman in the Cayuse territory east of the Cascades. Following the infamous "Whitman Massacre" in 1847 he relocated in Oregon's Willamette Valley where he reared his two sons, Edwin and Myron.

In the period 1867-1880, the federal government instituted a series of changes in its Indian policy that came to be known as Grant's Peace Policy. By 1869, when the Grant administration was installed, outrage over corruption and fraud in the administration of Indian Policy was at a peak, and the reputation of the Indian agent was at a low point. The system was perverted by political patronage and structured to encourage graft and corruption. Part of Grant's solution was to remove the responsibility for the nomination of Indian agents from the hands of politicians and turn it over to the religious missionary boards (Martin, 1969).

In 1871, acting through the American Missionary Association, the Congregational Church appointed Myron's brother Edwin as Indian agent for the 4,987 acre Skokomish Reservation on Hood Canal. His father and brother joined him there in 1874.

It had been almost twenty years since the Point No Point Treaty and there were approximately nine hundred Twana and Klallam technically subject to the treaty, but only about three hundred, mostly Twana, resided at Skokomish Reservation. In fact, the census taken by Myron in 1880 (see page 89) shows only six Klallam actually living on the reservation. Consequently, Myron's writings about the Klallam record his seasonal travels to places like Port Gamble, Elwha, and Jamestown, where the Klallam could be found.

Myron served as missionary to the Skokomish until his death in 1907. During this time he made ethnographic collections and wrote extensively about the Indians under his charge. These writings constitute a valuable record of the Puget Sound tribes in the midst of profound cultural change. Along with his brother Edwin, he was an active agent of this change committed to civilizing and Christianizing the natives. Like other reformers and missionaries of the day he viewed the native culture as barbaric and set about to dismantle traditional ways with the object of assimilating them into the mainstream of American life.

By the time Eells recorded his observations of Indians the traditional ways had largely disappeared. What he saw was a society under the command of outsiders. Tribal boundaries, political alliances, kinship systems and customs were in disarray. Traditional healing practices were banned and a system for identifying and punishing Indian "crimes" was in place. Tribal society was manipulated, with "Chiefs" appointed by agents and provided with salaries from federal coffers (Castile, 1985).

Though often distinctly paternalistic and ethnocentric in tone, this selection of Eells' writings also shows sympathy and often a kindly regard for his charges and gives a vivid picture of the times, the life of the Klallam people and the state of Klallam-white relations in the late 19th century.

TEN YEARS OF MISSIONARY WORK AMONG THE INDIANS AT SOKOMISH, WASHINGTON TERRITORY, 1874-1884

Rev. M. Eells

"Weeds will grow where nothing is cultivated."
From his introduction.

From: THE FIELD AND WORK

The work has been about as follows: At Skokomish there were about 200 Indians, including a boarding school of about 25 children. Services were held every Sabbath morning for them in Indian. The Sabbath-school was kept up immediately following the morning service. English services were held once or twice a month, on Sabbath evening, for the white families and the school children resident at the agency. On Thursday evening a prayer meeting was held regularly. It was in English, as very few of the non-

English speaking Indians lived near enough to attend an evening service, had they been so inclined.   Various other meetings were held, adapted to the capacities and localities of the people: as prayer meetings for school boys, those for school girls and those at the different logging camps.

Thirty miles north of Skokomish is Seabeck, where about 30 Indians live, most of whom gain a living by working in the saw mill there. For several years I preached to the whites at this place about eight times a year and when there also held service with the Indians.

Twenty miles farther north is Port Gamble, one of the largest saw mill towns on Puget Sound.   Near it were about a hundred Klallam Indians, most of whom became Catholics, but who have generally received me cordially when I have visited them two or three times a year.   They, however, have obtained whiskey very easily, and between this and the Catholic influence, comparatively little has been accomplished.

Thirty five miles farther on is Port Discovery, another saw mill town, where 30 or 40 Indians have lived, whom I have often called to see on my journeys; but so much whiskey has been sold near them and to them, that it has been almost impossible to stop their drinking, and hence, very difficult to make much permanent religious impression on them.   By death and removal for misconduct, their number has diminished so that at one time there were only one or two families left. But the opportunity for work at the mill has been so good that some of a fair class have returned and bought land and settled down.

Forty miles from Port Gamble, and 17 from Port Discovery, is Jamestown, near Dungeness, on the Straits of Fuca.   This is the center of an Indian settlement of about a 140.   Previous to 1873 these Indians were very much addicted to drinking - so much so that the white residents near them petitioned to have them removed to the agency, a punishment they dreaded nearly as much as any other that could be inflicted on them.   The threat of doing this had such an influence that about 15 of them combined and bought 200 acres of land.   It has been laid off into a village; most of the Indians have reformed and they have settled down as peaceable, industrious, moral persons.   I have generally visited them once in six months, and they have become the most advanced of the Klallam tribe.   A school has been kept among them, a church organized, and their progress has been quite interesting - so much so, that considerable space will be devoted to them in the following pages

Once a year I have calculated to go farther: and 20 miles beyond is Port Angeles, with about 30 nominal Indian residents. But few of them are settlers, and they are diminishing, only a few families being left.

Seven miles further west is Elwha, the home of about 70 Indians. It was, in years past, the residence of one of the most influential bands of the Klallam tribe, but they are diminishing, partly from the fact that there have been but few white families among them from whom they could obtain work, and, with a few exceptions, they themselves have done but little about cultivating the soil. As they could easily go across the straits to Victoria in British Columbia, about 20 miles distant, where there is little restraint in regard to their procuring whiskey, because they are American Indians, they have been steadily losing influence and numbers. Four or five families have homesteaded land, but as it was impossible for them to procure good land on the beach, they have gone back some distance and are scattered. Hence they lose the benefits of church and school. Still the old way of herding together is broken up, and they obtain more of their living from civilized pursuits.

Thirty five miles farther is Klallam Bay, the home of about 50 more. This is the limit of the Indians connected with the Skokomish Agency. They are about 150 miles from it, as we have to travel. In 1880 they bought 160 acres of land on the waterfront, and are slowly following the example of the Jamestown Indians. This is the nearest station of the tribe to the seal fisheries of the northwest coast of the Territory; by far the most lucrative business, in its season, which the Indians follow.

From: DIFFICULTIES IN THE WAY
OF RELIGIOUS WORK

One great difficulty in the missionary work is the number of languages used by the people. The Klallams have one, the Twanas another; about one sixth of the people on the reservation had originally come from Squaxin, and spoke the Nisqually; the Chinook jargon is an intertribal language, which is spoken by nearly all the Indians, except the very old and very young, as far south as Northern California, north into Alaska, west to the Pacific Ocean, and east to Western Idaho. It was made by the early traders, especially the Hudson's Bay Company, out of Chinook, French, and English words, with a few from several other Indian languages, for use in trade. It serves very well for this purpose, and is almost universally used in intercourse between the whites and Indians. Very few whites, even when married to Indian women, have learned to talk any Indian language except this. But it is not very good for conveying religious instruction. It is too meager. Yet so many different languages were spoken by the seven or eight hundred Indians connected with the agency that it seemed to be the only practicable one, and I learned it. I have learned to preach in it quite easily, and so that the Indians say they understand me quite well. The Twana language would have been quite useful, but it is said to be so difficult to learn that no intelligent Indian advised me to learn it. The Nisqually is said to be much easier, and one educated Indian advised me to learn it, but it did seem to me to be wise, for while nearly all the Twana Indians understood it, as, in fact, nearly all the Indians on the upper Sound do, yet it was spoken by very few on the reservation.

Hence I have often used an interpreter while preaching on the Sabbath at Skokomish, for then usually some whites, old Indians, and children were present who could not understand Chinook. At other times and places I constantly used the Chinook language. But a good interpreter is hard to obtain. "It takes a minister to interpret for a minister," was said when Mr. Hallenback, the evangelist, went to the Sandwich Islands and there is much truth in it. The first interpreter I had was good at heart, but he used the Nisqually language. While most of them understood it, yet this person had learned it after he was grown, and spoke it, the Indians said, much like a Dutchman does our language. Another one, a Twana, cut the sentences short, so that one of the school boys said he could have hardly understood all that I said had he not understood English. A third could do well when he tried, but too many times he felt out of sorts and was lazy, and would speak very low and without much life. Hence sometimes I would feel like dismissing all interpreters, and talking in Chinook, but then I was afraid that it would drive away the whites, who could not understand it, but whose presence, for their example's sake, I much desired. I feared also that it would drive away the very old ones, who sometimes made much effort to come to church, and also that the children, whose minds were the most susceptible to impressions, would lose all that was said.   So there were difficulties every way.

The medley of services and babel of languages of one Sabbath are described as follows: The opening exercises were in English, after which was the sermon, which was delivered in English, but translated into the Nisqually language and a prayer was offered in the same manner.   At the close of the service two infants were baptized in English, when followed the communion

service in the same language.   At this there were present 12 white members of the Congregational church here, and one Indian; two white members of the Protestant Methodist church; one Cumberland Presbyterian, and one other Congregationalist.   There were also present about 75 Indians as spectators.   The Sabbath school was held soon after, 75 persons being present.   First, there were four songs in the Chinook jargon; then three in English, accompanied by an organ and violin.   The prayer was in Nisqually, and the lesson was read by all in English, after which the lessons were recited by the scholars.   Five classes of Indian children and two of white children were taught in English and one class partly in English and partly in Chinook jargon.   There was one Bible class of Indian men who understood English, and were taught in that language, a part of whom could read and a part of whom could not, and another of about 40 Indians of both sexes whose teacher talked English, but an interpreter translated it into Nisqually; and then they did not reach some Klallam Indians.   Next followed meeting of the Temperance Society, as six persons wished to join it.   A white man, who could do so, wrote his name and five Indians, who could not, touched the pen while the secretary made their mark.   Three of these were sworn in English and two in Chinook.   The whole services were interspersed with singing in English and Chinook jargon.

The Potlatch is the greatest festival that the Indian has.   It is a Chinook word, and means "to give," and is bestowed as a name to the festival because the central idea of it is a distribution of gifts by a few persons to the many present whom they have invited.   It is generally intertribal, from 400 to 2,000 persons being present, and from one to three, or even ten thousand dollars in money, blankets, guns, canoes, cloth and the like are given away. There is no regularity to the time when they are held.   Three have been held at Skokomish within fifteen years, each one being given by different persons, and during the same time, as far as I know, a part or all of the tribe have been invited to nine others, eight of which some of them have attended.

The mere giving of a present by one person to another, or to several, is not in itself sinful, but this is carried to such an extreme at these times that the morality of that part of them becomes exceedingly questionable. In order to obtain the money to give they deny themselves so much for years, live in old houses and in so poor a way, that the self-denial becomes an enemy to health, comfort, civilization and Christianity. If they would take the same money, buy and improve land, build good houses, furnish them and live decently, it would be far better.

But while two or three days of the time spent at them is occupied in making presents, the rest of the time, from three days to two and a half weeks, is spent in gambling, red and black tamahnous, and other wicked practices, and the temptation to do wrong becomes so great that very few Indians can resist it.

When some of the Alaska Indians, coveting the prosperity which the Christian Indians of that region had acquired, asked one of these Christians what they must do in order to become Christians, the reply was: "First give up your potlatches." It was felt that there was so much evil connected with them that they and Christianity could not flourish together. Among the Twanas, while they are not dead, they are largely on the wane. Among a large part of the Klallams they still flourish.

Intemperance is a besetting sin of Indians, and it is about as much a besetting sin of some whites to furnish intoxicating liquors to the Indians. The laws of the United States and of Washington Territory are stringent against any body's furnishing liquor to the Indians, but for a time previous to 1871 they had by no means been strictly enforced. As the intercourse of the Indians with the whites was often with a low class, who were willing to furnish liquor to them, they grew to love it, so that in 1871 the largest part of the Indians had learned to love liquor. Its natural consequences, fighting, cutting, shooting and accidental deaths, were frequent.

From: TEMPERANCE

In 1871 the agent began to enforce the laws against the selling of liquor to the Indians, and, according to a rule of the Indian Department, he also punished the Indians for drinking. Missionary influence went hand in hand with his work, and good results have followed. For years very few Indians on the reservation have been known to be drunk. Punishment upon the liquor-drinker as well as the liquor-seller has had a good effect. Far more of the Klallams drink than of the Twanas. They live so far from the agent that he cannot know of all their drinking, and, if he did, he could not go to arrest them all; and many of them live so close to large towns where liquor is very easily obtained, that it has been impossible to stop all of their drinking. Still his occasional visits, the aid of a few white men near them, and of the better

Indians, together with what they see of the evil effects of intemperance on themselves, have greatly checked the evil. Very few complete reformations, however, have taken place among those away from the reservation, except those who have become Christians. In addition, a good share of the younger ones have grown up with so much less temptation than their parents had, and so much more influence in favor of temperance, that they have become teetotalers.

For a long time, beginning with 1874, a temperance society flourished, and nearly all the Indians of both tribes joined it. Each member signed the pledge under oath, and took that pledge home to keep, but in time it was found that the society had no penalty with which to punish offenders sufficient to make them fear much to do so again. The agent alone had that power - so the society died. But the law and gospel did not tire in the work and something has been accomplished.

The agent could tell many a story of prosecuting liquor-sellers; sometimes before a packed jury, who, when the proof was positive, declared the prisoner not guilty; of having Indians witnesses tampered with, and bought either by money or threats, so that they would not testify in court, although to him they had previously given direct testimony as to who had furnished them with the liquor; of a time when some of the Klallam Indians became so independent of his authority that they defied him when he went to arrest them, and he was obliged to use the revenue cutter in order to take them, and when, in consequence, his friends feared that his life was in danger from the white liquor-sellers, because the latter feared the result of their lawlessness; of a judge who, although a Christian man, so allowed his sympathies to go out for the criminal that he would strain the law to let him go; or, on the other hand, of another judge who would strain the law to catch a rascal; of convicting eight white men at one time of selling liquor to Indians, only to have some of them take their revenge by burning the Indians' houses and all of their contents. Still, in a few years he made it very unsafe for most permanent residents to sell intoxicating liquors to the Indians, so that but few except transient people, as sailors and travelers, dared to do so.

"For ways that are dark and tricks that are vain" the Indian and the liquor-seller can almost rival the "heathen Chinee." A saloon is on the beach, and so high that it is easy to go under it. A small hole is in the floor under the counter. A hand comes up with some money in it: after dark a bottle goes down, and some Indians are drunk, but nobody can prove anything wrong. An Indian takes a bucket of clams into a saloon and asks the bar-tender if he wishes them. "I will see what my wife says," is the reply, and he takes them to a back room. Soon he comes back and says: "Here, take your old clams, they are bad and rotten." The Indians takes them, and soon a company of Indians are "gloriously drunk," a bottle having been put in the bottom of the bucket. Sometimes a part of a sack of flour is made of a bottle of whiskey.

An Indian, having been taken up for drunkenness, was asked in court, in Port Townsend, where he obtained his liquor. "If I tell, I cannot get any more," was the blunt reply. Others have found theirs floating in the river or lying by a tree, which may all have been true, yet some man who understood it was the gainer of some money, which perhaps he found. Many an Indian, when asked who let him have the liquor, has said: "I do not know;" or, "I do not know his name."

Yet there are stories on the other side which make a brighter picture....A subchief of the Klallam Indians at Elwha, 120 miles from the reservation, in 1878 found that an Indian from British Columbia had brought a keg of liquor among his people. He immediately complained before a justice of the peace, who arrested the guilty man, emptied his liquor on the ground, and fined him 64 dollars.

The head chief of the Klallams, Lord James Balch, has for nine years so steadily opposed drinking, and imprisoned and fined the offenders so much, that he excited the enmity of the Indians, and even of their doctors, and also of some white men, much as a good Indian agent does. Although he is not perfect, he still continues the good work. Fifteen years ago he was among the worst Indians about, drinking, cutting, and fighting.

In January 1878, I was asked to go 90 miles, by both Klallams and Twanas, to a potlatch to protect them from worthless whites and Indians who were ready to take liquor to the place. The potlatch was at Dungeness, given by some Klallams. I went, in company with about 75 Twanas, and it was not known that more than eight of them had tasted liquor within four years, although none of them professed to be Christians. During that festival, which continued nine days, and where more than 500 Indians were present, only one Indian was drunk.

More than once a whiskey bottle has been captured from an Indian, set out in full view of all on a stump or box, a temperance speech made and a temperance hymn sung, the bottle broken into many pieces, and the contents spilled on the ground.

The Indians say that the Hudson's Bay Company first brought it to them, but dealt it out very sparingly, but when the Americans came they brought barrels of it. They seem to be proud that it is not the Indians who manufacture it, for if it were they would soon put a stop to it; nor is it the believer in God, but wicked white men who wish to clear them away as trees are cleared from the ground.

Thus, when we take into consideration the condition of these Indians 15 years ago, and the present condition of some other Indians in the region who lie beastly drunk in open sight, and compare it with the present status of those now here, there is reason for continued faith in the God of the law and gospel of temperance.

From: INDUSTRIES

....The Klallams have done very little logging or farming. A number have obtained land at Port Discovery, Jamestown, Elwha and Klallam Bay, but only a little of it is first class land, and they have used it for gardens and as a place for a permanent home, so that they should not be driven from one place to another, more than for farming. At Seabeck, Port Gamble, Port Townsend and Port Discovery, they work quite constantly in the saw mills;

at Jamestown, for the surrounding farmers; at Port Angeles, Elwha and Klallam Bay, more of them hunt and fish than elsewhere. A number earn considerable money taking freight and passengers in their canoes. The obtaining of dog fish oil is something of a business, as logging camps use a large amount of it. In September there is employment at the Puyallup and surrounding region, about 90 miles from Skokomish, in picking hops. Hop raising has grown to be a large business among the whites, and Indians have been preferred for picking the hops, thousands of whom flock there every year for the purpose, from every part of the Sound, and even from British Columbia and the Yakama country. Old people, women and children do as well at this as able bodied men. It has not, however, always been a healthy place for their morals, as on Sundays and evenings gambling, betting and horse racing have been largely carried on. At one time "The Devil's Playground," in Puyallup Valley was noted as the place where Indians and low whites gathered on the Sabbath for horse racing and gambling, but it became such a nuisance to the hop growers, as well as to the agents, that they combined and closed it. A part of the Klallams earn considerable money by sealing, off the northwest coast of the Territory, a very profitable business generally from January to May. In 1883 the taxes of those Klallams who live in Klallam County were $168.30.

FROM: TITLES TO THEIR LAND

"The plow and the bible go together in civilizing Indians," is the remark of Rev. J.H. Wilbur, who for more than 20 years was one of the most successful workers among them: but neither Indians nor whites feel much like clearing land and plowing it unless they feel sure that the land is theirs.

When the treaty was made in 1855 it was the understanding that whenever the Indians should settle down on the reservation, adopt civilized habits, and clear a few acres of land, good titles would be given to them by the government. With this understanding, not long after Agent Eells took charge, he had the reservation surveyed and divided, so that each head of a family whose home was on the reservation should have a fair portion. He gave them papers, signed by himself, in 1874, describing the land, with the expectation that the government in a short time would give them good titles, he having been thus assured by his superiors in office. Other agents did the same. But new movements by the government with reference to the Indians are usually very slow, as they have no votes, and this was no exception.

Agent Eells, as well as others, pleaded time and again, to have this stipulation in the treaty fulfilled, but for a long time to no purpose. Often he had no reply to his letters. People of both political parties put this as a plank into their platform; those of all religions and no religion; those who opposed the peace policy as well as those who favored it, signed petitions to this effect, but in vain. This delay was the source of much uneasiness to the Indians, more, I think, than any other cause, for men were not wanting who told them that they would be moved away; there were plenty of people who coveted their land, and examples were not wanting of Indians who had been moved from place to place by the government. It has been the only thing which has ever caused them to talk about war. Some Indians left the reservation because they feared they would be moved away. "I am not going to clear land and fence it for the whites to use," was what one said and others felt.

When the treaty was made it was believed by the Indians that they possessed all the land, and that they sold all except the reservation, to which they supposed they had a good title, at least as good as the United States had, and white people believed the same; but a decision of the Supreme Court of the United States in 1873 reversed this idea, and they learned that they had sold all the land, and that the government graciously allowed them to stay on the reservation according to its will. In the spring of 1875 they were forbidden to cut a log and sell it off of the reservation, and found that they had no rights to the land which the government was bound to respect, but if she wished to remove them at any time she could do so.

The question came up early in missionary work. The Indians said: "You profess to be Christians, and you have promised us titles to our land. If these titles come we will believe your religion to be true, but if not it will be evidence that you are deceiving us...."

In March 1881, certificates of allotment were sent to the Indians. They were not wholly satisfactory. The title to the land still remained in the United States. They said that each Indian is entitled to take possession of his land, "and the United States guarantees such possession, and will hold the title thereto in trust for the exclusive use and benefit of himself and his heirs so long as such occupancy shall continue." It prohibited them from selling the land to anyone except other members of the same tribe.

These certificates, however, proved to be better than was at first feared. It was decided that under them the Indians had a right to sell the timber from the land. The Indians were satisfied that they would not be removed, and were quieted.

The Klallam Indians have bought their land or taken it by homestead, and so have not had the same difficulty in regard to titles. One incident, however, was rather discouraging.   Four of the Klallam Bay Indians, in 1879, determined to secure, if possible, the land on which their houses stood. They were sent to the clerk of the Probate court, who knew nothing about the land, but told them that it belonged to the government, and offered to get it for the usual fee, $19 each. They paid him the $76, and he promised to send it to the land office and have their papers for them in two weeks. They waited the two weeks but no papers came. In the meantime they learned that the man was not to be trusted, although he could lawfully attend to the business, and that the land had been owned by private individuals for 15 years. He, too, on writing to the land office, found the same to be true. But the difficulty was to get the money back.   This man was an inveterate gambler, and the evidence was quite plain that he had gambled the money off very soon after he received it. I saw him soon afterward, and he told me that it had been stolen, that he would soon get it, and the like. One Indian spent three weeks, and two others two weeks each, in trying to recover it, but failed to do so.   Then the agent took it into court, but through an unjust ruling of the judge, or a catch in the law, he was neither compelled to pay it nor punished for his deed. The Indians received about the amount they lost, as witness fees and mileage for their attendance on court. Yet that man, at that time, was also postmaster, United States Commissioner, and deputy sheriff, and had offered $50 dollars to the county treasurer, to be appointed his deputy.

This was a strange contrast to the action of the Indians. I felt very sorry for them. For four years we had been advising them to obtain land, and they were swindled in their first attempt. When I saw them, before the case was taken to the court, I was fearful lest they should become discouraged, and offered them $10, saying "If you never get your money, I will lose this with you: but if you do obtain it, you can then repay me."   One tenth of my income has long been given to the Lord, and I felt that thus much would do as much good here as anywhere. When I first mentioned this to them, they refused to take it, saying that they did not wish me to lose my money, if they did theirs; but two weeks later, when I left the last one of them, he reluctantly took it.

From: EDUCATION

There was no provision in the treaty for more than one school, and that on the reservation. But after the Klallams at Jamestown had bought their land, laid out their village, built their church, and become somewhat civilized, they pleaded so hard for a school, offering the use of the church building for the purpose, that the government listened to them, and in 1878 sent them a teacher. This was a day school, because funds enough were furnished to pay only a teacher, and nearly all the children lived in the village within less than a half mile from the school. A very few of the children walked daily five or six miles to school, and some of the better families of the village did nobly in making sacrifices to board their relations, when the parents would not furnish even the food for their children. This school has varied in numbers from 15 to 30 children, and has been conducted in other respects mainly onthe same principles as the one on the reservation. It has been of great advantage to the settlement.

A few of the rest of the Klallam children, whose parents were Catholics, have sent their children to a boarding school at Tulalip, a Catholic agency, and others have not gone to school, there being difficulties in the way which it has been almost or quite impossible to overcome.

FROM: VARIETY

On one tour among the Klallams, I find the following: When three miles from home, the first duty was to stop and attend the funeral of a white man. Forty five miles on, the evening of the next day until late at night, was spent in assisting one of the government employees in holding court over four Indians, who had been drunk; a fifth had escaped to British Columbia and was safe from trial. This kind of business occasionally comes in as an aid to the agent. I seldom have anything to do with it on the reservation, as the agent can attend to it; but when off from the reservation, where neither of us can be more than once in six months or thereabouts it sometimes saves him much trouble and expense, and seems to do as much good as a sermon. It is of but little use to preach to drunken Indians, and a little law sometimes helps the gospel. The agent reciprocates by talking gospel to them on the Sabbath on his trips.

On reaching Jamestown, the afternoon was spent in introducing an Indian from British Columbia, who had taken me there is his canoe, to the Klallam Indians and the school; and in comforting two parents, Christian Indians, whose youngest child lay at the point of death. The next day she died, and, as no minister had ever been among these Indians at any previous funeral, they needed some instruction. So it was my duty to assist in digging the grave and making the coffin, comfort them and attend the funeral in a snow storm.

The Sabbath was spent in holding two services with them, one of them being mainly a service of song; and, as there was a part of the day unoccupied, at the request of the whites nearby I gave them a sermon. The next day I found that "Blue Monday" must be adjourned. Years ago the Indians purchased their land, but owing to a mistake of the surveyor, it was necessary that the deeds should be made out again. So, in order to get all the Indians together who were needed, with the proper officer, I walked 14 miles, rode six in a canoe, and then, after half past three o'clock, saw that 19 deeds were properly signed, which required 62 signatures, besides the witnessing, acknowledging, and filing of them, which required 76 more signatures. The plat of their town - Jamestown - was also filed and recorded. When this was done, I assisted the Indians to obtain two marriage licenses, after which we went to the church, where I addressed them on two different subjects, and then the two weddings took place, and by nine o'clock we were done.

The monotony of the next day was varied by a visit to the school; helping the chief to select a burying-ground (for their dead had been buried in various places); a walk of ten miles and a wedding of a white couple, who have been very kind to me in my work there, one of them being a member of the Jamestown church.

On my way home, while waiting for the steamers to connect at Port Gamble, I took a trip of about fifty miles, to Port Madison and back, to help in finishing the Indian census of 1880 for General F. A. Walker and Major J.W. Powell; and then on my way home, by the kindness of the captain of the steamer, who waited half an hour for me, I was able to assist the chief in capturing and taking to the reservation the fifth Indian at Port Gamble who had been drunk, and had, by that time, returned from the British side.

The variety of another trip in 1878 is thus recorded: as to food, I have done my own cooking, eaten dry crackers only for meals, been boarded several days for nothing, and bought meals. As to sleeping, I have stayed in as good a bed as could be given me for nothing, and slept in my own blankets in an Indian canoe, because the houses of the whites were too far away and the fleas were too thick in the Indian houses. They were bad enough in the canoe, but the Indians would not allow me to go farther away, for fear that the panthers would catch me. As to work, I have preached, held prayer meetings, done pastoral work, helped clean up the streets of Jamestown, been carpenter and painter, dedicated a church, performing all the parts, been church organist, studied science, acted for the agent, and taken hold of law in a case where whiskey had been sold to an Indian, and also in making a will. As to traveling, I have been carried 90 miles in a canoe by Indians, free, paid an Indian four dollars for carrying me twenty miles, have been carried 20 more by a steamer at half fare, and 20 more on another for nothing, have rode on horseback, walked 50 miles, and "paddled my own canoe" for 45 more.

I have never had a vacation since I have been here, unless such things as these may be called vacation. They are recreation, work, and vacation, all at once. They are variety, and that is rest, the vacation a person needs, with the satisfaction that a person is doing something at the same time.

FROM: MARRIAGE AND DIVORCE

The Indian idea of the marriage bond is that it is not very strong. They have been accustomed to get married young, often at 14 or 16 years of age, to pay for their wives in money and articles to the value of several hundred dollars, and the men have had, oftentimes, two or three wives.

When they married young, in order that two young fools should not be married together, often a boy was married to an elderly woman, and a young girl to an elderly man, so that the older one could take care of the younger, with the expectation that when the younger one should grow older if they did not like each other they should be divorced.

Such ideas naturally did not suit the government, the agent, or the Bible. The agent has had about all the children of school age in school, and thus had control of them, so that they could not get married as young as formerly. In 1883 the government sent word to prevent the purchase of any more wives, and this has been generally acquiesced in by the Skokomish Indians. Some of the Klallam Indians, however, are so far from the agent, and are so backward in civilization, that it has not been possible to enforce these two points among them as thoroughly as among the Twanas.

The Commissioner of Indian Affairs, in his report for 1878, recommended the passage of a law compelling all Indians who were living together as man and wife to be married. The law has not been made, but the agent worked on the same principles long before 1878 - indeed ever after he first took charge in 1871. He urged them to be married, making for a time special presents from government annuities to those who should consent, as a shawl or ladies' hat, and some consented. Only two couples had been thus married when I went there. It seemed rather comical on the Fourth of July, 1874, when I had been on the reservation only about two weeks, to be asked to join in marriage seven couples, some of whom had children. One Sabbath in 1883 a couple stood up to be married, the bride having a baby in her arms, and she would probably have held it during the ceremony had not my wife whispered to a sister of the bride to go and get it. During the ten years I have married 26 couples among the Twanas, and 29 couples among the Klallams, and a number of other Klallams have been married by other persons. Some very comical incidents have occurred in connection with some of these ceremonies. In 1876 I was called upon to marry 11 couples at Jamestown. All went well with the first ten, the head chief being married first, so that the others might see how it was done, and then nine couples stood up and were married with the same set of words. But the wife of the other man was sick with the measles. She had taken cold and they had been driven in, but had come out again, so that she was as red as a beet. Still they were afraid that she would die, and as I was not to be there again for several months they were very anxious to be married so as to legalize the children. She was so near death that they had moved here from their good house to a mat-house, which was filled with smoke. The fire was thrown out, and soon it became less smoky. She was too sick to stand, and only barely able to sit up. This, however, she managed to do in her bed, which was on the ground.

Her husband sat beside her and took her hand, and I married them, measles and all. She afterward recovered.

FROM: THE CENSUS OF 1880

In the fall of 1880 the government sent orders to the agent to take the census of all the Indians under him for the United States decennial census. To do so among the Klallams was the most difficult task, as they were scattered for a 150 miles, and the season of the year made it disagreeable, with a probability of its being dangerous on the waters of the lower Sound in a canoe. I was then almost ready to start on a tour amongst a part of them and the agent offered to pay my expenses if I would combine this with my missionary work. He said that it was almost impossible for him to go; that none of the employees were acquainted either with the country or the large share of the Indians; that he should have to pay the expenses of someone; and that it would be a favor if I could do it. I consented, for it was a favor to me to have my expenses paid, while I should have an opportunity to visit all of the Indians; but it was December before I was fairly able to begin the work and it required four weeks.

In early life I had read a story about taking the census among some of the ignorant people of the Southern States and the superstitious fear that they had of it, and I thought that it would not be strange if the Indians should have the same fear. My previous acquaintance with them and especially the intimacy I had with a few from nearly every settlement who had been brought to the reservation for drinking and had been with us for some time and whose confidence I seemed to have gained, I found to be of great advantage in the work. Had it not been for these, I would have found it a very difficult task.

The questions to be asked were many - 48 in number including their Indian as well as "Boston" names, the meaning of these, the age and occupation; whether or not a full blood of the tribe; how long since they had habitually worn citizen's dress; whether they had been vaccinated or not; whether or not they could read and write; the number of horses, cattle, sheep, swine, dogs, and firearms owned; the amount of land owned or occupied; the number of years they had been self supporting, and the percent of support obtained from civilized industries and in other ways.

I began the work at Port Gamble one evening and after much talk secured names, but the next forenoon I only obtained six. The men were at work in the mill, and the women, afraid, were not to be found. I then hired an interpreter, a boy who had been in school, and after talking a while had no more difficulty there. The best argument I could use why it was required was that some people said they were nothing by worthless Indians, and that it was useless to try to civilize them; that some of us thought differently and wished for facts to prove it, and when found, that they would be published to the world. And this I did in the Port Townsend Argus and American Antiquarian. One man refused to give me any information because that, years before, a census had been taken and soon after there had been much sickness, and he was afraid that if his name were written down he would die. But I easily obtained the information most needed from others. I was almost through, and was at Seabeck, the last town before reaching home, when I found the only one who was at all saucy. He gave me false names and false information generally, as I soon learned from another Indian present and it was afterward corrected. The ages of the older ones were all unknown, but the treaty with the tribe was made 25 years previous, and every man, woman and child was present who possible could be, and I could generally find out about how large they were then. When I asked the age of one man he said two years, but he said he had 200 guns. He was about 43 years old and had only one gun. To obtain the information about vaccination was the most difficult, as the instructions were that they should show me the scars on the arm if they had been vaccinated, and many of them were ashamed to do this. As far as I knew, none of them made a false statement. When about half way through I met Mr. H. W. Henshaw, who had been sent from Washington to give general information about the work, and he absolved them from the requirement of showing the scar. He said that all that was needed was to satisfy myself on the point. On this coast, a dime is called a bit, although in reality a bit is half a quarter, and the Indians so understand it. In finding how nearly a pure Klallam one man was, I was informed that he was partly Klallam and partly of another tribe. But when I tried to find out how much of the other tribe I was told: "Not much; a bit, I guess."

I was instructed to take the names of not only those who were at home, but of a number who were across the straits on the British side, whose residence might properly be said to be on this side. In asking about one man I was told that he had moved away a long time ago, very long, two thousand years, probably, and so was not a member of the tribe.

It struck me that some pictures of myself, with descriptions of them would have adorned Harper's Monthly as well as any of Porte Crayon's sketches. With an old Indian man and his wife I sat on the beach in Port Discovery Bay all day waiting for the wind to die down, because it was unsafe to proceed in a canoe with the snow coming down constantly on one of the coldest days of the year, with a mat up on one side to keep a little of the wind off, and a small fire on the other side; and, at last, we had to give up and return to Port Discovery, as the wind would not die. I waked up one morning on the steamer *Dispatch* to have a drop of water come directly into my eye, for there was a hard rain, and the steamer overhead (not underneath) was leaky. I got up to find my shirt so wet that I dared not put it on, while the water in the stateroom above me was half an inch deep and was shoveled out with a dustpan. I walked from the west to the east end of Klallam Bay, only two miles, but while trying to find a log across the Klallam River I wandered about a long time in the woods and brush, wet with a heavy rain, and when I did find it it reached just not across the river, but within a few feet of the bank, and I stood deliberating whether it was safe or not to make the jump; trying to jump and not quite daring to run the risk of falling into the river, sticking my toes and fingers into the bank and the lake, but at last made the crossing safely. It took half a day to travel those two miles. I ate a Sunday dinner at Elwha, between church services, of some crumbs of sweet cake out of a 50 pound flour sack, so fine that I had to squeeze them up in my hands in order to get them into my mouth. An apple and a little jelly finished the repast - the last food I had. At Port Angeles I rode along the

beach on horseback at high tide, and at one time in trying to ford a slough I found we were swimming in the water. I partly dried out at an Indian house nearby, taking the census at the same time. Again, the steamer *Dispatch* rolled in a gale, while the water came over the gunwales, the food and plates slid off the tables, the milk spilt into gum boots, the wash dish of water upset into a bed, and ten minutes after I left her at Dungeness the wind blew her ashore, dragging her anchors. But there were also some special providences on the trip. "He who will notice providences will have providences to notice," someone has said, and I was reminded of this several times. I came in a canoe from Klallam Bay to Elwha, the most dangerous part of the route, with the water so smooth that a small skiff would have safely rode the whole distance, 35 miles, to have a heavy storm come the next day, and a heavy gale, when I again went on the water, but then a steamer was ready to carry me. The last week, on coming from Jamestown home, in a canoe, I had pleasant weather and a fair north wind to blow me home the whole time, only to have it begin to rain an hour after I reached home, the commencement of a storm which lasted a week. Strange that a week's north wind should bring a week's rain. I have never noticed the fact at any other time.

The statistical information obtained in this census is as follows:

In the Klallam tribe there were then 158 men, 172 women, 86 boys, and 69 girls; a total of 485 persons. Six were on or near the reservation, 10 near Seabeck, 96 at Port Gamble, six at Port Ludlow, 22 at Port Discovery, 12 at Port Townsend, 18 at Sequim, 86 at Jamestown, 36 at or near Dungeness. (Those at Sequim and near Dungeness were all within six miles of Jamestown). Fifty seven at Port Angeles (but a large share of them were across the straits on the British side), 67 at Elwha, 24 at Pyscht, and 49 at or near Klallam Bay. There were 290 full-blooded Klallams among them, and the rest were intermingled with 18 other tribes. Fifteen were part white. During the year previous to October 1, 1880, there had been 11 births and nine deaths. Forty one had been in school during the previous year, 49 could read and 42 write; 135 could talk English so as to be understood, of whom 69 were adults; 65 had no Indian name; 33 out of 123 couples had been legally married.

They owned 10 horses, 31 cattle, five sheep, 97 swine, 584 domestic fowls, and 137 guns and pistols, most of them being shotguns. Thirty four were laborers in saw mills; 22 were farmers. There were 80 fishermen, 23

laborers, 17 sealers, 15 canoe men, six canoe makers, six hunters, three policemen, 11 medicine men, four medicine women, one carpenter, two wood choppers, one blacksmith, and 40 of the women were mat and basket makers. Twenty eight persons owned 576 acres of land with a patented title, four more owned 475 acres by homestead, and twenty two persons, representing 104 persons in their families, cultivated 46 acres.

During the year they raised 2,036 bushels of potatoes, 14 tons of hay, 26 bushels of oats, 258 bushels of turnips, 148 bushels of wheat, 20 bushels of apples, five of plums, and four of small fruit. They had 113 frame houses, valued by estimate at $5,650, four log houses, worth $100, 29 outhouses, as barns, chicken houses, and canoe houses, two jails, and two churches. They cut 250 cords of wood; received $1,994 for sealing, $646 for salmon, and $1,000 for work in the Port Discovery mill. I was not able to learn what they had earned at the Seabeck and Port Gamble sawmills. Two hundred and eleven of them were out of the smoke when at home. I estimated that on an average they obtained 72 percent of their living from civilized food, the extremes being 50 and 100 percent.

FROM: COOK HOUSE BILLY

He will always be known by this name, probably, though on the church roll his name is written as William House Cook. He is a Klallam Indian, of Jamestown. His early life was wild and dissipated, he being, like all the rest of his tribe, addicted to drunkenness. At one time, when he was living at Port Discovery, he became quite drunk. He was on the opposite side of the bay from the mill, and, wishing for more whiskey, he started across in a canoe for it; but he was so drunk that he had not gone far before he upset his canoe, and had it not been for his wife, who was on shore and went to his rescue, he would have been drowned.

In his early life he mingled much with the whites. He lived with a good white family some of the time; worked in a cook house at a saw mill for a time, where he gained his name; and once went to San Francisco in a ship. Thus he learned to speak English quite well, and he knew more about civilized ways, and even of religion, than any of the older Indians at Jamestown. He entered willingly into the plan to buy land, and soon after the people there first began to hold some kind of services on the Sabbath, they selected him as the one to pray, hardly because he was better than all the rest, though he was better than all with two or three exceptions, but because he had been more with the whites, and knew better how to pray. Soon after this, and long before he joined the church, a report, which was probably true, was in circulation that he had once or twice secretly drank some. Thereupon the chief took him and talked strongly to him about it.

The chief did not wish him to be minister to his people if he was likely to do in that way, and at last asked him if he thought he had a strong enough mind to be a Christian for one year. The reply was, Yes. Then the questions were successively asked if he was strong enough to last two years, five years, 10 years, all his life, and when he said Yes, he was allowed to resume his duties as leader of religion.

After this he remained so consistent that he was one of the first two in Jamestown to unite with the church, in December 1878, when he was supposed to be about 33 years old. The road supervisor in his district sent his receipt for road taxes to him one year, addressing it to Rev. Cook House Billy.

When the church was organized at Jamestown in 1882, he was unanimously elected as deacon, and he has ever since filled that position.

Once, five or six years ago, when in Seattle, he was asked by a Catholic Indian of his own tribe, belonging to Port Gamble, to drink some whiskey, but he declined. When urged time and again to do so he still refused, giving as his excuse that he belonged to the church. "So do I," said his tempter; "but we drink, and then we can easily get the priest to pardon us by paying him a little money." "That is not the way we do in our church," said Billy.

But afterward, two years ago, he was very strongly tempted, and yielded, while at Seattle. It was known, and soon after his return home he made his acknowledgement to the church. On my next visit to them in the fall he was reprimanded, and suspended as deacon for five weeks. He often spoke of this fall of his, and seemed to be very sincere in his repentance. In 1883, just before he and nearly all the Indians of his village were going to Seattle, again, either to fish or on their way to pick hops, he sent me a letter in which was written: "One day I was talking in meeting to them and said I hoped they would none of them follow my example last summer about drinking, for I had never got over it. I feel ashamed and feel bad every time I think about it, and hoped none of them would have occasion to feel as I did.

He is of a bright, sunny disposition, always cheerful, and has done more for school and church than any of the rest of his tribe, unless it may be the head chief, Balch. Sometimes he has boarded three children free of cost, so that they might go to school, whose parents, if alive, lived far away.

In 1881 two of his children died, a fact of which the opponents of religion made use against Christianity, and he was severely tried, but he stood firm. In 1883, with two others, he went to Klallam Bay with me to preach the gospel to those Indians, the first actual missionary work done by either Indian church. When he left his wife was sick; but, as he had promised to go, she would not keep him back, and he was willing to trust her with God. When we returned she was well.

His wife is a true helpmeet to him. She did not join the church for a year and a half after he did; but he afterward said that she was really ahead of him, and urged him to begin and to stand fast. When I examined her for reception into the church, I noticed one expression of hers which I shall always remember. In speaking of her sorrow for her sins, she said that her "heart cried" about them. An expression was in use, which I also often used, that our hearts should be sick because of our sins; but I had never used her expression, which was deeper. She is the foremost among the women to take part in meeting, often beseeching them with tears to turn into the Christian path.

FROM: LORD JAMES BALCH

A few years previous to the appointment of Agent Eells, in 1871, this person was made head chief of the Klallams, although, until about 1873, he could get drunk and fight as well as any Indian. At that time he took the lead in the progress for civilization near Dungeness...and, although once after that, on a Fourth of July, he was drunk, yet he has steadily worked for the good of his tribe. He has had a noted name, for an Indian, as an enemy to drunkenness, and his fines and other punishments on his offending people have been heavy. He gave more than any other one in the purchase of their land, and, in 1875, it was named Jamestown in honor of him. He has taken a stand against potlatches, not even going six miles to attend one when given by those under him. For a long time he was firm against Indian doctors, though a few times within about three years he has employed them when he has been sick, and no white man's remedies which he could obtain seemed to do him any good. He was among the first three Indians to begin prayer, a practice which he kept up several years. But when, in 1878, the other two united with the church, Balch declined to do so, although I had expected him as much as I had the others. He gave as his excuse that as he was chief he would probably do something which would be used as an argument against religion - an idea I have found quite common among the Indian officers. In fact, a policeman once asked me if he could be a policeman and a Christian at the same time. Balch said that whenever he should cease being chief, he would "jump" into the church. He has continued as chief until the present time, and his interest in religion has diminished. At, one time he seemed, in the opinion of the school teacher, to trust to his morality for salvation. Then he turned to the Indian doctors, gave up prayer in his house, and now by no means attends church regularly. Still he takes a kind of fatherly interest in seeing that the church members walk straight; and the way in which he started and has upheld civilization, morality, education, and temperance will long be remembered both by whites and Indians, and its influence will continue long after he shall die.

FROM: TOURING

Once I was obliged to stay in one of their houses in the winter, a thing I have seldom done, unless there is no white man's house near, even in the summer, when I have preferred to take my blankets and sleep outside. The Indians have said that they are afraid the panthers will eat me; but between the fleas, rats, and smoke (for they often keep their old fashioned houses full of smoke all night), sleep is not refreshing, and the next morning I feel more like a piece of bacon than a minister.

Traveling in February with about seventy five Indians, it was necessary that I should stay all night in an Indian house to protect them from unprincipled white men. The Indians at the village where we stayed were as kind as could be, assigning me to their best house, where there was no smoke; giving me a feather bed, white sheets, and all very good except the fleas. Before I went to sleep I killed four, in two or three hours I waked up and killed 14, at three o'clock 11 more, and in the morning I left without looking to see how many there were remaining.But Indian houses are not the only unpleasant ones. Here we are at a hotel, the best in a saw mill town of four or five hundred people; but the barroom is filled with tobacco smoke, almost as thick as the smoke from the fire which often fills an Indian house. Here about fifty men spend a great portion of the night, and some of them all night, in drinking, gambling, and smoking. The house is accustomed to it, for the rooms directly over the barroom are saturated with smoke, and I am assigned to one of these rooms. Before I get to sleep the smoke has so filled my nostrils that I cannot breathe through them, and at midnight I wake up with a headache so severe that I can scarcely hold up my head for the next 24 hours. It is not so bad, however, but that I can do a little thinking on this wise: Who are the lowest – the Indians, or these whites? The smoke is of equal thickness: that of the Indians, however, is clean smoke from wood; that of the whites, filthy from tobacco. The Indian has sense enough to make holes in the roof where some of it may escape; the white man does not even do that much. The Indian sits or lies near the ground, underneath a great portion of it; the white man puts a portion of his guests and his ladies' parlor directly over it. Sleeping in the Indian smoke I come out well, although feeling like smoked bacon, and a thorough wash cures it; but sleeping in that of the white man I come out sick, and the brain has to be washed.

INDIAN SHAKERS

Commentary

The Indian Shaker Church should not be confused with the Euro American Shakers, a Christian group in the eastern United States which originated in England in 1772. The Indian Shaker Church is a blend of Christian and native religion that originated in lower Puget Sound in the 1820s. It was founded by John Slocum, a Puget Sound Squaxin man in his 40s who, it is claimed, died and came back to life.

After his resurrection, Slocum claimed he was reborn to instruct his people how to live the right kind of Christian life so they could enter heaven. He also promised that God would send them some powerful medicine.

About a year later Slocum fell ill and almost died a second time. His wife, in her distress, tried to help him. At one point something "hot came over her and she started to shake" (Gunther, 1949). With this shaking came the power to heal, and when Slocum recovered he knew that this was the promised medicine.

This curing function was probably the most important feature of the Indian Shaker Church in that it restored the old "Indian curing" outlawed in 1871 by the Superintendent of Indian Affairs of Washington Territory. White doctors were usually remote, expensive and basically inaccessible to most native people.

Shakerism replaced the traditional shaman doctor with a collective spirit that revived the magical, ecstatic, visionary kind of healing formerly practiced by shamans, and now banned.

> The sick or ailing person (man, woman or child) is put in a chair or a bed, and the operators gather about. A general situation appropriate for a cure is brought about by arranging candles, crosses and religious pictures, and by singing and praying. The assumption on the part of the believers is that sickness is produced by sin, sin being something that can be bodily removed from a person by manipulation. When the

patient...is in the proper frame of mind, they pass their hands over his body, gradually working the sinfulness *to his extremities and then* gathering it in their hands and "throwing it away"...the people who treat the sick...very often have the shaking visitation to such a degree that they are completely lifted out of themselves, becoming suffused with religious emotion, and ringing the bells in a perfect fury, and not seldom losing their senses (Waterman, 1922).

This is clearly a survival of the shamanistic method of curing through taking out the disease, believed to be a substance within the patient which the medicine man is able to draw out and remove. The overlay of Christian doctrine gave the church respectability in the surrounding white society and allowed this healing function to flourish, despite some official opposition.

Stories of curing and of finding lost people and objects abound in contemporary accounts by church members. But while the old Indian doctors charged for their work and could also use their medicine against people, Shakers never charged for their curing services and would not use it negatively; believing God sent this medicine so that all people could benefit. Slocum declared that, unlike shamanism, Shakerism was free for all to practice and entirely benevolent (Gunther, 1949).

The Shaker Church was a curious amalgam of the new and the old, the modern Christian and old shamanistic Indian religions. Slocum's death, resurrection and revelations parallel in some ways the traditional spirit quest, but resulted in possession by the God of Christianity rather than a guardian spirit. It was an "extraordinary blend of old shamanistic performances with Catholic ritual and Protestant doctrine" (Gunther, 1949).

Unlike other Messianic reform cults which sprang up across the west, including the Plains Ghost Dancers, the Plateau Prophet Dance and the Smohalla movement, the Shaker religion had more Christian elements and also lacked any anti-white feeling. The church ritual combined elements of the Catholic mass and the Congregational prayer-meeting, including an altar covered with white cloth, cross and hand bells, pictures of Mary, the Savior and the Sacred Heart, sermons and prayers.

One researcher declared that the Shaker Church may have been of considerable historical importance because it was probably the "first Native institution that successfully defied White authority, particularly the religious authority of the orthodox Christian churches" (Suttles, 1987). But another researcher (Castile, 1990) has shown how a supposed friend of the Shakers, one Judge James Wickersham, capitalized on this aspect. His efforts in behalf of the Shakers were actually "part of a long campaign to discredit the agent [Edwin Eells] and promote the opening of the Puyallup reservation to whites."

Despite the best efforts of the Rev. Myron Eells, Christianity never enjoyed much acceptance by the Klallam. After twenty years of missionary work on the Skokomish Reservation his congregation was still meager.

> It would appear that he had only 65 members after 20 years and not all of these were Indians. Writing in 1898 he estimated that the Shaker Religion had six hundred to eight hundred members, a startling contrast to his own limited success....Myron in some ways seems to have approved of the [Shaker] Church and...credits it repeatedly with achieving the aims of promoting and sustaining temperance as well as discouraging gambling....and other forms of debauchery (Castile, 1985).

Meanwhile, the Indian Shaker Church won converts as far north as southern British Columbia, as far south as the Klamath Reservation in Oregon and extended even to some Columbia Plateau tribes such as the Yakima.

A PORTFOLIO OF KLALLAM PHOTOS

The following selection of photographs is from the collection of the Jefferson County Historical Society. Several feature the work of Joe McKissick and William Wilcox. Both men have provided a rich legacy of images and insights into Klallam life in the late 19th and early 20th centuries.

A people of dignity and beauty gaze at us from these photos. Here are the elders who witnessed the transition from aboriginal to post-contact times, and their children born into a radically different world.

In each photo the influence of the white culture is evident: modern dress, milled lumber and glass windows, stoves and utensils, coffee pots, oarlocks and canvas sails, often with Victorian sea ports of Port Townsend or Port Angeles in the background.

Born near the town of Sequim in 1869, Joe McKissick spent his entire life as a photographer. He maintained a studio in Dungeness and had a tent studio that he would take to Sequim, furnished with a cylinder phonograph to play music for his customers. He died in 1939 leaving behind a unique record of community life in the early days of the Sequim-Dungeness area.

William Wilcox was a quiet Victorian man who lived simply and had a passion for photography. Although his work is virtually unknown by the public, he is considered one of the most talented amateur photographers of his time. In 1895 he moved to Port Townsend where he roomed a few blocks from James G. McCurdy, a banker and himself an excellent amateur photographer. Together they went on photographic outings and developed their skills in McCurdy's basement darkroom. Wilcox remained in Port Townsend over twenty years and died in 1940.

INDIAN FAMILY AT PORT TOWNSEND, 1899.

Photo by William Wilcox.
Collection of the Jefferson County Historical Society

CANOE WITH SAILING SHIPS IN THE BACKGROUND
IN PORT TOWNSEND BAY.

Photo by Joe McKissik.
Collection of the Jefferson County Historical Society

"MRS. WHITE" WEAVING A BASKET AT POINT HUDSON IN
PORT TOWNSEND.

Collection of the Jefferson County Historical Society

NATIVE FAMILY NEAR CHIMACUM CREEK, WASHINGTON.
Photo by Torka's Studio
Collection of the Jefferson County Historical Society

CARVING A CANOE.
Collection of the Jefferson County Historical Society

CHET-ZE-MOKA'S SON, THE PRINCE OF WALES,
PICTURED WITH HIS SECOND WIFE NELLIE, AT THEIR
LOWER HADLOCK CABIN.

Photo by Joe McKissick..
Collection of the Jefferson County Historical Society

"GRANDMA NEWMAN" DRYING FISH ON PORT TOWNSEND
BEACH.

THE MAKAH CARVER, ATTLU, WITH A CEREMONIAL
DANCE MASK.

INDIAN CANOE BEING TOWED BY A STEAM TUG.
SHIP IN BACKGROUND.

WEAVING ON THE BEACH WITH THE MARINE HOSPITAL
IN PORT TOWNSEND IN THE BACKGROUND.

MRS. STRAND OF THE SNOHOMISH TRIBE MAKING A
BASKET IN CHIMACUM.

FAMILY AT POINT HUDSON, PORT TOWNSEND.
Photo by Katherine McCurdy.
Collection of the Jefferson County Historical Society

NATIVE HOME ON CHIMACUM CREEK, PUGET SOUND,
WASHINGTON.

Photo by Torka Studio.
Collection of the Jefferson County Historical Society

"LIGHTHOUSE JIM" AND A WOMAN WEAVING A BASKET.
SALMON DRYING. BRINNON, WASHINGTON.

Photo by Fannie Gilson Brown.
Collection of the Jefferson County Historical Society

WOMAN SITTING ON THE EDGE OF A CANOE AT POINT
HUDSON, PORT TOWNSEND, WASHINGTON

SON OF CHIEF CHETZEMOKA (DUKE OF YORK) AND
SEEHEIMETZA (QUEEN VICTORIA). CHIMACUM BEACH.
CLASSEN CHEMICAL PLANT IN THE BACKGROUND.

INDIAN BASKET WEAVER "ELSA" AT LA PUSH, WA

Photo by Ellis Studio.
Collection of the Jefferson County Historical Society

NATIVE GROUP AT POINT HUDSON, PORT TOWNSEND, WASHINGTON, 1905.

Photo by Katherine McCurdy.
Collection of the Jefferson County Historical Society

CHET-ZE-MOKA, CHIEF OF THE KLALLAMS AND FRIEND
OF PORT TOWNSEND SETTLERS, SHOWN WITH HIS WIFE,
SEE-HEM-ITZA.

Photo by Lathrop Bros. photographers.
Collection of the Jefferson County Historical Society

INDIAN WARS IN PUGET SOUND

Commentary

War broke out in the aftermath of the treaties. The fiercest fighting occurred east of the mountains and involved the plateau tribes, primarily the Yakima, but the conflict spilled over into Puget Sound. Historian Murray Morgan summarized the long-term effects of the war:

> The Indian wars that grew out of Governor Isaac Stevens' treaty-making efforts in 1854-55 profoundly influenced the early development of Washington Territory. They slowed immigration, interrupted economic development, and left tangles of antagonisms, not all of them racial.
>
> Federal and territorial officials, military and civilian, were at odds about strategy during the war and about responsibility for war debts afterwards. Whigs and Democrats differed as to whether the war had been necessary. The territorial judiciary wanted the territorial governor punished for declaring martial law and imprisoning the chief justice. Rivalry between the Protestant missionaries who were predominantly American, and the Catholic missionaries who were predominantly French Canadian or European, was embittered. American-born settlers believed many of the Hudson's Bay Company employees had helped the hostiles. And the Indians remembered who had taken the field and who had not.
>
> The war affected the growth of the Puget Sound towns. Seattle, although the target of the only attack on a settlement, benefited by the influx of refugees from the farms along the Duwamish, White and Black rivers; benefited too from the sense of a common cause that developed among people protected by a log palisade of their own construction. On the other hand the folk who had settled near Nicholas Delin's mill on Commencement Bay scattered to Steilacoom and Olympia during the war. Tacoma did not take shape as a community for more than a decade and remained a generation behind Seattle is developing a civic leadership (Eckrom, 1989).

The Klallams maintained their neutrality during this conflict and credit for keeping them out of war is given to the reigning chief of that period: Chet-ze-moka, also known as the Duke of York.

Peter Simpson's essay, "We Give Our Hearts To You" explores the life and personality of this well-known figure in Indian-white relations, revered by the Port Townsend community to this day.

WE GIVE OUR HEARTS TO YOU
A View of Chet-ze-moka

Peter Simpson

Whenever cultures clash over issues of supremacy, the leaders who emerge in the shaping of events later serve to perpetuate the out-comes of the struggle. Whether the private thoughts and desires of such men and women match the eventual interpretation is unknown. Because the resulting view often turns mythological, the descendants of these struggles rarely hold, if they ever knew, the original motivations of their ancestors. Through the stories and tales passed on generation to generation, the dreams of the old leaders, once full-blooded creatures governed by the complex realities of their day, are molded into new and different purpose. They become heroes whose reworked motivations give rationale to the justification of victory, and the celebration of their sacrifice helps to atone for any brute force required in the pursuit.

Consider, then, the life of T'chits-a-ma-hun, a chief of the Klallams, whose story has been told essentially by victorious white men with motivations of their own.

T'chits-a-ma-hun, a name reportedly meaning "fine young man," emerged in the view of his white contemporaries as a friend to the invading settlers. Called Chet-ze-moka by whites, his intervention among his own and neighboring tribesmen was credited with single-handedly protecting Port Townsend settlers from massacre during the Indian Wars of the 1850s. As a result, the white victors in the struggles of nearly a century and a half ago, and their succeeding generations, have kept his name in the forefront. Indian leaders of the resistance, such as Leschi of the Nisqually, who was hanged - many then and now believe unjustly - for killing a white during wartime, often were held with respect, but rarely were they regarded with the warmth or held with the generosity of spirit reserved for Chief Chet-ze-moka.

Had the result of the conquest been different, had those small bands of resisting Indians in the 1850s prevailed, Chet-ze-moka's name likely would not have been revered; indeed, he might well have been considered a traitor. But such speculation is hypothetical. The fact is that he possessed great insight, made a courageous decision, acted upon it, and then clung to it through a series of trials that ended in the diminution of his own people.

Here, then, is T'chits-a-ma-hun, the white man's friend.

Two differing lineages are offered for the Klallam chief. McCurdy (1937) says the chief's father was a member of the Skagit tribe and that his mother was a Klallam. Marrying a member of a neighboring tribe was consistent with the marital customs of upper class Klallams, but Mary Ann Lambert (1960), who was Chet-ze-moka's distant cousin, contradicts that version with her more romantic account.

Obtaining her information from descendants of what she called the "the house of the seven brothers," Lambert says that Chet-ze- moka's Klallam ancestry was patrilineal. In her version, Ste-tee- thlum, a Klallam chief lived in a village of the same name located halfway between the present day Jamestown and the mouth of the Dungeness River. Ste-tee-thlum's favorite of his three wives had died and he wished to replace her with "a woman of high standing."

One day, accompanied by his son, the old chief canoed across the Strait of Juan de Fuca to the land of the rival Nanaimo tribe on what is now called Vancouver Island. His intent was to steal the daughter of the chief. After hours of steady paddling, Ste-tee-thlum observed "a beautifully decorated touring canoe." In it were the Princess of Nanaimo and two slave girls on a journey to a nearby village where the princess' mother's people lived. Ste-tee-thlum intercepted the princess and pulled her into his canoe. He instructed the slave girls to return to their village and inform their chief that "the chief of the (Klallams) of the House of Ste-tee-thlum has taken his daughter with honorable intent of marriage."

On their return to the southern shore of the strait, no word was exchanged between the old chief and his son. "The silence was broken only by the suppressed sobbing and occasional sniffing of the captive princess, which caused the chief's son to do a little private thinking...."

Upon arrival at the village, Ste-tee-thlum stood before his tribesmen to present his captive bride-to-be when his son stepped forward and said, "My father, my honorable, I desire this maiden. Only today I realize I have reached manhood. I would take the daughter of the House of Nanaimo to wife. I am young. She is young. You are old, my father, yes, old and vigorless."

Without hesitation the elder Ste-tee-thlum acquiesced, "My son, you speak wisely, you speak words of truth. I am old – yes, I am old. I realize that now. Take the daughter of Nanaimo. Take also my title, my chieftainship. This day I bestow upon you the honor of my ...name. Now and from henceforth you shall be known as Chief Ste-tee-thlum the Younger, Chief of all the (Klallams). Yes, yes, this I say."

The old chief walked to the family longhouse and disappeared inside. The young Ste-tee-thlum took the hand of his new bride and before the assembled members of the tribe, who had watched this transfer of power and possession between father and son, the couple followed the elder chief into the longhouse. Next day a feast began that lasted several days celebrating the union of rival tribes from both sides of the vast Strait of Juan de Fuca.

The young Ste-tee-thlum and the Nanaimo Princess had seven sons, the last being Lah-ka-nim, who married Qua-tum-a-low. Whether Qua-tum-a-low was a member of the Klallam tribe or of another, Lambert does not venture, but given the exogamous practices of the Klallams - if the Lambert version is correct - she would have had to have been from another, perhaps neighboring tribe. They had four sons and four daughters. Chet-ze-moka was to become the most famous, but most of his siblings also were well regarded. Aside from conflicting opinions about the eldest, Chet-ze-moka's brothers were respected, "ordinary men, living harmoniously...and producing large families." The daughters of Lah-ka-him and Qua-tum-a-low were "ambitious women, all having married white men." One married a

U.S. Customs inspector for the San Juan Islands, two were wedded to Port Townsend men, and one married farmer Tom Brinnon for whom the Hood Canal community later was named (Lambert, 1960).

Chet-ze-moka was born sometime in the first or second decade of the 19th century at Kah-tai, the Indian name for what whites were to call Port Townsend. Nothing is known of his childhood; likely it was spent in preparation for the roles and responsibilities of Klallam adulthood. Daily activities would have included rising early to greet the sun, swimming each morning every day of the year, personal grooming. He would have played with girls until he reached the age of 12. Endurance training would have begun about four years earlier. Gunther reports that children were frequently "given food, a little dried salmon, only once in five days." Mothers would warn other tribesmen to not feed a child if he begged; denial helped to make him strong.

At the onset of adolescence, Chet-ze-moka would have been sent from his home to seek a vision and thereby be joined by a guardian spirit. These spirits often were animals or birds, but sometimes they appeared in the form of the sun, a spider web, thunder, "something from far out in the water." Guardian spirits gave Indians special powers in hunting and for gathering, in war or for bravery, of farsightedness or for prophecy. Sent out during the stormiest weather of winter in which the spirits were believed to run about, a child remained for days, even weeks. Upon return from the quest, the child did not speak of the experience immediately for fear of losing its power. No evidence has been uncovered to determine what spirit Chet-ze-moka acquired, but because of his status it is likely that it was a powerful one. Chet-ze-moka inherited his chieftaincy from his older brother, Klows-ton, who, according to one report, was unhappy with the coming of the white settlers and left in his canoe one day, never to return. Although ascendancy to the position of chief was normally from father to son or from older brother to younger brother, the primary requisite for leadership was wealth, not succession. A man who could distribute wealth through numerous potlatches was recognized by his village as its leader, or *ssia'm*. It was not uncommon for a member of the lower class to rise to the chieftaincy.

Klallam leaders lacked the authority of their European and American counterparts. A chief's essential role was to give advice, and he had only tribal opinion to give it substance. He served as little more than an interlocutor and considerably less than a judge when hearing quarrels between families or married couples. He offered solutions or punishments that were carried out, if at all, by members of the family in conflict. The chief functioned in issues of retribution between tribes by counseling and offering opinions that were "valued, but not always followed. If the visiting (tribe) demand(ed) too high a price the chief might help by collecting funds from his relatives in order to avoid war. If the demands for some reason (could not) be met and the issues (came) to war, the chief would call on neighboring villages for help in fighting. If, on the other hand, a party of Klallams (went) out to collect blood money, the chief generally accompanie(d) them provided the person injured (was) important socially. The chief...accompan(ied) the expedition only to give advice, he (would) not talk with the opposite group, but leave that to the messengers who (went) along or to his speaker." Nor was a chief automatically a warrior; he joined war parties only when personally interested (Gunther, 1937).

A Klallam chief held no command over the movements of his people. Because of the Indian's communal view of land usage, tribe members were free to move about as they wished. Although there were lands and certain beaches traditionally dedicated to specific tribal use, there was no notion of individual property rights, and thus it did not require protection. A chief's permission was not required to begin the fishing season, to hunt, or to gather other foods.

As a wealthy tribesmen Chet-ze-moka could afford more than one wife, but the fact that Chet-ze-moka did have two wives and therefore held status among his clan does not further suggest that Chet-ze-moka was necessarily a desirable catch.

> ...the Duke...was...inclined strongly toward the opposite sex. He was a sort of dandy, and a flirt as well, in his own particular way, but not being handsome, and being already married, he was avoided by the ladies. Nevertheless he took his pick of womenfolk of his tribe. The fact that he already had a wife made little or no difference to him. (See-hem-itsa) knew her man; anything he did was all right with her, even helping him choose the youthful Chill-lil as her lord and master's number two wife...(Lambert, 1960).

Contact between Chet-ze-moka's elders and the European explorers was quite likely. McCurdy (1937) offers the first record, stating that Chet-ze-moka recalled his father's memory of the arrival of Captain George Vancouver in May 1792:

> The boy often heard his father relate how startled the Indians were when they first beheld two large vessels gliding over the surface of the inland sea, like immense birds.

> Not knowing whether these mysterious white winged visitants boded good or evil, the natives kept hidden in the dense underbrush along the shore, while watching with keen eyes their every movement.

> Later, they found that those in charge of the "great canoes" were men who differed from themselves only by the color of their skin. As no hostile intent toward them was manifested, Chet-ze-moka's forefathers established communication with the strange vessels.

> The Indians were courteously received by the "White Chief" in command, and considerable barter took place. For years Chet-ze-moka's father proudly displayed a knife he had received from one of Vancouver's men, in exchange for a watertight basket.

Vancouver's account of the first contact shows that on May 2, when he sailed into Port Discovery, which he named after his flag-ship, he and his crew "found a deserted village capable of containing a hundred inhabitants." The structures appeared not to have been recently inhabited, "...their insides were over-run with weeds; amongst which were found several human skulls, and other bones, promiscuously scattered about." It is possible that the site had been abandoned after an outbreak of smallpox that afflicted the Klallams on several occasions.

Vancouver's crew spent the next three days repairing and altering sails and rigging, inspecting casks, stopping leaks, drying gunpowder, gathering provisions, cutting wood, brewing spruce beer, and caulking the ship's sides. On Sunday, May 6, Vancouver granted shore leave "for some recreation and exercise." He wrote in his journal:

A few of the natives in two or three canoes favored us with their company, and brought with them some fish and venison for sale. The latter was extremely good, and very acceptable, as we had not hitherto obtained any....These people, in their persons, canoes, arms, implements, &c. seemed to resemble chiefly the inhabitants of Nootka; though less bedaubed with paint, and less filthy in their external appearances. They wore ornaments in their ears, but none were

observed in their noses; some of them understood a few words of the Nootka language; they were clothed in the skins of deer, bear, and some other animals, but principally in a woollen [sic] garment of their own manufacture, extremely well wrought. They did not appear to possess any furs. Their bows and implements they freely bartered for knives, trinkets, copper, &c; and, what was very extraordinary, they offered for sale two children, each about six or seven years of age, and, being shewn [sic] some copper, were very anxious that the bargain should be closed. This, however, I peremptorily [sic] prohibited, expressing, as well as I was able, our great abhorrence of such traffic (Lamb, 1984).

On May 8, when Vancouver and a small crew he had assembled for further exploration rounded Point Hudson and sailed toward Indian Island, the company sighted a deserted village, decayed in much the same way as the one at the head of Port Discovery.

At what may have been Kala Point, Vancouver and his men saw with fascination two "rudely carved" poles, about 15 feet tall. "On the top of each was stuck a human head, recently placed there. The hair and flesh were nearly perfect; and the heads appeared to carry the evidence of fury or revenge, as, in driving the stakes through the throat to the cranium, the sagittal, with part of the scalp, was borne on their points some inches above the rest of the skull (thus giving the scalp a tentlike appearance). Between the stakes a fire had been made, and near it some calcined bones were observed...."

Returning to Point Hudson by the Kah-tai lagoon a series of tall poles was seen for which Vancouver could not discern a purpose but which was identified by later explorers as the framework for holding high nets to catch low-flying fowl. Next day, near Port Ludlow, Vancouver met up with a group of Chemakum Indians with whom they "courteously...and cordially traded."

The novelty of the white men in their great sailing canoes, Vancouver's store of trade goods and the gentleness of his crew, combined with their light complexion - a mark of distinction among the Klallams - likely were determinate factors in the cordiality between the early explorers and the Indians.

Noted for their warlike behavior, the Klallams were not always cordial, as witness their killing of five members of the Hudson's Bay Company more than 30 years later. Though reference to individual members of the Klallam tribe were not included in Ermaringer's account (see page 4) of the Hudson's Bay Company's 1828 expedition to gain revenge, Chet-ze-moka and his family likely were witnesses to at least some of the brutal chase. The expedition resulted in the death of up to 20 Klallams and the burning of villages at Dungeness and Kah-tai, or Port Townsend as it was fast becoming known to traders and explorers. Undoubtedly, these varying encounters had strong and mixed impact on the later Indian view of the uninvited white man.

For 30 years following 1820, the Klallams' contacts would have been mostly with traders from Hudson's Bay Company. It was not until 1851 that settlers appeared in any number. On April 24 of that year, Alfred A. Plummer and Charles Bachelder arrived in Port Townsend Bay intent on settling and claiming land as homesteads, although the United States government had not yet discussed the matter with the Klallams, nor for that matter, with any Northwest tribe.

Plummer and Bachelder, and the soon-to-follow Loren B. Hastings and Francis W. Pettygrove were the advance guard, heralding the ambitions and willfulness of the fateful national bent on realizing "Manifest Destiny." Considered by many as "more truculent than most of their neighbors," some Klallams" looked upon the arrival of white people who began to cut timber, build houses, and give other indications of an intent to remain permanently in their country, with evident displeasure, and they early served notice on them not to cultivate the ground and to cease cutting their trees." Yet, the Klallams "offered no violence...though their conduct gradually became more annoying" (Snowden, 1909).

Klows-ton, Chet-ze-moka's older brother, who was known to the whites as King George, was said by some to have "...adopted a quarrelsome attitude toward the settlers.....He was usually under the influence of liquor....He had, moreover, a very annoying habit. Going into the trading post he would select something that took his fancy; then he would refuse to settle for it, calmly telling the trader to regard it as a slight advance payment on the land that the settler had taken from him" (McCurdy).

In the summer of 1851, a survey steamer, the "Active," arrived at Port Townsend. She sported a "brightly polished cannon, displayed on the upper deck, (and) perhaps recalled to (the Klallams') minds their experience with Ermatinger" (Snowden, 1909).

On October 1851, Loren B. Hastings and Francis W. Pettygrove arrived from Olympia to examine Plummer's and Bachelder's claims to see if they might join these two settlers. Immediately convinced of the efficacy of the place, they returned to Portland to close their business affairs and assemble their families.

Before their departure, the new settlers made arrangements to send Chet-ze-moka to San Francisco, fully paying his fare and expenses. This was not a trip where the "noble savage" was offered as a curiosity to the white world, as had been the case of Omai, the Tahitian who had accompanied Capt. James Cook's party for the education and amusement of the English court in 1775. Sending Chet-ze-moka to San Francisco in 1851 had a more practical and calculated purpose.

"Early settlers (to the Northwest)...while courageous enough, were never to be caught napping. They were greatly outnumbered...for a number of years. And the ways of Indians...were at times mysterious. Their very willingness to give up their lands to the whites was looked upon with some misgivings. So, (Chet-ze moka) was treated, by the 'graciousness' of his white neighbors, to (the) trip to San Francisco...." (Pioneer Project).

Although Hastings was to become friendly with the Klallam chief, his experience on the Oregon Trail four years earlier no doubt influenced the decision to send Chet-ze-moka to San Francisco. After several days of skirmishes with the Pawnee Indians along the Platte River, Hastings wrote in his journal on June 13, 1847: "The...Indians are the greatest thieves I ever saw - the best way I think to civilize or Christianize Indians is with powder and lead, & this (is) the way we shall do hereafter" (Hastings).

Chet-ze-moka was sent in the charge of a Capt. Felker on board the brig "Franklin Adams." In San Francisco, Capt. Felker turned Chet-ze-moka over to James G. Swan, a Massachusetts-born adventurer who was to become the first and foremost ethnographer of Northwest Indian culture. Swan was engaged by the ship chandler where Felker traded. He took Chet-ze-moka in hand and escorted "...him all over the city. He saw the crowds of people, the soldiers, the shipping in the harbor, and visited the great ocean steamers. He was impressed with the great concourse of white people and their evident strength and superiority," Swan recalled years later. Chet-ze-moka was introduced to a bustling, gold-frenzied world he could never have anticipated from the experiences and stories of his childhood. Seeing San Francisco must have altered his traditional concepts and view of the future. He was taken from an ancient cultural and spiritual pattern that rarely varied and set down in the middle of a zone totally unknown to him.

But the Klallam chief was an astute observer. He returned to Port Townsend "with very enlarged views of the number and power of the white man..." (Swan, 1859). "Upon his return, he was quietly informed that all of the people of San Francisco, and all of the vessels he had seen there in the harbor and at sea, were manned by 'brothers' of the Port Townsend settlers who, in case of any trouble, would all come in a body to aid, or if necessary, to avenge their Port Townsend kin" (Trotter, 1937).

> Later, when the tribe began to complain to their chief about the encroachments of the white settlers, (Chet-ze-moka) was greatly perturbed. It is said that he stepped into his canoe one evening and rowed to a lonely inlet where he spent the night in thought. When he returned next morning, he called together the disgruntled faction of the (Klallams) and made a speech in which he told of the great number of white people more numerous than the trees in the forestand the vast armada of 'flying birds' manned with armed forces that would swoop down upon them and exterminate them if any harm came to his friends, the white settlers. The speech was effective, and such fear and respect was implanted in the hearts of the Klallams that no further talk of driving the settlers away was heard.

In justice to Chet-ze-moka, however, it must be said that once impressed with the strength of the white race he did become a friend and was so considered by all during his lifetime (Trotter, 1937).

On Feb. 21, 1852, when Hastings and Pettygrove returned to Port Townsend with their families, the Klallam welcome was warm. Arriving in a schooner, the two families accompanied by four passengers arranged for two large Indian canoes and crews to bring the party ashore.

After the...women had landed, a number of Indians rushed into the water and raised upon their brawny shoulders the canoes which still held the children, bore them with great pomp into the large council house, where a general conference was to take place.

Oregon (Columbus) Hastings was...a sturdy boy of six years, with a mop of flaming red hair. Red, to the Indians, was the color of royalty and this was the first time they had ever seen hair of that color. They began to whisper among themselves:

"Yakah tenas sochalie tyee!" meaning in the Chinook vernacular, "That child's a little God!" He was lifted from the canoe and placed at the right hand of the chief where he remained in state while various matters were discussed by the whites and natives. The boy was subsequently given the Indian name "En Squiawk" meaning "Red Head" (McCurdy, 1937).

At the confab between the new settlers and the Klallams, Plummer promised without authority that the U.S. government would pay "liberally" for the lands they were going to cultivate. Pettygrove offered an "assortment...of beads, mirrors, needles, pipes, and fishhooks" that were received by the Indians "with great delight. The pow-wow ended amicably..." (McCurdy, 1937).

In 1853, the new settlement celebrated its first wedding.

This marriage, at which the entire group of settlers was present, was typical of the pioneer days. There was no wedding gown of satin, no soft church music, no lovely home furnished with gifts. The music was provided by fiddlers playing the favorite airs of the period. The wedding supper consisted of a pig roasted whole, together with pies, doughnuts, fruits, and coffee. After a season of merrymaking and we give congratulations, the newly wedded pair proceeded to a new log cabin which the groom had been for some time preparing for occupancy....

It had three rooms, with a big fireplace and a roof of hand-split shakes. Much of the furniture was home made....There was a little rocker of split-maple with a seat of rawhide. (Chet-ze-moka) presented the bride with a clock which must have been of the alarm variety as he called it his "make-music" (McCurdy, 1937).

Described by McCurdy as "short and thickset, with a large head, deep set but expressive eyes, and very powerful," the affable Chet-ze-moka developed a liking for white man's clothing. He requested of the settlers an outfit, "so the women set to work to make him a suit. The coat and pants were made of blue blanket cloth, with red stripes running down the sleeves and legs, cut from a petticoat. This suit he prized very highly and he wore it upon all important occasions, topped with a cap which some captain had given him" (McCurdy, 1937).

In preparation for establishing treaties with the Indians, the U.S. government appointed Isaac Stevens as Superintendent of Indian Affairs in 1853 in addition to his responsibilities as Governor of Washington Territory. Although no treaties had been signed, nor even discussed with the Indians of the inland waters, the government and its agents nevertheless had taken de facto possession of the land and had assumed the moral position of an occupying force. On April 19, 1854, Stevens issued the following appointment:

To all Persons whom it may concern: Whereas T'chitz-a-ma-hun, otherwise called Duke of York (1), an Indian of the 'Clallam Tribe...has been this day recognized as Head Chief of the same; now, therefore, this paper is given to him that he may be known and treated accordingly. The said chief is held responsible for the good behavior of his people and is required to inform the Superintendent of Indian Affairs or the Agent of all offences [sic] committed by Indians against the citizens of the territory and to deliver upon demand all persons accused thereof. In so doing he will be assisted by the subchief appointed to Counsel with him, and will be supported by the Government and the military. He is also on behalf of his people to make complaint of injuries done by citizens or others against them and particularly of the sale of liquor to Indians. In this the faith of the government is pledged to sustain him, and do them justice. Should he said Chief fail to perform his duty honestly, the Superintendent will remove him and make another chief.

T'chits-a-ma-hun's name had been corrupted by whites into the more easily pronounced Chet-ze-moka, but he was called the "Duke of York" by most - even Swan - who found it difficult to mold their tongues to Indian phonetics, choosing instead to give Indian leaders the names and titles of their white counterparts. As noted, Chet-ze-moka's older brother, Klows-ton, was known as King George, named presumably for George III, then reigning

monarch of England. The Duke's first wife, See-hem-itsa, was called Queen Victoria, and his second wife, Chill-lil, became Jenny Lind, after the popular Swedish-born British coloratura soprano who made a successful tour of the United States in 1850 and 1851 under the auspices of P.T. Barnum. Chet-ze-moka's youngest son, Lah-ka-nim, was dubbed Prince of Wales. (2)

The phrase, "...held responsible for the good behavior of his people," was literally enforced by representatives of the U.S. government. Early in March 1854, an outbreak of hostilities between Army troops and Klallam tribesmen at Dungeness left four killed, two Klallams and an Army captain and a lieutenant. Three Klallams were arrested for the murder and three others were flogged for an apparently related theft. In October, just months after Chet-ze-moka had been recognized by the whites as "Chief of the Klallams," the three tribesmen accused of the murder escaped from Fort Steilacoom. In December soldiers proceeded to a Klallam camp on Hood Canal and demanded surrender of the prisoners; the tribe refused. In response the soldiers destroyed the camp and the winter supply of salmon. The accompanying cutter fired shots into the woods reportedly killing five Klallams. The army contingent, led by Indian Agent Michael Simmons encountered Chet-ze-moka farther down the canal and took him hostage. Eventually the tribe surrendered the escaped prisoners and Chet-ze-moka was released (Bancroft, 1890). By this stage in Indian-white relations, there was no going back.

Indian life had been irrevocably altered. First, smallpox, measles, and syphilis accompanied explorers and early traders and, lacking any natural immunity, the Indians were devastated. It is possible that half the Indian population succumbed to the diseases before the settlers ever arrived. Many explorers noted in their journals the ravages of the pox on native faces. With the traders, Indians were able to take advantage of, and indeed, increase their wealth by trading for the white man's conveniences, and enhanced their skills with the white man's often superior *ictas* (things). Yet the trade had had little initial impact on Indian customs. It was to the traders' benefit that Indian life continue as unchanged as possible; Indians provided traders and some early, isolated settlers with furs, food, and wives. It was important to keep a balance of power between the trader and the Indian so that their exchange could continue and prosper. The traders' view of land usage was compatible with the Indians' so conflict was rare and when experienced was usually the response to differences between individuals, not cultures.

Nevertheless, a toll was exacted. Item by item, the Indians began to discard their own goods. First to go probably were bone and stone in favor of iron for tools and weapons. The metal preceded the arrival of the explorers when it floated ashore as flotsam from far off shipwrecks. With the arrival of the Hudson's Bay Company and their even-then-famous blankets, the tribes neglected their isolated breeding of "wool dogs" which soon became mongrelized and their fur unworkable. While most of the white man's food was considered inferior to the fresh catch available within minutes after the first hunger pangs, the Indians soon favored the potato as a convenient, easily cultivated, replacement for indigenous roots that required laborious digging for harvest and had to be steamed for days to be edible.

Encouraged by the prim customs of the whites, Indians soon began to turn yard goods into European-style clothing, discarding the worked cedar bark and furs that protected them from wet and cold but did not cover their genitals to the distress of the settlers and missionaries. With the ships that called for Douglas fir and western red cedar to fuel San Francisco's building boom, came whiskey by the barrelful, and the Americans were less concerned about its impact than had been the largely-British traders. The effect of liquor was no less severe than the dreaded pox; it may have been worse. With the doctrine of Manifest Destiny as the nation's guide, there was no stopping, no slowing the encroachment of whites onto land the Indians had occupied for millennia. Just as inevitably, resentment among the Indians was building, and Chet-ze-moka soon was faced with reaffirming or discarding his stand on behalf of the settlers and their government. The evidence suggests that he was seldom in doubt.

In 1854, a conference of chiefs from both sides of the mountains gathered at the Snohomish village of Heb-Heb-O-Lub, near Tulalip. Representatives from the Yakimas came to urge their Puget Sound brethren into action against the settlers. Chiefs from among the Nisqually, Duwamish, Skagit, Lummi, and Skykomish tribes were present; Chet-ze-moka represented the Klallams. Owhi, brother of the Yakima chief, Kamiakin, "urged immediate action by all natives of the Oregon country to drive (the settlers) out, making

it so uncomfortable that they would never again attempt to settle. He reasoned that the numbers were small now, while in a few seasons they might be great enough to overwhelm the native warriors. By uniting now, the campaign would be successful" (Stock and Pembroke, 1979).

Chet-ze-moka disagreed, stating that he had lived among the whites for years and "found them interesting and friendly." Patkanim, who was of Yakima ancestry but who represented his Snoqualmie tribe at the conference, cautioned the warriors of "the great numbers (of settlers) already on the coast. "A Yakima representative erupted in anger over Patkinim's caution, calling into question his bravery and honesty; "...the whites (make) promises they (fail) to keep. They cut the trees, and drive the natives from their homes."

Chet-ze-moka countered by blaming the interior Indians for skirmishes with whites who had become angered as the result of Indian hostility.

"Whose coats are you wearing? (Chet-ze-moka added.) Whose guns are you using? Whose tobacco are you smoking? You get them all from the white men. They buy your fish and skins and you buy their small *ictas*. We should be friends and not try to kill each other. If you wanted to kill off the whites, you should have struck long ago. Now it is too late.

"In the big city I visited the people are as thick as the leaves on the trees. They are like the grass which is cut down by the mower. It soon springs up thicker than before. Some years ago my people made a treaty on Port Townsend beach with Plummer, Pettygrove, and Hastings, and we agreed to be friendly with each other. We have all lived up to that promise and I and my people will not break it" (3) (McCurdy, 1937).

WE GIVE OUR HEARTS TO YOU 139

Chief Sealth also spoke in favor of harmonious relationships.

But Leschi, who was the war chief for the Nisqually tribe, argued back. He opposed extending friendship to the new settlers. Leschi related the story of his father, a chief of the Nisqually, who initially had befriended the white men and encouraged close relationships with them. Leschi's sister had married a young soldier. They lived happily until the troops were ordered to another station and the white military commanders would not allow her to accompany him. Having no place to go, she returned to her father who, because of Indian custom, was disgraced by the incident. "He crept like a dog instead of walking erect, and howled continually. Soon he died," Leschi relayed, and reaffirmed his vow to drive out white soldiers and other newcomers. Only older settlers who were "tried and accepted" would be spared (Stock and Pembrok, 1979).

One Yakima representative hailed Leschi's position and called those who would not fight "cowards." Chet-ze-moka again pleaded for accommodation and extracted promises of peace from Chiefs Sealth, Patkanim and Kitsap (who later changed his views and fought against the settlers).

Openly angry, the Yakima representatives accused their brethren "of having sick minds, of having had too much...whiskey. (They)...were walking in darkness, or if they could see, they were lame. They feared to go out and meet the Pastuds (whites) in battle, but preferred to hide in the field like mice. (Their) hearts were actually against the invaders, but (their) bodies were cowardly." The Yakima representatives vowed to unite and assemble tribes from over the mountains to attack the whites on the coast.

As host, the Snohomish chief brought the conference to a close by declaring it impossible to reach agreement. Chet-ze-moka's experience with the whites and his arguments on behalf of peace were considered the greatest influence in forestalling the Yakima from an immediate call to war (Stock and Pembroke, 1979).

Having been raised in a culture where disagreements were settled mostly by avoidance or by fighting with reparations made afterward, Chet-ze-moka seems to have been offering a new paradigm in furthering relationships with whites. He proposed friendship and trade as the basis for dealing with these new people and their pervasive culture. The subsequent treaties offered by the whites likely seemed to him the best solution.

For a short time - only a matter of months - the Indian treaties of 1855 delayed major confrontation in the Puget Sound region. In a series of four negotiations between Christmas Day 1854, and Jan. 31, 1855, Stevens signed treaties with all tribes in the northwestern section of the territory.

In the third of these gatherings, the Klallams and their neighbors, the Chemakums and the Skokomish (or Twana) began to assemble at Hahdskus, or Point No Point, on Wednesday, Jan. 24. Chet-ze- moka represented the

Klallams; Kul-kah-han, or General Pierce, was representing the Chemakums; and Dah-whil-luck, the Skokomish. Negotiations began on Thursday amidst a major winter storm. Stevens began with what had become his standard opening speech delivered in a style that openly reflected his and the government's paternalistic view of the Indian, but he cut it shorter than usual because of the foul weather.

The treaty then was read in Chinook, the limited jargon that Stevens insisted on using during the conduct of negotiations. The major provisions of the treaty called for the three tribes' relocation from 438,430 acres of ancestral lands to a 3,840-acre tract of Skokomish land at the elbow of Hood Canal within one year after ratification by the "Great Father." It gave the Indians the "right of taking fish at usual and accustomed grounds" and the "privilege of hunting and gathering roots and berries on open and unclaimed lands" with the exception of shellfish "from any beds staked or cultivated by citizens."

In exchange for the land, a sum of $60,000 was offered in decreasing payments over a 20-year period, with the "Great Father" reserving the right to "determine at his discretion upon what beneficial objects to expend the same." Additionally, $6,000 was to be provided for cultivation of the reservation, "to be laid out and expended under the direction of the President." The U.S. government promised to establish an agricultural and industrial school and to employ a blacksmith and carpenter. A farmer and a physician also would be provided for 20 years to instruct and care for the Indians. In addition to ceding their land, the Indians were to "exclude from their reservation the use of ardent spirits," to "free all slaves" (which the

U.S. government had yet to do with black Americans), and to "not trade at Vancouver Island, or elsewhere out of the dominions of the United States, nor shall foreign Indians be permitted to reside in their reservations without consent of the superintendent or agent."

After several strong objections were answered by members of Stevens's party, Chet-ze-moka offered support to the treaty. Witnesses to the treaty negotiations reported that because of a "pronounced stutter" the Klallam chief asked that a member of his tribe speak for him. Through this intermediary Chet-ze-moka professed to be happy about the treaty since it specified that his people could seek food from throughout the land and the water, that only their residences were confined to the reservation. He said

that the Indians were no longer poor nor did they quarrel so much since the coming of the white man. He said to Stevens: "I am glad to acknowledge you and the Great Father as our Fathers." He was greeted, according to the white recorder, by cheers from the assembled crowd. One of the earlier speakers recanted his objections and two more Klallams spoke in support of Chet-ze-moka's position (Gibbs, 1855).

The chief of the Skohomish, however, asked for a delay in signing the treaty until the next day so that tribal representatives could "talk it over and understand it thoroughly." The negotiations were adjourned for the day.

Whatever occurred that night among the assembled tribes remains known only to the stones and whatever spirits that may have been present on the beach at Point No Point. Next morning the Indians returned to Governor Stevens bearing white flags.

Chet-ze-moka spoke: "(My) heart (is) white, so (are) those of (my) people and (I) will never stain it with blood or blacken it." Dah-whil-luk, the Skokomish chief, concurred: "(My) heart too (has) become white and (I give) it to (Governor Stevens). (I) put away all (my) bad feelings. (I will) be a good man, not stealing or shedding blood. (I send) this word to the Great Father."

The Chemakum chief, Kul-kah-han, added, giving voice to an expectation of the white men they were not to honor: "We talk to you, but what should we say? We can say nothing but what this flag tells. We give our hearts to you with it, in return for what you do for us. We were once wretched, but since you come you have made us right....Formerly other Indians did wrong to us. Since the whites (have) come, we are free and have not been killed". (8)

The chiefs were unanimous in their support. Hands were shaken, presents were distributed, and in the afternoon the negotiators returned to their various homes, their hearts as pure as they would ever be. The killings were about to begin.

Gov. Stevens was satisfied with the results of the four treaties. He believed he had been an honorable negotiator during his forty-day tour of the northwestern section of the territory. He had gained nearly one-fourth of what was to become Washington state in exchange for a few thousand acres set aside for an Indian reservation and for several hundred thousand dollars

that the Indians would have to fight for more than a century to obtain. He alerted the tribes that the treaties would have to be ratified by the "Great Father" in Washington D.C. before their provisions could take effect, and no doubt he saw as generous the provision to delay relocation to the reservations for one year after that ratification.

For all his confidence, however, Stevens apparently did not discern how little the Indians had understood the provisions of the treaty nor how much resentment he had engendered by pursuing them to sign it.

Sixty years later, in October 1915, an ancient See-hem-itsa (Queen Victoria), who had attended the treaty negotiations with Chet-ze-moka at Point No Point, recalled that it had been her band's belief that they would be allowed to reside at Dungeness, not Skokomish as the treaty read.

For Leschi of the Nisquallys, the resentment remained in check only months until it erupted. Moving into the hills, Leschi assembled a band of angry Indians who roved about the thick brush over the next few months, attacking settlements and bringing the whites and the Indians to a general state of war.

The harsh realities of the fighting in Puget Sound during the wet and cold waning months of 1855 and of early 1856 generally escaped the settlers at Port Townsend, but the stories of attacks on isolated settlements in the White River valley and of face-to-face combat in Seattle created fears strong enough to band them together to build a blockhouse and to assemble a local militia under the command of one of the settlement's founders, Alfred Plummer.

And one year later, Indian Agent Michael T. Simmons wrote to Gov. Stevens expressing fear that lack of ratification of the treaties would create even more unrest. "They have waited so long for the fulfillment of our promises in vain that they are beginning to look upon all Indian Agents as liars, and they already exhibit symptoms of dissatisfaction and bitterness. Were it not for an acquaintance and intimacy with these Indians of 12 years I would not consider myself safe among them" (Simmons, 1858).

The winter of 1856 - 1857 was bitterly cold and food supplies were low. In December 1856, Simmons undertook to distribute goods to "the destitute Indians" in the Puget Sound region. When he reached Port Gamble where

Chet-ze-moka and others were in temporary residence, the Indians responded with "appropriate expressions of thanks for the kindness and consideration of the white Chiefs in making provision for the old, decrepit and helpless among (them)."

Simmons reported to Governor Stevens further that the "Duke of York...an intelligent man, said that he had been told by cultus (bad) white men that the food and presents which they had received was their payment for the lands they had agreed to sell the whites. He said he did not believe these stories himself, but he had experienced great difficulty in making his people reject them, many of whom had not the same confidence in the white man's faith which he had. He said he had endeavored to persuade his people that the cause of so much delay on the part of the whites in fulfilling their treaty stipulations was owing to the war (with) the ...tribes of Indians (who) had been waging against us, and that the blame should fall upon the hostiles and not the whites. He desired me to urge upon the proper authorities the urgent necessity and the great desire on the part of the Indians that their treaties be speedily ratified" (Simmons, 1858).

The settlers of Port Townsend were, however, more fearful of the northern Indians, as tribes above the Canadian border were generally called. These Indians were feared not only by the settlers, but also by the tribes of the U.S. waters. Skirmishes and raiding parties among them were not uncommon, the northern Indians the initiators more often than the southern tribes. Generally, the northern tribes were belligerent toward everyone. On one occasion during this period, Port Townsend authorities engaged the steamer "Hancock" to assist them in driving away a band of northern Indians, "who, by their constant thieveries, had made themselves unbearable..." (Kellogg, 1976).

In October 1856, more than100 Haidas from the Queen Charlotte Islands were encamped at Port Gamble. The captain of the government steamer, the "Massachusetts," asked their leaders to leave but the request was ignored. Next morning, a lieutenant from the steamer went ashore carrying a flag of truce; once more the request was made, but still the Indians refused. Men from the ship then hauled a howitzer to the beach, aimed the cannon at the Haida camp, and fired. The camp was destroyed. Twenty-seven Indians were killed, including several leaders, and 21 injured (Kellogg, 1976). The Haidas "departed in a very ugly mood," and vowed revenge (McCurdy, 1937).

In the spring of 1857, McCurdy states, combined forces of warriors from Barclay Sound on the west coast of Vancouver Island and the Snohomish Indians from across Puget Sound established a pincer movement: one tribe approaching from Port Discovery, the other from Port Townsend Bay, to annihilate the Chemakum tribe at its tribal grounds in the midsection of the Quimper Peninsula. Several hundred, perhaps as many as 400, were slaughtered in a nighttime battle that sent Port Townsend settlers scurrying for safety in their recently-built blockhouse. Only a handful of the Chemakums survived.

A few months later, on the night of Aug. 11, 1857, a group of northern Indians approached the home of Col. Isaac N. Ebey on Whidbey Island across Admiralty Inlet from Port Townsend. Ebey was the Collector of Customs for the Puget Sound district and had arranged the relocation of the port of entry from Olympia to Port Townsend in 1853. He was a member of the Oregon territorial legislature. He had had no involvement in the Port Gamble episode of the year before, but he was a leader among the white men, a man important enough to serve as a sacrifice.

The Ebey dog, Rover, had barked throughout that Tuesday night, causing the colonel to move out of doors as was his pattern whenever the creature was restless. Ebey returned to the house and asked his wife for clothing. Others in the house awoke. At that point Ebey spotted Indians in the yard. He went outside to ask them what they wanted. There was a response that no one in the house could understand, then two shots were fired. Holding his head, Ebey ran around the side of the house, turned, as if escaping from some other assailant, and ran back. Two more shots were fired.

Mrs. Ebey, her two children, a visiting U.S. Marshall and his wife escaped out a window as the Indians invaded the other end of the cabin. As they scrambled over a fence a shot was fired in their direction, but it missed. The marshall's wife reached safety at a near-by cabin; Ebey's widow and children and the U.S. Marshall huddled barefoot in the woods, covered with one blanket, until they were found next morning.

Ebey's brother, Winfield was alerted to the scene where he found the colonel, beheaded:

> ...I came in the yard and beheld him in his gore (Winfield wrote in his diary two days later). His Headless trunk lay on its side near the end of the porch - Apparently where he had fallen - When I knelt by his side & took his rigid hands in mind there was no room for doubt as to identity.
>
> Although the head was not there I could have recognized him among a thousand. Could I have looked on that face once more, where I have so often got encouragement. Could I have read the feeling in that agitated...bosom, I could have derived some consolation - But no - nothing was left that could ease one pang of heart rending agony - We wraped [sic] him up & carried him in the house & layd [sic] him on his bed from which he had arisen to meet his death...(Kellogg, 1976).

Within a couple of days, a captain of the U.S. Revenue Service based in Port Townsend had rounded up seven northern Indians. A party of Indian women was gathered by white authorities and dispatched to the San Juan Islands where it was believed the guilty party had fled. The women were instructed to tell the marauders that the seven Indians in Port Townsend were being held hostage and would be hanged at noon, Saturday, Aug. 15, if the murderers were not produced. As the deadline neared, settlers in their fear and frustration continued to hand over Indians to Port Townsend authorities; soon there were 18 hostages.

On Saturday morning, 50 Whidbey Island residents sailed into Port Townsend "where they passed a resolution to kill all Northern Indians who might come into the country from that time on." But by noon, the Indian women sent to the San Juans had not returned, and the judge released eight of the hostages. Eventually all were released (Kellogg, 1976). That three large canoes of Indians friendly to the whites attempted to find the northern murderers was of little consolation. They returned empty-handed, and tensions heightened. Settlers in Port Townsend began to leave their homes. A U.S. Treasury agent, sent to Puget Sound to investigate the impact of the Indian Wars, encountered the Hastings and Pettygrove families two miles from Olympia in full retreat; how long before they returned is not known (Dillon, 1965).

The dates are not certain, but it was at sometime in this period that Chet-ze-moka fully extended his friendship to the settlers. According to McCurdy (1937), not all Klallams had united behind Chet-ze-moka's accommodation of the white settlements. Many of those who resided on the western end of the Strait of Juan de Fuca felt wronged by the new settlements and wished to rid the land of them. Assembling at what is now called North Beach, a "large company...crazed by quantities of bad whiskey, resolved to exterminate the entire settlement of Port Townsend."

Chet-ze-moka talked with these men and attempted to dissuade them, but soon he could see that they no longer trusted him. Late that night he sought out Pettygrove and Hastings. He alerted them to the danger and explained his plan:

> If I am seen coming to you I will not be able to help you further. But each morning I will sit on top of the big rock on the east side of Kah Tai Valley. If you are still in danger I will keep my blanket over my head and then you will know that you must have your guns handy and place your women and children where they will be safe, for they are apt to be captured and held as slaves. If the danger passes I will stand up, throw off my blanket and give a great shout. Then you will know that you are safe.

Each day Chet-ze-moka and others friendly to the settlers argued with the assembled war council, and each morning he would mount the rock as the settlers watched from the other side of the valley. For nine days Chet-ze-moka kept his head enshrouded. Finally, on the 10th morning, he

...came to the rock and after squatting down for a few seconds, rose to his full height, dramatically threw off his blanket and gave an exultant shout, thereby proclaiming that the (Klallams) had given up their purpose and the danger was over. (4)

From that day in late summer or fall of 1857, the threat of war between the two races in Port Townsend was over. The balance of power had shifted: the whites with their ascendant ambitions and the Indians with their culture slowly and inexorably eroding. Port Townsend settlers soon referred to the site where Chet-ze-moka had kept his vigil as Sentinel Rock and they were forever grateful to him. But for the rest of his tribe, that gratitude must have been cold comfort.

Chet-ze-moka and his tribe were now a diminished people. Having agreed to the white man's treaties, they seemed bent on self-destruction. As the Indians swallowed the white man's liquor, so it seemed they became swallowed by the white man's greed. Having given up their land, the Indians now gave up their bodies and their minds.

Noting the Klallam's shrinking population after the turn of the 19th century, Professor Edmond S. Meany wrote in the Sunday edition of the Seattle Post-Intelligencer on Oct. 22, 1903:

"Whiskey has killed them."

In her interview 12 years later, Chet-ze-moka's aged widow, See-hem-itsa, agreed. Whiskey killed more than disease, she said (See page 68).

Whiskey did not kill Chet-ze-moka but it played a major part in his life, giving him an unsavory reputation that was featured in West Coast newspapers and a national magazine in the late 1850s and in a best-selling book during the Civil War years. How the notoriety affected the chief is not known, but it was upsetting to the white citizens of Port Townsend who were held publicly accountable for Chet-ze-moka's drunkenness and the depressed state of the Indians.

There was much truth to the charge.

The Hudson's Bay Company had maintained a policy not to distribute whiskey to the Indians, nor to trade it for their goods. With some lapses, the policy was effectively followed. But with the coming of the American lumber ships and the merchants who supplied them, whiskey became more available. Missionaries and Indian agents from the U.S. government discouraged its sale and use, but they could not be everywhere. Laws were passed and treaty provisions were framed to eliminate the traffic, all to little effect.

From 1874 until his death in 1907 The Rev. Myron Eells worked as a missionary among the tribes, including the Klallams, who by treaty had been assigned to the Skokomish reservation. Eells wrote in 1886 of the "tricks" of the Indian and the liquor seller.

Reminiscing at the turn of the century, the publisher of the *Puget Sound Argus*, wrote about the reputation Port Townsend developed during its early years. In an article in the January 1900 edition of *The Washington Historian*, Allen Weir remembered that Port Townsend was so well known for its liquor traffic that, at a temperance meeting many years later, "it was solemnly declared that in digging on the sand spit you could smell whisky for ten feet below the surface" (Weir, 1900).

In 1854, J. Ross Browne, a U.S. Treasury agent, visited the three-year-old settlement, which he found to be a rough-and-tumble town with a few cabins and a lot of shacks. Three years later, in August 1857, he returned to investigate the effects of the Indian wars. In this pursuit, he met Chet-ze-moka and his two wives. His impression both of Indians and whites was not flattering. "From what I saw...I formed the opinion that the Duke of York and his amiable family were not below the average of the white citizens residing at that benighted place. With very few exceptions, it would be difficult to find a worse class of population in any part of the world." He backed his opinion by noting that six murders had been committed in the town in the previous eight months. Port Townsend "is notorious as a resort for beachcombers and outlaws of every description."

He blamed the residents of the new town for the plight of the Indians, which he described in the most degrading of conditions:

> The palace and out buildings of the Duke of York are built of driftwood...and are eligibly located near the wharf so as to be convenient to the clams and oysters and afford his maids of honor an

opportunity of indulging in frequent ablutions. There is somewhat of an ancient and fish-like odor about the premises of his highness, and it must be admitted that his chimneys smoke horribly, but still the artistic effect is very fine at a distance....

The principal articles of commerce (in Port Townsend), I soon discovered, were whisky, cotton handkerchiefs, tobacco, and cigars, and the principal shops were devoted to billiards and the sale of grog. I was introduced by the Indian Agent to the Duke, who inhabited that region and still disputed possession of the place with the white settlers. If the settlers paid him anything for the land upon which they built their shanties, it must have been in whisky, for the Duke was lying drunk in his wigwam at the time of my

visit. For the sake of morals, I regret to say that he had two wives, ambitiously named Queen Victoria and Jenny Lind, and for the good repute of Indian ladies of rank it grieves me to add that the Queen and Jenny were also very tipsy, if not quite drunk when I called to pay my respects.

The Duke was lying on a rough wooden bedstead, with a bullock's hide stretched over it, enjoying his ease with the ladies of his household. When the agent informed him that a Hyas Tyee, or Big Chief, had called to see him with a message from the Great Chief of all the Indians, the Duke grunted significantly, as much as to say, "that's all right."

The Queen, who sat near him in the bed, gave him a few whacks to rouse him up and by the aid of Jenny Lind succeeded, after a while, in getting him in an upright position. His costume consisted of a red shirt and nothing else, but neither of the royal ladies seemed at all put out by the scantiness of his wardrobe. There was something very amiable and jolly in the face of the old Duke, even stupefied as he was by whisky. He took me by the hand in a friendly manner and, patting his stomach, remarked, "Duke York, belly good man!"

Browne complimented the Duke on his reputation and gave a small speech, "derived from the official formula," about the President of the United States as the "Great Chief" of all and whose white children "were as numerous as *the leaves on the trees and the grass on the plains.*"

"Oh, damn!" said the Duke, impatiently, "him send any whisky?" No, (Brown replied), on the contrary, the Great Chief had heard with profound regret that the Indians of Puget's Sound were addicted to the evil practice of drinking whisky, and it made his heart bleed to learn that it was killing them off rapidly and was the principal cause of all their misery. It was very cruel and very wicked for white men to sell whisky to the Indians....

"Oh, damn!" said the Duke, turning over on his bed and contemptuously waving his hand in termination of the interview, "dis Tyee no'count." While this wa-wa, or grand talk, was going on, the Queen put her arms affectionately around the Duke's neck and giggled with admiration at his eloquence. Jenny sat a little at one side, and seemed to be under the combined influence of whisky, jealously, and a black eye. I was subsequently informed that the Duke was in the habit of beating both the Queen and Jenny for their repeated quarrels, and when unusually drunk was not particular about either the force or direction of his blows. This accounted for Jenny's black eye and bruised features, and for the alleged absence of two of the Queen's front teeth, which it was said were knocked out in a recent brawl (Dillon, 1965).

Browne's report, printed by an order of Congress, appeared to Northwest citizens first in an Olympia newspaper. Port Townsend's settlers were outraged and wrote to him in San Francisco, stating, in part:

"Sir, it may be that on the occasion of your visit here the Duke of York and his wives were drunk; but the undersigned are satisfied, upon a personal examination, that neither Queen Victoria nor Jenny Lind suffered the loss of two front teeth...and they are not aware that Jenny Lind's eyes were ever blacked by the Duke of York, nor do they believe it...." Not to be outdone, Browne responded with "an apology" that appeared in the San Francisco papers.

When I alluded to the beachcombers, rowdies, and other bad characters in Port Townsend, I had no idea that respectable gentlemen like yourselves would take it as personal....You may deny positively that either Queen Victoria or Jenny Lind had her front teeth knocked out by the Duke of York. Well, I take that back, for I certainly did not examine their mouths as closely as you seem to have done. But when you deny that Jenny Lind's eye was black, you do me great injustice. I shall insist upon it to the latest hour of my existence that it was black-deeply, darkly, beautifully black, with a prismatic circle of pink, blue, and yellow in the immediate vicinity. I cheerfully retract the tooth, but gentlemen, I hold on to the eye. Depend upon it, I shall stand by that eye as long as the flag of freedom waves over this glorious republic ! (Dillon, 1965)

Letters flew back and forth, appearing at least in Olympia and San Francisco newspapers, before quieting months afterward. But the account was later printed in the national magazine *Harper's Weekly* and ultimately as a chapter under the title of "The Great Port Townsend Controversy, Showing How Whiskey Built a City" in an anthology of Browne's writings. Port Townsend and Chet-ze-moka became the laughing stock of the nation.

The comic notoriety was reinforced in 1863, during the weariness of the Civil War, when Theodore Winthrop's picaresque *The Canoe and The Saddle* was published.

A grandson of Connecticut's first governor, John Winthrop, the young Theodore was only 25, fresh out of Yale University, when he arrived Port Townsend on Aug. 21, 1853. His two days with Chet-ze-moka served as the beginning of a book that was brought out in dozens of editions and sold untold thousands of copies. Published first in 1863, two years after Winthrop's death as a major in the Civil War, the book seldom has been out of print.

Its burlesque portrait of Chet-ze-moka is brutal. Winthrop began his "Adventures Among the Northwestern Rivers and Forests" with this alliterative thrust:

"The Duke of York was ducally drunk."

He continued: "His brother, King George, was drunk - royalty may disdain public opinion, and fall as low as it pleases, but a brother of the throne, leader of the opposition, possible Regent, possible King, must retain at least a swaying perpendicular."

There was more. "In the great shed of slabs that served them for palace sat the Queen, - sat the Queens - mild-eyed, melancholy, copper-colored persons, also, sad to say, not sober. Etiquette demanded inebriety. The stern rules of royal indecorum must be obeyed. The Queen Dowager succumbed to ceremony; the Queen Consort was sinking; every lesser queen, - the favorites for sympathy, the neglected for consolation, - all had imitated their lord and master."

Winthrop sought a canoe and paddlers to transport him to Fort Nisqually where he was to mount a horse and saddle for an overland trek to The Dalles on the Columbia River. He could find none among Klows-ton's, or King George's, immediate entourage to accommodate him. Chet-ze-moka was, however, available and willing.

> Fortunately, without I found the Duke of York, only ducally drunk....It was a chance festival that had intoxicated the Klallams, king and court. There had been a fraternization, a powwow, a wah-wah, a peace congress with some neighboring tribe, - perhaps the Squaksnamish, or Squallyamish, or Sinahomish, or some other of the Whulgeamish, dwellers by Whulge, - the waters of Puget's Sound. And just as the festival began, there had come to Port Townsend, or Kahtai, where the king of the Klalams, or S'Klalams, now reigned, a devilsend of a lumber brig, with liquor of the fieriest. An orgie followed, a nation was prostrate (Winthrop, 1863).

Winthrop began a coy exchange with Chet-ze-moka, bargaining blankets and rum for his fare. Conversing in the Chinook jargon, the translation of his offer reads roughly: "Drunk lie the King George, a beggarly majesty at that. A mighty prince art thou, (Duke of York,) and knowest how robustly to ply paddle. I would with speed canoe it to Squally (Fort Nisqually). Store of blankets will I give and plenteous sundries."

Chet-ze-moka responded favorably, "grasping" Winthrop's "hand, after two drunken clutches at empty air." Winthrop quotes the Indian: "Yea, friend. Tender is my heart toward thee, O great Yankee don. (King George) indeed is drunk - not I - no loafer-man, the Duke of York. Got canoe, and heartily do I wish to go to Squally."

According to Winthrop, Chill-lil encouraged Chet-ze-moka, offering to join him as "the solace of thy voyage." She also hoped that her reward would be a string of beads and a pocket mirror. "Then (Winthrop writes) she smiled enticingly, her flat-faced grace, and introduced herself as Jenny Lind, or as she called it, 'Chin Lin.' Indianesque, not fully Indian was her countenance.

There was a trace of tin in her copper color, possibly a dash of Caucasian blood in her veins. Brazenness of hue was the result of this union, and a very pretty color it is with eloquent blushes mantling through it....Her forehead was slightly and coquettishly flattened by art...."

Getting Chet-ze-moka prepared for the trip provided Winthrop with more gaudy paint for his blatantly colored portrait.

"Where is my cleanest shirt, Chin Lin?" (the Duke) asked. "Nika macook lum; I buy grog with um," replied the Duchess. "Cultus mamook; a dastardly act," growled the Duke, "and I will thwack thee for 'it."Jenny Lind sank meekly upon the mud-floor, and wept, while the Duke smote her with palm, fist, and staff.

"Kopet! Hold!" cried I, rushing forward. "Thy beauteous spouse has brought the nectar for thy proper jollity. Even were she selfish, it is uncivilized to smite the fair. Among the Bostons, when women wrong us, we give pity or contempt, but not the strappado." Harangues to Indians are traditionally in such lofty style.

The Duke suffered himself to be appeased, and proceeded to dress without the missing article. He donned a faded black frock-coat, evidently a misfit for its first owner in civilization, and transmitted down a line of deformed wearers to fall amorphous on the shoulders of him of York. For coronet he produced no gorgeous combination of velvet, strawberry-leaves, and pearls; but a hat...also of civilization, wrinkled with years and battered by world-wandering, crowned him frowzily. Black dress pantaloons of brassy sheen, much crinkled at the bottom, where they fell over moccasins with a faded scarlet instep-piece, completed his costume. A very shabby old-clo' Duke. A virulent radical would have enjoyed him heartily, as. an emblem of decay in the bloated aristocracy of this region. Red paint daubed over his clumsy nose and about the flats surrounding his little, disloyal, dusky eyes, kept alive the traditional Indian in his appearance (Winthrop, 1863).

Chet-ze-moka, according to Winthrop, offered papers, "greasy documents" for him to inspect. Supposedly written by "Yankee skippers, by British naval officers, by casual travelers, (the letters were) all unanimous in opprobrium. He was called a drunken rascal, a shameless liar; a thief; called each of these in various idioms, with plentiful epithets thrown in, according to the power of imagery possessed by the author."

Displaying also a photograph that had been taken of him in San Francisco, Chet-ze-moka offered Winthrop the certificates "gravely, and with tranquil pride. He deemed himself indorsed by civilization, not branded. Men do not always comprehend the world's cynical praise. "

Winthrop's description of the overnight trip to Fort Nisqually continues with the same blatant stereotypes that made fun of Chet-ze-moka and turned him and his companions into fools.

While extreme in its portrayal, Winthrop's view of Chet-ze-moka and his tribe was not unusual. It simply exaggerated the paternalistic and misconceived white view of the native American culture. Gov. Stevens' position offered the ultimate example. In his speeches to the summoned

tribes for the so-called negotiation of treaties in 1855, Stevens repeatedly used the analogy of the whites as parents and the Indians as children. Recounting that he had been sent by "the Great Father" the year previously to ascertain the needs of the Indians, he said: "We went through this country this last year, learned your numbers and saw your wants. We felt much for you, and went to the Great Father to tell him what we had seen. That Great Father felt for his children. He pitied them and he has sent me here today to express those feelings and to make a treaty for your benefit" (Richards, 1979).

Certainly, in comparison to the vast power of the white man, the Indians were relatively helpless. But the notion of European supremacy - successful and as accurate as it proved to be in material possessions and sheer brute force was nevertheless developmentally rooted in an immature, vainglorious belief that became clearer as the decades passed.

This is easily observed in the labeling of Chet-ze-moka as "the Duke of York," his brother as "King George," and his wives as "Queen Victoria" and "Jenny Lind." Not only was there a certain smirky superiority to this practice, but it also allowed the whites to thumb their noses at their own grandees. It is behavior one might expect of sophomores, not of grown men and women who had labored hard and long to make new lives for themselves and their families in the wilderness, this last frontier.

One thing should be said for Winthrop, however: he knew well what was happening to the Indians, and he, along with Browne, was among the first to say so. "It seems a sorry thing...that we should first distinguish in people their faults and deformities," he offered as something of an apology for his cruel portrait of Chet-ze-moka. Describing the Klallam chief as "drunken, idle, insolent, and treacherous," he nevertheless observed:

> Civilization came, with step-mother kindness, baptized him with rum, clothed him in discarded slops, and dubbed him Duke of York. Hapless scarecrow, disreputable dignitary, no dukeling of thine shall ever become the Louis Philippe of Klallam revolutions. Boston men are coming in their big canoes over sea. Pikes (men who crossed the Rocky Mountains) have shaken off the fever and ague on the banks of the muddy Missouri, and are striding beyond the Rockys. Nasal twangs from the east and west soon will sound thy trump of doom. Squatters will sit upon thy dukedom, and make it their throne.

By the time *The Canoe and The Saddle* was published in 1863, 10 years after its incidents were experienced, that prophecy had become history.

The charges against Chet-ze-moka weren't only drunkenness and buffoonery; they included murder. In 1895, James Allen Costello claimed that it was a "death-dealing Duke of York" who plotted the massacre of the Chemakums 40 years earlier, not a northern tribe as McCurdy had reported. In the Costello account, Chet-ze-moka allegedly enlisted the Skagit tribe as decoys against the unsuspecting Chemakums, then led the attack himself.

> The (Chemakums) at the time were encamped upon the beach fishing and merry-making all unconscious of the terrible fate so soon to overtake them. They were there with all their ictas, their papooses scampering about the white sands, or scudding through the woods in the rear while the...Duke of York was planning their destruction. The Skagit Indians brought on the attack by appearing in front of the peaceful (Chemakum) camp in canoes, yelling and hooting to attract the(ir) attention...and bring them all out and down to the beach. The old Duke of York and his warriors, who were hidden in the woods in the rear, rushed out of their hiding places and the

slaughter began. The Skagit warriors landed and the battle was soon raging fiercely. The attacking parties were too strong and the (Chemakums) were soon at their mercy. The battle lasted but a short time and soon there was not a (Chemakum) brave left.

Costello's account, however, is suspect. Of the three extant accounts of the Chimacum massacre, none of them recorded by witnesses, only Costello implicates Chet-ze-moka. His source for this accusation was a colorful Port Townsend raconteur who was noted for the tallness of his tales and the shortness of his accuracy.

Though he offered no details, Winthrop also reported that Chet-ze-moka had murdered at least two men, a piece of information that added an element of danger to his account of the trip from Port Townsend to Fort Nisqually, but the charge has been seriously questioned. McCurdy, for one, did not believe a word of it. An early edition of "*The Canoe and The Saddle*," housed in Port Townsend's Carnegie Library, contains marginal notes by McCurdy. At the

first mention of Chet-ze-moka's involvement in a murder, McCurdy wrote in pencil, "False. J.G.M." Later, when Winthrop describes Chet-ze-moka as "beguiled into murders," McCurdy scored the passage and wrote in the margin, "All pioneers hold this to be a falsehood. J.G.M. "The truth of this matter likely is never to be known. Port Townsend settlers revered the memory of Chet-ze-moka and well may have not wanted to believe the stories. But one should also note that murder of an enemy or someone who had committed a grave offense was not unusual in tribal life at that time.

The reconstruction of Chet-ze-moka's reputation began on St. Valentine's Day, 1859, when James G. Swan sailed into Port Townsend Bay. Swan and Chet-ze-moka had met eight years earlier in San Francisco. Upon his return to Port Townsend, Chet-ze-moka had sent Swan an Indian canoe as a thank-you gift and extended an invitation to visit him at Kah-tai. Swan finally was responding to the Klallam chief's hospitality. In the interim he had lived for three years at Shoalwater Bay (now called Willapa Bay), about which he wrote the first book about life in Washington, *The Northwest Coast*. Later, he had joined Gov. Stevens, a fellow native of Massachusetts, in the conduct of the Indian treaty negotiations with southwestern Washington tribes. In 1857, Stevens was elected as the territory's Congressional representative in Washington, D.C. and Swan joined him as secretary for several months, broadening his understanding of white and Indian relationships in the

Northwest. Swan followed with interest the controversy that engaged J. Ross Browne, Port Townsend, and Chet-ze-moka, and was advised by Stevens to "Go to Port Townsend. It's going to be a situation of commercial importance" (McDonald, 1972). In San Francisco, he made arrangements with the publisher of the *Bulletin* to write articles about the Puget Sound region and then he sailed north.

Chet-ze-moka had served to protect the founders and their families against the Klallams, and Swan returned the favor by restoring Chet-ze-moka's and Port Townsend's stature with the white nation. Swan's first article appeared in the May 10, 1859 edition of the *Bulletin* where he took the issue head on.

> Those persons who have formed an opinion of Port Townsend and its inhabitants from the report of J. Ross Browne...will find matters far different at the present time. If Mr. Browne's report was correct, there certain has been a wonderful change for the better.

He noted that "the 'beach-combers' and 'outlaws'...with very few exceptions" had left. He witnessed no rioting or drunkenness and found that the conduct of citizens and visitors was "law-abiding" and "order-loving."

As for Chet-ze-moka, he found the chief "an intelligent and very reliable Indian, formerly much addicted to whiskey drinking; but of late, he has been very sober, as all the rest of the tribe have been. In fact, during a residence at Port Townsend of nearly six weeks, I have not seen a single drunken Indian."

Swan spoke a bit too soon.

Entries in his diaries during the next two years cite numerous instances of Chet-ze-moka's drunkenness, though it must be noted that two of them were the kind of ceremonies that white men also considered worthy of alcoholic celebration. One of these occurred less than two weeks after Swan's initial report appeared in the *Bulletin*.

On Saturday, May 21, Swan reported that "this morning the Duke of York bought a squaw for a his son, 'Mr. Mason,' a young man of some seventeen years."

The (wedding) ceremonies consisted of a sort of procession of the Duke's friends bringing blankets and guns. After several songs they proceeded to the lodge where the girl was and offered their presents. Two old men then made speeches and the whites retired. The bride all this time was busily engaged rolling out dough with a bottle into cakes, to be baked and appeared to take the least interest of anyone present. During the night most of the party got drunk.

Next morning, the wedding party was still "drunk and disorderly...the Duke of York particularly so, but I coaxed him away to his house where he soon went to sleep."

On March 30, 1860, Chet-ze-moka indulged on the occasion of the birth of his daughter, Ellen. The following report appeared in the April 4 edition of the "Port Townsend Register":

BIRTHS IN HIGH LIFE - Queen Victoria, the amiable spouse of the Duke of York, gave birth to a fine little princess of the House of Clallams...The same day the lady of General Washington was delivered of a son....Both infants are doing well, and were taken out...the following day for an airing on the hill. A grand banquet was given in honor of the event by the Duke of York at his palace on Water Street and a sumptuous repast of clams, halibut, salmon, skate, squid, hard bread and whiskey were served up. The Duke accompanied by Jenny Lind (and others) made a formal visit to Capt. Fay, our local Indian Agency, to announce the event. The Captain responded by giving good advice, and several yards of cheap calico.

Though frequent for a period of time, Chet-ze-moka's drinking does appear to have been episodic, stimulated either by special celebration or surprise at the unexpected availability of sporadic supplies. Further, these episodes were punctuated by long periods of sobriety when his duties as chief required that he be in control of his faculties (5).

Part of his duties were social ones that he bestowed upon Swan. On April 3, nearly two months after Swan's arrival, Chet-ze-moka invited his old friend from San Francisco to join him, his wives, and other members of his family on a fishing trip to Chimacum Creek. Passing several canoes that had been fishing, the party was offered gifts of a variety of fish so that "before we were half way to the Chemakum we had fish enough to last us a week."

Upon landing at the mouth of the creek, several of the women began harvesting clams while Chet-ze-moka, Chill-lil (Jenny Lind) and Swan began fishing for trout. "We soon had our lines in the water and had very good luck, but the place where we stood was so small that the lines were continually tangled, and at last a big trout caught the hooks of my line and that of Jenny Lind in his mouth at one time, and we both pulled the fish out together, much to the merriment of the whole party. The question now arose as to which of us the fish belonged, but Jenny soon settled that by cutting my line off close to the fish's mouth and declaring the prize to be hers."

The proprietor of the sawmill at the mouth of Chimacum Creek approached the party to invite Swan to dine with him, but Swan declined. "I preferred to dine Indian style." Their menu included clams-roasted and boiled, broiled salmon, roasted trout, mussels, oysters, and barnacles, "the last a dish I never ate of before, but which I found delicious."

Dessert was a roasted skate, eaten by

> ...grasping a handful of hot fish, and after giving it a rinse in a pan of cold water, conveying it to the mouth. Queen Victoria presided over the skate, and never was greater misnomer than to bestow the name of royalty on the amiable spouse of the Duke of York. Jenny Lind, who had served up to me my first repast of clams, and roasted trout, had the grace to blow away the ashes and sand that might adhere to the food, and place the viands in a clean tin pan, and hand one clean clam shell to use as a spoon to drink clam water with; but the Queen, bless her dirty face! is certainly, of all squaws, the Queen of Dirt, with face begrimed, hands thick with dirt, her dress all full of grease and ashes, and her hair matted and uncombed, she sat and bade me eat.

> Her first operation was to give me a pan of dirty water, which I threw away, and told her to give me good. She did so with a very pleasant laugh, for she is as good-natured as she is dirty, and when her face is washed, she is quite goodlooking. I had eaten but a few handfuls of the roasted skate, when the redoubtable General Walker (her youngest son) came toddling along, having soiled his shoes by stepping into some filth. The Queen no sooner discovered this, than she took them off and commenced to wash them in the very pan of water I was using to cool my fish in. This was rather too much for my appetite, so I concluded my repast very abruptly (Swan, 1971).

This was the most critical comment Swan ever wrote about Chet-ze-moka or his family. Betrayed for the moment by his own cultural patterning, Swan's relationship with Chet-ze-moka was solid and if Swan ever held a sense of superiority over the Klallam chief and his wives, he kept it to himself. As noted, he privately lamented and occasionally expressed frustration in his journals over Chet-ze-moka's fondness for whiskey, but that was the extent of his criticism.

At the end of April, Chet-ze-moka invited Swan and several Port Townsend residents to observe portions of their tamanawos, an initiation ceremony, into the secret society the Klallams called xun- xani'te. This elaborate, several-days event, involved placing initiates into a death-like trance, slaughtering a dog which may have been eaten raw, singing and drumming and dancing, complete with masks, headdresses, costumes and face and body paint. Its purpose, according to Swan (1971), was to "(avert)...evil, and...(to) obtain plenty of food for the ensuing year."

The strangeness of the ceremony evoked in its white witnesses both fear and nervous laughter. At one point, on the second night of the ceremony, fires were burning dimly in each corner of the long house while light was provided by a "bright fire of fir bark" in the center. Opposite the white visitors, a section on the left side of the lodge was screened with red blankets to hide the performers during costume changes. Directly opposite them were 20 men and boys, their faces blackened, their hair powdered with goosedown. While singing they accompanied themselves with rattles, and drums, "thumping the roof, and shaking in the air bunches of shells, and waving fans made of white geese wings." Their chorus was followed by a single Indian who "rushed out from behind the screen with a gun, ran round the fire two or three times, and then, pointing his gun at the opening of the screen, awaited the approach of something." Three Indians appeared

,...crawling on their hands and knees, having masks on resembling huge lizards' heads. They were perfectly hideous. Painted up with black and red, with great glass eyes, and an erect mane of hair, they certainly looked like some of the dragons of old, pictured out by the fertile imagination of ancient painters.

This performance was followed by other imitations of bears, then owls, "look(ing) like the devil...moping and bowing about."

Swan noted that several in the white audience "had to give vent to their feelings by laughing. This gave great offence to the Indians, to whom all this mummery was of grave importance; and so as soon as the maskers retired, the old chief rose and gave the Duke of York a reprimand for not keeping better order among the white people...." The old chief shortly declared the ceremonies closed and instructed the whites to leave, although the ritual continued for another three days, ending with a potlatch. Not all of Chet-ze-moka's duties as chief were social or ritualistic. On many occasions recorded by Swan and others he served as translator, escort, or as an intermediary. Mostly he accompanied the whites in their adjudications with Indians, but sometimes he spoke on behalf of Indians before the whites. He successfully interceded on behalf of his tribes-men who were sentenced to hard labor shackled by "ball and chain" for their part in the Dungeness massacre; his action secured their freedom. And as Lambert notes in her account (entitled *Circumstantial Evidence* on page 207), Chet-ze-moka saved the life of a tribes-man about to be hanged by a lynch mob in Port Townsend.

Although Indian agent Michael T. Simmons had complained in his June 1858 report to the Secretary of the Interior that "the Duke of York has not the influence that a chief should have with his people," Chet-ze-moka's impact was not immeasurable. When a young Makah chief was killed in 1861 by a member of the Klallams' Elwha band who was carrying goods from Port Townsend to a white trader at Neah Bay, Chet-ze-moka accompanied Swan to find the murderer. Chet-ze-moka was not to bring him to justice, because the matter was a personal one between the two Indians, but to recover the white man's goods. Chet-ze-moka's intervention was critical to Swan's success.

He had mixed results in his appeals before the white society. His joint plea with Chief Sealth in 1858 to spare the life of Chief Leschi was unsuccessful (Meeker, 1905), but he later thwarted a mob of angry whites who wanted to lynch an Indian for the alleged killing of a mail carrier. Chet-ze-moka later was credited with searching out sufficient evidence to clear the young Indian and secure his release (McCurdy, 1937).

Simmons' complaint of lack of influence was not just of Chet-ze-moka. Not comprehending the role of a chief in Indian culture, Simmons saw a pattern that was "...characteristic of all the Indians west of the Cascade mountains."

"There are none," he said, "that actually deserve the name of chief. This is to be regretted, for if one of them had mind and courage enough to obtain great influence among his people, he would be able to see the advantages of civilization, and the chief, if he is really a chief, would carry his people with him." Evidently, blaming the victim is not a recent phenomenon in cultural criticism.

With the treaty signed by Congress and proclaimed by President Buchanan in early 1859, relocation to the new Skokomish reservation on Hood Canal loomed for the Klallams and surviving Chemakums. The treaty provision allowed for the transfer to occur within one year of the treaty's ratification. The record is sketchy on the matter. Some (white) historians believe that it

never happened (Eells), but Lambert, who was Chet-ze-moka's cousin, provided an account in her privately printed booklet, *Dungeness Massacre and Other Stories*, written nearly 100 years later (see page 66).

According to tales passed down by members of the tribe, 50 Klallam canoes assembled in Port Townsend Bay, probably in the early 1860s, and were towed by steamboat around Marrowstone Point down Hood Canal to Skokomish. As they looked back at their Kah-tai homeland, they saw their village in flames. Once at Skokomish they were set loose and drifted ashore, but their new home was intolerable. Within five days they began, canoe by canoe, to return. Keeping a distance, Chet-ze-moka and his family established residence across the bay on Indian Island.

With this act, the conquering was effectively complete. Although the Klallams returned to their homelands, the 12 villages listed in the 1855 Point No Point Treaty soon became only three and two of these were not historic sites. In being hauled away, the Indian claim to their traditional homes was destroyed. It was now the white man's land and not until the early 1960s did the U.S. government fully settle up with the Klallams for what they had taken.

At this point, Chet-ze-moka falls out of frequent view in the literature of the period. This was due, in part, to Swan's relocation to Neah Bay and his growing interest in the Makahs and the northern tribes. With threat of Indian war over, and the recovery of the national economy after the Civil War, the white settlements began to expand and to burgeon. When Swan returned to Port Townsend in the late 1860s, his attention was consumed by his attempts to interest the Northern Pacific Railway in siting its terminus in Port Townsend. To the white community, the Indians and their culture were a part of a past they wished to release.

In June 1870, Swan recorded in his journal that Chet-ze-moka had met with the territory's Congressional representative in an attempt to have Indian Island declared a reservation. According to Lambert, promises were made in writing but nothing came of it.

Whiskey re-enters the picture in 1876.

On Sunday, Jan. 9, Chet-ze-moka, his two wives, and daughter, visited Swan to sell a basket, but "Jenny (Lind) was drunk and I cleared them out and told the Duke to come tomorrow." Subsequent entries made no mention of a follow-up visit.

On July 24, Swan wrote:

> Frank Tucker wedding. This was the funniest wedding ever on Puget Sound. I was invited but it being...court day I (couldn't) leave. Rev. Mr. Rea officiated. The party went down from here in two or three steamers and schooners, Hunt, Pettygrove, Maj. Van., Geo. Howell and half the town. It was to be a Good Templars wedding, but the boys smuggled some liquor on board and the whole party had a glorious (time). The occasion of old Frank's wedding will never be forgotten, by those who were present. The Duke of York was invited but the steamer went off and left him. He was very angry about it. The party returned late at night, pretty tired.

On Oct. 12, 1880, Port Townsend streets were planted with evergreen trees and an arch with a large sign reading Welcome was erected at the head of Union Wharf. A banner hoisted across Water Street boasted, "We Honor the

President." At 5 p.m. as the party of Pres. Rutherford B. Hayes eased into its berth at Union Wharf, bells rang, cannons boomed, and the gathered citizens of Port Townsend cheered its first and only visit by a sitting president.

The President was escorted to the nearby wood-frame Central Hotel where he mounted the balcony and spoke to the throng. He expressed pleasure at the assembly of citizens and encouraged the crowd by saying that Port Townsend had a "great future," but that its citizens "must be willing to labor for the common good and exercise patience. He seemed touched by seeing so many children present and spoke words of encouragement to them, advising them to persevere in their studies and reminded them that they would be the citizens of tomorrow" (McCurdy, 1937).

The presidential party was driven about town in open carriages as bonfires blazed to light the way. At 7:30 p.m., according to newspaper reports of the day, 500 people crowded into the Central Hotel for a public reception. The "Puget Sound Argus," based in Port Townsend, bragged: "...everybody, old and young, rich and poor, filed in to shake the hands of our distinguished guests. The occasion...will long be remembered. The President and those with him were delighted...they were especially pleased because those who attended their reception included ALL instead of those from higher walks of life only."

The *Argus* didn't mention it, but the *Seattle Weekly Intelligencer* reported that among the guests was "the Duke of York, who was introduced by a special committee."

After all that had gone on before and was still unresolved - the promises of the treaties not having been fulfilled, the Great White Father and the Klallam chief were face to face. What they said to one another was not reported.

In 1884, Chet-ze-moka's chieftaincy was reduced in authority by the Superintendent of Indian Affairs to that of sub-chief. Why this was done is not clear; likely, there were probably too few Indians remaining in the Port Townsend area - most having moved to Jamestown - to warrant a full chief.

Two years later, Swan recorded that a large family of touring performers had played at Learned's Opera House on Dec. 1, 1886, "to a large and delighted

Indians to dance and sing." The child performers watched carefully "learning some of the songs and dances and afterward repeated them...with great success."

Ten months later, Swan jotted in his journal: "(The) Prince of Wales caught 1000 salmon last night so (the) Duke of York and Queen Victoria were selling them today."

And that was the end of him. Within another 10 months, he was dead.

On June 21, 1888, Chet-ze-moka's two sons, the Prince of Wales and Charlie Swan York (13), crossed the bay from Indian Island to announce their father's death, "giving vent to their heartfelt lamentations," according to the *Puget Sound Argus*. Once again, the whites took command.

Frank Pettygrove, a son of one of the town's founders, immediately began a fund drive "to give the old fellow a decent white man's burial." He obtained a suit of clothes, a plot at the cemetery, a "substantial" coffin, the free use of

a hearse, a team of horses to pull it, and he began a subscription list to help pay other costs. By the end of the day, he had raised $50 for the services. The "Argus" also established a fund for "a suitable monument...in recognition of the debt of gratitude which all pioneers and their successors owe to his memory."

Two days later his body was laid out for viewing at the county courthouse. He was then buried at what is now called Laurel Grove Cemetery. The *Seattle Weekly Intelligencer* reported that "no Indian in Washington Territory, and very likely none in the United States, ever received so flattering a funeral as did the Duke of York...." According to their report, his cortege was escorted from the courthouse to the cemetery by the port of entry guards and "22 carriages, filled with our oldest and wealthiest citizens following the hearse." (The *Argus* reported 15 carriages.) The service was read by the vicar of St. Paul's Episcopal Church. Before Chet-ze-moka's body was "consigned to the earth," a salute was fired by the guards.

But for all the regard, genuine as it no doubt was, the newspaper accounts, read 100 years later, still are steeped with the cliches of white supremacy.

Said the *Argus*: "Altogether it was an event in the history of Port Townsend and was a fitting sequel to the lifelong friendship of (the) deceased for the paleface."

And the *Weekly Intelligencer* concluded: "Although the chief was undoubtedly sincerely mourned by Queen Victoria, his wife, and the rest of the tribe, not a tear was shed at the funeral, illustrating the stoic nature of the redmen."

It was Swan who, once again, felt and was able to best express the poignancy of the complex relationship between the settlers and the Indians. Writing from Massachusetts where he was on what turned out to be the final visit to his own family, Swan sent $5 to the "Argus's" memorial fund. He wrote:

> The Duke of York was a man of more than average intellectual capacity and had a full understanding of justice and integrity, and during the many years of our personal acquaintance, I never knew him to wrong or defraud any one.   What he promised he performed, and the early pioneers can tell many a tale of kindness shown by him to distressed white persons....Though an untutored Indian he had a manly sense of right which showed by his acts that he had an intuitive conception of better things. I am one of those, as Longfellow beautifully expresses it,
>
> > *Who have faith in God and Nature,*
> > *Who believe, that in all ages*
> > *Every human heart is human.*
> > *That in every savage bosom*
> > *There are longings, yearnings, strivings*
> > *For the good they comprehend not,*
> > *That the feeble hands and helpless*
> > *Groping blindly in the darkness*
> > *Touch God's right hand in that darkness*
> > *And are lifted up and strengthened.*

By the time he reached his own reward, Chet-ze-moka had seen both the coming of the settlers and the death of their founders. Hastings had died in 1881 at age 67. Plummer died in 1883; he was 61. Pettygrove died at age 75 in 1887. For all the benefits of the white culture, Chet-ze-moka had lived to a riper old age. Clearly, theirs had been a march of heroes, their destiny intertwined by circumstance and unthinking choice. The cost to the Indian was near annihilation, a loss of wealth and a way of life. The cost to the white man was a few lives. But to the men and women of Port Townsend the experience with Chet-ze-moka and the Klallams offered something of a heightened conscience. Though not fully appreciating and certainly not acknowledging what they had done to the Indians, they understood the gratitude they owed Chet-ze-moka.

The grave marker was fully subscribed and was quickly installed.

It read:

CHETZEMOKA
June 21, 1888
(The Duke of York)
"The White Man's Friend"
We honor his name

The atonement continued. In 1893, when Port Townsend's massive federal building was completed, the sandstone capitals on the entry columns had been carved in likenesses of Chet-ze-moka and members of his family. In 1904, a women's civic group selected some land on Admiralty Inlet not far from the old Klallam encampments at Point Hudson, held a work party consisting of husbands and brothers, and established the city's first park, naming it in honor of Chet-ze-moka. In 1937, the Lucinda Hastings Parlor No. 1 of the Native Daughters of Washington installed a bronze plaque on Sentinel Rock to commemorate his saving of the white people from massacre.

These memorials are carefully maintained to this day.

And in 1989, 101 years after Chet-ze-moka's death, Port Townsend sculptor Paco Mitchell proposed to cast a bronze bust of the Klallam chief for installation at Chet-ze-moka Park as "an invitation to consider the reality of our past,...a tacit acknowledgment of the terrible truth of European supremacy and...a grain of moral weight toward a balancing of the scales."

NOTES

1. It is not known who first called Chet-ze-moka the "Duke of York." Gregory (1966) says that it was Oregon Columbus Hastings, but the red-headed first son of Port Townsend's first white family was only about six years old when the family arrived in Port Townsend, so the credit probably does not belong to him, but to Hudson's Bay Company men. In the polyglot 500-word Chinook jargon that developed from various Indian languages, English, and French, men associated with the Hudson's Bay Company were called "King George's men" by the Indians while they called the Americans "Boston men," each moniker accurately reflecting their origins, most American settlers of that time having originated from New England. It is likely that "King George's men" used their own royalty as names for Indian leaders and their families, and the same may have been true for the "Boston men" who probably were responsible for such Indian nicknames as "General Washington" and "General Gaines." However, the first recorded uses of the name "Duke of York" were made by "Boston men" (Browne, Simmons, Swan, Winthrop).

2. The Prince of Wales continues, in diminutive form, as the family name. When the Klallams began to discard their Indian names, Lah-ka-nim's children chose "Prince" as their surname. After the death of the Prince of Wales in the early 1940s and after the U.S. Navy purchased Indian Island where they had lived on Scow Bay, the family moved to Jamestown.

3. McCurdy says that this speech by Chet-ze-moka was made in "the fall of 1855 at Port Madison." That is possible, although no other record of such an assembly at that time and place has been found by this writer. Nevertheless, the arguments used by Chet-ze-moka to justify his position in the McCurdy account likely were similar in content to those that he would have made at Heb-Heb-O-Lub, and are used here as representative of his view. Although they offer few specifics to substantiate their claim, Stock and Pembroke say (on page 70) that "the reasoning of Chet-ze-moka had been the greatest influence (at Heb-Heb-O-Lub) in preventing agreement to wage war." The quotations from McCurdy's so-called Port Madison account are probably a good example of Chet-ze-moka's "reasoning."

4. It is possible that McCurdy's and Trotter's accounts are the same event, attributed to different times and circumstances. Certainly they are similar in content. Eells (1886) confirms Trotter's story. "After (Chet-ze-moka's) return (from San Francisco) the Indians became very much enraged at the residents of Port Townsend, who were few in numbers, and the savages were almost all ready to engage in war with them. Had they done so, they could easily have wiped out the place, and the white people knew it. The Indians were ready to do so, but the Duke of York stood between the Indians and the

whites. For hours the savage mass surged to and fro, hungry for blood, the Duke of York's brother being among the number. For as many hours the Duke of York alone held them from going any farther, by his eloquence, telling them of the numbers and power of the whites; and that if the Indians should kill these whites, others would come and wipe them out. At last they yielded to him. He saved Port Townsend and saved his tribe from a war with the whites."

5.   Swan's public silence about Chet-ze-moka's affinity for alcohol may have been tempered by his own weakness for the beverage. Known to go on periodic binges himself, Swan - at age 65 - was declared by the local courts in 1884 to be "a habitual drunkard" (McDonald, 1972).

JAMESTOWN

Commentary

The Jamestown Klallam are unique among Indian groups in western Washington, having purchased a land base more than 100 years ago, residing there as a community and maintaining their tribal identity to the present.

The Point No Point Treaty contained two inconsistent provisions: on one hand, the Klallam secured the right to fish in their "usual and accustomed grounds and stations." On the other hand, they were assigned to a reservation 100 to 180 miles away from their usual and accustomed fishing places along the Strait of Juan de Fuca.

Edwin Eells, the agent in charge of the Skokomish Reservation, and Michael Simmons, the first Indian agent for the Puget Sound District, advised the Superintendent of Indian Affairs of the Klallam dilemma and Simmons even assured the Klallam that one or more reservations would be made for them in their own territory.

Despite efforts of Simmons and others, and in spite of repeated requests by Klallam leaders, no action to establish official reservations in Klallam territory was taken until 1981.

In 1874, a band of Klallams under the leadership of Lord James Balch, whose father had signed the 1855 treaty, raised $500 in gold coin and purchased 210 acres near Dungeness, Washington Territory. In so doing they refused relocation or extinction and concentrated on survival.

The people who formed this community came mainly from villages in the vicinity of the Dungeness River and what is now known as Sequim Bay (formerly Washington Harbor). Other Jamestown families came from Clallam Bay to the west and from Port Discovery (now Discovery Bay) to the east.

Today the old neighborhood community of Jamestown is unrecognizable. The late 19th century Klallam settlement of 200 people belongs to the past. Fewer than half of the 224 enrolled tribal members still reside in the old

neighborhood (enrollment requirements specify a minimum of one-quarter traceable Jamestown Klallam blood for eligibility); but, as a cultural entity, the Jamestown community is alive and well, a strong economic and political presence on the Olympic Peninsula.

What follows is a history of this amazing community reprinted from Lewis Langness' master's thesis written in the 1950s while he was an undergraduate at the University of Washington. The selection relates the history and development of the Jamestown community. The original thesis also examines that history within the context of anthropological theories of native reform movements, and raises questions about the relation between the psychological states engendered by different contact situations, and particular responses to those states.

After reviewing the pre-contact ethnography of the Klallam and tracing the history and development of Jamestown, Langness compares their history with the Makah, the Skokomish, and the Quileute, their neighbors to the west, south and southwest.

In the 1860s treaty terms were enforced on the Makah, Quileute and Twana and they began reservation life. Most of the Klallam were never placed on reservations. In order to exercise their treaty fishing rights they remained in their traditional territory and continued to fish there and as always, depending upon their traditional leaders to direct economic activity, religious functions, and settle disputes.

While the reservation tribes actively resisted being forced to accept Christianity, schools and agriculture, the people at Jamestown were making a conscious and inspired effort voluntarily to bring about these same changes. In fact, Jamestown embraced change.

During the years preceding Jamestown the Klallam culture broke down and native people were increasingly subordinate to white society. Whites circulated petitions to relocate Klallams to the Skokomish Reservation. Known as "Siwash," they were criticized, punished, exploited, despised and sometimes murdered.

The Klallam were a highly class conscious people now relegated to the lowest possible class; their numbers plummeted because of disease and

alcohol, although they recognized liquor as one of the chief sources of their dilemma; they were aware of conditions on the reservations and the futility of resistance - all are factors Langness identifies that apparently combined to bring about the Jamestown reform.

Jamestown was forward looking.   The people involved did not want to perpetuate or revive any traditional customs or beliefs. The first generation born into Jamestown continued what their parents had started, teaching children to avoid use of the native language, clearing land to plant crops and gardens, adjusting to neighboring whites, creating a school, and even introducing the first Christian church to the region, complete with white paint, church bell, and prayer meetings.

The Jamestown Klallam received federal recognition in 1981, and now have a small reservation at the head of Sequim Bay.

A CASE OF POST CONTACT REFORM AMONG THE KLALLAM

L.L. Langness

In 1874, one group of Klallam Indians embarked upon a rather extensive reform program and founded the community of Jamestown on the Olympic Peninsula....This is an attempt to record and analyze the Jamestown movement, to determine the conditions which may have precipitated it, and to see how well it fits current hypotheses pertaining to culture change.

It is not my intention to discuss Klallam acculturation in general. I have chosen to restrict this thesis to the investigation of Jamestown and the events surrounding its inception and development. Jamestown is only one of the three remaining Klallam settlements. It is not typical of the acculturation process experienced by most Puget Sound groups. It is interesting and instructive because it does present a contrast to the typical situation.

... Many of the Klallam were never placed on reservations and have never been wards of the government. Those who are now on reservations were established there only recently and have a somewhat different contact history than the Makah, the Skokomish, or the Quileute, their neighbors to the west, south, and southwest, respectively. This may well have had significant effects upon personality and the rate of assimilation....

When Juan Perez reached Nootka in 1774, he found the Indians there already in possession of bits of iron and copper, presumably taken from wrecked vessels which had drifted in to the coast.

Captain James Cook had touched the northwest coast by 1778 and also during these years several others touched upon it (Meany, 1916). In view of the extensive and frequent contacts among the Indians of Puget Sound it is doubtless the case that the Klallam knew of the presence of whites before they came into direct contact with them.

The first violence of any kind on the Olympic Peninsula between whites and Indians was probably the fight between Captain Quadra and the Quinault 1775, the next between Captain Barkley and the natives near Destruction Island in 1787 (Sperlin, 1917). There is some evidence to indicate that by 1790, some of the Indians on Cape Flattery had been contacted by missionaries and had been baptized (Sperlin, 1917). The first settlement in Washington was made by the Spaniards at Neah Bay in March 1792. This establishment was abandoned in October of the same year (Sperlin, 1917). There is every reason to believe that the Klallam had heard of these contacts, they quite possibly visited the Spanish settlement (Gibbs, 1877).

It is equally probable that the Klallam had been contacted directly by 1789.

> So far as the records at present available disclose Captain Gray in the "Washington" in March, 1789, marked the furthest advance of the trader within the Straits of Fuca when he reached Klallam Bay. In 1790 Quimper reached Port Discovery; in 1791, Elisa made his way into the Gulf of Georgia and examined its shores as far as Cape Lazo; but these were Spanish exploring expeditions. Vancouver's expedition (1796) appears to have been the first of any kind to enter Puget Sound (Howay, 1915).

There were Klallam settlements at both Port Discovery and Klallam Bay. According to statements given to Gibbs (1877) one of these ships did contact the Klallam and gave them presents of knives, buttons and copper.

Vancouver contacted the Klallam in 1792 and remarked upon their indifference to him (he, of course, believed himself the first to visit there). He traded them copper, trinkets, and knives. They offered to sell him two children (Gibbs).

These first contacts served to introduce some European goods to the Indians, acquainted them with whites, and opened the way for the fur trade which was to follow. It is interesting to note that at this time these Indians did not possess an abundance of furs. (Vancouver, as quoted by Gibbs, 1877) They did have some, of course, but probably only those used for their own clothing. Within two years of this time other ships had come and the Indians had been introduced to muskets, shot and powder, iron hoops, broken iron, looking glasses, and other trinkets (Gibbs, 1877). All of these ships traded for furs as well as for curios such as bows and arrows and Indian blankets. From this time on more and more ships called, all wanting furs, which the Indians soon learned to supply. These fur trading ships continued to call for several years.

In 1825, Fort Vancouver was established on the Columbia as a trading post (Meany, 1916). The Klallam knew of its existence but it is unlikely that there was extensive traffic between the Klallam and this fort.

The only serious military incident between the Klallam and the whites seems to have been in 1828, when a number of Klallam, two of whom had been serving as guides for five white men, murdered them and took possession of their equipment. This apparently was sparked by the ill treatment accorded the two Klallam guides by one of the whites. (Curtis, 1913) In any event a party of approximately 60 men from Fort Vancouver visited the Klallam and attacked the first Klallam house they found, murdering seven people (men, women and children) and burning the house. Then, in conjunction with a ship they attacked with cannon fire and muskets the Klallam village at Dungeness and destroyed it by burning. They also made away with several canoes and other Indian property. A total of 25 Klallam were reported killed (Ermatinger, 1914, also Dye, 1907).

This action perpetuated suspicion and ill feeling between the Klallam and whites but evidence as to how long it lasted is lacking.

In 1832, a trading post and agricultural settlement was established at Nisqually. It is recorded in the records of Nisqually House that the Klallam were trading skins and game there by 1833 (Farrar, 1915). The records kept between May 1833 and April 1835 show that Klallam visited there at least nine times, in every case to trade furs. Also one trading expedition was made to Klallam territory by this company during this same period. These records indicate that on several occasions the Klallam did not go through with the trade because they believed the rate of exchange to be unfair. On these occasions they retained their furs and expressed their intention to wait for some competitive trader.

On one of these trips a rumor was received at Nisqually that the Klallam were preparing to attack because of the destruction of their village six years previously. This proved to be unfounded but it does indicate that there was some suspicion between the Klallam and the whites. It is also the case, however, that one Klallam, reportedly the son of the chief slain at Dungeness, was at this time a trusted messenger for the whites between Nisqually, Fort Vancouver, and other places. The only trading mentioned in this report was beaver and sea otter skins for blankets, but no doubt many other items were being traded also (Farrar, 1915).

A census was taken by the Hudson's Bay Company in 1845, which showed the Klallam to number then about 1,500 (Gunther, 1927). This may not have been accurate but there is no reason to believe that the population had diminished appreciably by this time.

By 1847, when Paul Kane visited Nisqually House, there were 6,000 sheep and 2,000 cattle and as an agricultural station it had proved very successful (Kane, 1925). We can assume that the Klallam traded extensively with Nisqually House for this entire period and by this time were serving occasionally as guides for visiting travelers. They also must have been impressed by the increasing wealth in the form of cattle, goods, and agricultural products.

Kane's book indicates clearly that slavery was still practiced, that the Klallam by this time had largely given up bows and arrows and were in possession of guns, that duck netting was still common, shamanism was being practiced, and that shell money was still valued. He gives an excellent account of the performance of a shaman curing a Klallam girl (Kane, 1925).

At least one of the Klallam villages he visited was still fortified and was inhabited by approximately 200 Klallam. He was received there with cordiality and made sketches of some of the inhabitants (Kane, 1925).

Just prior to his arrival a battle had been fought between the Makah and the Klallam in which the latter had suffered a loss. This had come about because of an argument over the possession of a whale killed by the Makah which drifted into Klallam territory and was claimed by them (Kane, 1925).

In 1850 the first settler arrived at Port Townsend. In the same year a Klallam chief, the Duke of York, was taken to San Francisco by a ship captain. He returned very impressed with what he had seen of the whites there (Swan, 1859). In 1851 four more settlers arrived at Port Townsend and the first one arrived on the Sequim prairie at Dungeness. By 1853 sawmills were already in operation at Port Gamble and Port Ludlow and two more settlers were in the vicinity of Dungeness. The settlement at Dungeness was known as "Whiskey Flats," and for good reason. Liquor was sold freely to the Indians, who were numerous, far outnumbering the whites. There could not have been more than three or four cabins at this time and these were of crude construction, little better than those of the Indians (Meany, 1916, and the *Sequim Press*, 1951).

In 1853 the Klallam were visited by General A.V. Kautz. I have not been able to ascertain where the village he described was located. It could have been any one of three or four. He writes:

> Visit to Klallam - The Indians at this place are more primitive than those at the head of the Sound. They are less nomadic and have seen little of the whites and crowded with great curiosity about our camp. They have no range, except on the water, for the country behind is quite impenetrable. Their abodes are permanent, for they live in extensive

houses, reminding me of the tobacco sheds in the east. They are formed of large posts, supporting beams, some of them so large that it is a source of wonder how they are handled. The sides and roofs are formed of huge slabs of cedar fastened together with strong twigs. An elliptical hole through one of these slabs forms the door, and often the entrance consists of a passage-way of rough boards. The posts are decorated with carvings and drawings of men, animals and faces, ornamented with black and red paint. On the wall inside hang the mats on which they sleep. A horizontal beam is fastened to the posts, from which provisions are hung. There is room enough in such a structure for several families. They seem to be great lovers of size, for I saw a canoe this evening at least fifty feet long and six feet wide. It is doubtless used for the migration of the tribe, for it would hold a family or half a tribe. They are evidently poor, for they offer no food for sale, and when I tried to buy fish or game from them they asked high prices. Fortunately I had some of the venison from a buck the doctor had killed. The clams are accessible to us as well as to the Indians, besides which among our regular supplies we have bread, coffee and sugar. The Indians themselves live mainly on salmon and clams. They have a few potato patches, and I presume they also kill some game, but although it is quite abundant it is very difficult to get on account of the timber. I noticed a number of fish weirs at the mouth of the small streams. They are made of sticks placed about two inches apart, inclining downstream and forming a complete dam. Connected with this dam, similar sticks are placed up stream so as to form little pens. The salmon leaps over the dam, falling into the pen, and is readily caught by the Indian who is on the watch sitting on a mat placed on a slab on the pen. On the sand spits nets have been suspended from tall poles for the purpose of catching wild ducks and geese at the time of their annual flights. They fly against them in the night and kill themselves (Kautz, 1899).

At the time the whites first came to Dungeness (1851) Lord Jim Balch was the chief at Dungeness and the Duke of York was also a high ranking chief. That both of these Indians were well acquainted with liquor is well documented, and it is undoubtedly true that many of those who had much contact with the whites were similar in their drinking habits.

It seems that during this time there was a practice of giving "letters of recommendation" to the Indians.

> Lord Jim is very intelligent and can speak English quite well. He took a great deal of pride in showing me some papers he had received from different whites, principally sea captains. I was very much amused at their contents, for most of them abused him without reserve, calling him a liar, a thief, a drunkard and a gambler. Some of them were curious literary productions, abounding in flowers of speech. Lord Jim, of course, imagined these certificates of his rascality to contain nothing but praise and begged me to add mine to the number, which I think will help him as much as any of the others (Kautz, 1900).

Another traveler, Theodore Winthrop, visited the Klallam in 1853. In his somewhat suspicious account he describes a trip with the Duke of York and the Duke's wife, Jenny Lind, both of whom were intoxicated and caused him some trouble. They guided him to Nisqually and were paid in blankets for their trouble. Winthrop also describes some "certificates" which were possessed by the Duke of York and which were similar in tone to those described above (Winthrop, 1913).

According to E. A. Sterling, an early Indian agent, the Klallam were trading mostly in Victoria at this time. Also, like the other tribes of the sound, they were emulating the behavior of the whites to a certain extent.

> As a general rule, the characters of all these Indians are similar. They all depend upon fish, berries, and roots for a subsistence, and all evince a desire to copy after the whites. The pride they take in dressing in cloth, and in being thought to have dropped their savage customs, and to have approached, distantly, to the manners and appearance of the whites, forms a most marked difference between them and the Indians formerly inhabiting the eastern part of the United States (Starling, 1854).

There was at least one case of a white man being murdered by an Indian in Dungeness at this time. Several Indians were detained until the murderer was surrendered (MacDonald, 1958).

It is interesting to compare statements about some of these Indians for the insight they offer into the interpersonal relations between whites and Indians. General Kautz, a brief visitor, writes:

> I was introduced to the Duke of York and Lord Jim, both of whom are superior to any Indians I have yet met....Lord Jim is very intelligent and can speak English quite well (Kautz, 1900).

Allen Weir, one of the earliest settlers in Dungeness writes some-what differently:

> ...Lord Jim was one of the principal chiefs. He was saucy, cunning, and utterly unscrupulous.   When George Davidson first arrived at Dungeness, Lord Jim undertook to make him pay two bits for a drink out of the Dungeness River. Davidson's foot came up rather suddenly and collided with Mr. Indian's chin, and the latter recovered consciousness an hour or two afterward (Weir, 1900).

A more sophisticated observer, the ethnographer George Gibbs, visited the Klallam in 1855. According to his report (1877) the Klallam numbered 926 at the time of his visit. This census is believed by Eells (1866) to have been too low.   Even so, it is probably the case that their numbers had been significantly decreased because of intemperance and disease.   Gibbs states that this was the case. From Gibbs' report one gains the impression that in 1855, raiding was still going on between the Klallam and some of their neighbors; bows and arrows and the war club were almost entirely gone; the potato was being cultivated by all the sound tribes, but not extensively; the fur trade was almost extinct; slavery still existed; the potlatch was still widespread among the Klallam; flattening of the head was still practiced, but not on the children of mixed marriages.

> ...For a different reason, it is not performed on the offspring of whites by Indian mothers, it being a matter of pride to assimilate them to their fathers (1877).

Puberty ceremonies for girls were still practiced in 1855. The Indians were now familiar with money and almost all of them were dressed in the manner of the whites. Gibbs goes onto say that many tools and utensils of European manufacture were being used. At that time there were still Indians living who could remember the first ships which had contacted the Klallam (Gibbs, 1877).

In 1855 the Klallam along with the Skokomish and Chemakum signed a treaty with the whites in which they agreed to give up their land in return for reservations and governmental support. They were to be moved to the Skokomish reservation (at the southern tip of Hood Canal) at government

expense and given aid in the form of rations and instruction. This move was never carried out, however, and most of the Klallam simply remained where they were. They did begin to receive some rations from the government which were distributed at Skokomish from time to time. These were never extensive. Under the terms of the treaty they were forbidden to trade on the Canadian side of the strait.

In 1856 there were numerous Indian difficulties around Puget Sound and Fort Townsend was established about three miles from the town of Port Townsend. There were no great disturbances after this time, however, and the troops garrisoned there took part in only a few minor incidents connected with Indian affairs (Cowell, 1925).

In 1859 there were only 300 whites in Port Townsend. Some attempt was made to curb Indian drunkenness. The Duke of York was chief of about 200 Klallam in Port Townsend. The Duke, whose trip to San Francisco had so impressed him with the strength of the whites, did much to promote peaceful relations (Swan, 1859).

In 1857 a lighthouse was built at Dungeness and at this time there were approximately 35 settlers in the vicinity of Dungeness. Five years later Dungeness was still hardly an impressive settlement, there were a few white residents all living in crude cabins, only two horses and wagons in the community, and even oxen were still rare (Lotzgesell, 1933, and Weir, 1900).

Consistent dominance-subordinate relations between Indians and whites were still in the process of being established. For example, Mrs. Lotzgesell writes:

Bands of Indians would pay visits to the early settlers, go through their homes and fields and anything that attracted their attention was taken without opposition. If a farmer grew potatoes the band would dig a sack for each member and walk off with the usual 'ugh' (1933).

Caroline Leighton reports:

> Yesterday, as we sat there, we received a call from two Indians in extreme undress. They walked in with perfect freedom, and sat down on the floor (Leighton, 1884).

Allen Weir, reminiscing about the same period of time says:

> John Allen went to Victoria in 1861 and while away his squaw wife at Dungeness was killed. On his return, blaming the Indians for the death of his squaw, Allen shot an Indian. The next day the Indians were arranged in war paint on one side of the Dungeness River, and the white men of the settlement (a little more than a handful compared with the
>
> Indians) were gathered on the opposite bank prepared for the worst. Fortunately the affair was patched up without further bloodshed by John Allen paying the relatives of the dead Indian a sum of money (1900).

Also according to Weir there was smallpox among the Klallam at about this time. There is no account of how serious it was (1900). In 1859 Clallam County was formed. In 1860 the first election was held with a total vote of 90. In 1861 the first school was held for three months at Dungeness. In 1863 the first Sunday school class was held and the first building of real lumber was erected. In 1864 a road was cut 12 feet wide from Port Angeles to Sequim. The first postmaster was appointed in Sequim in 1866. At this time there were only two buildings there, a post office and a school. In 1867 Dungeness was the county seat and the largest community in Clallam County. In 1867 an election was held and in this one, 116 votes were cast. In 1866 the first school district was established with a total of 69 pupils (all persons over four and under 21) (Lauridson and Smith, 1937, *Sequim Press*, 1951, and MacDonald, 1952).

At about this time, perhaps a few years earlier, slavery was given up completely by the Klallam. It is known that some slaves belonging to Lord Jim, were sent out as prostitutes among both Indians and whites, and also that there were two slaves at Clallam Bay just prior to this time (Gunther, 1927).

A census taken in 1862 indicted that there were 1,300 Klallam. This census figure is probably not accurate, of course. If we assume, as Eells did, that Gibbs figure of 926 taken in 1855 was too low, it would indicate that the population was declining, although relatively slowly (Gunther, 1927).

In 1869 the last act of intertribal warfare involving the Klallam occurred. A band of over 30 Tsimshian, men, women, and children, were massacred on the Dungeness spit by a group of approximately 20 Klallam men. The rationalization for this massacre was the abduction of two Klallam women by the Tsimshian several years earlier. After some hesitancy, and some discussion of what the whites would think about it, the raid was carried out following the traditional pattern. The Tsimshian were all murdered and mutilated with the exception of one woman who pretended to be dead. One Klallam was killed and this brought about a great deal of bickering between the murderers who finally threw away their trophies and went home in dejection.

These men were apprehended and placed at hard labor on the Skokomish reservation (Curtis, 1913). They were not detained there very long, however, and the punishment was not considered by them to have been severe.

It is no doubt true that from the initial contact period to the year 1862 the number of Klallam decreased somewhat, but the census figures do not indicate a rapid decrease (Gunther, 1927) up to this time. From the years 1862 to 1875 this decrease became much more serious, or so the figures for 1862 to 1875 would indicate. The number declines from 1,300 in 1862 to only 597 in 1878. During the years 1862 to 1875 a large group of Klallam lived near Dungeness and it is known that liquor and disease were taking a heavy toll. It is impossible to estimate the actual size of this group, my guess is that it varied from time to time between 300 and 600. By 1873 this group had degenerated to such a state of drinking, fighting and bickering that the white residents of Dungeness threatened to have them removed to the reservation. It is unlikely, of course, that all of the Klallam were drunkards but there is every reason to believe that many of them were. This was the lowest point in their history. Balch, the chief, is known to have been a heavy drinker prior to 1873, at which time he reformed (Eells, 1886). The reasons for his sudden reform are unknown.

During the years 1851 to 1875, some of the Klallams had worked for the white settlers. This must have been very slight at first but no doubt increased in frequency and importance as more settlers came in. There is no reason to believe that it had seriously interfered with their more traditional ways of making a livelihood up to this time. Much of the money earned in this way must have gone to the liquor dealers in Dungeness. Many of the people dug clams, fished for salmon, and did odd jobs for the whites in order to obtain money which they spent for liquor.

It is difficult to tell exactly what the situation was just prior to 1874 but there can be no question about the fact that relationships between the white residents of Dungeness and the Indians were seriously strained. This must have been over drunkenness and accompanying factors such as fighting and thievery. The only question is how serious this really was. In any case, the whites perceived it as serious enough to threaten the Klallam with removal to the reservation.

The threat of being removed to the Skokomish reservation seems to have been the factor which initiated a series of events that constituted a critical turning point in the lives of this group of Klallam. Apparently they feared this very much (Eells, 1866).

For two years previous to 1875 the Klallam in Dungeness had been living on a hillside just above the town. They were asked to move from that location, presumably by the owner, and they moved onto the sand spit north of the town. Then they were asked to move from there, and finally were threatened with removal to the reservation. James Balch, the chief, knew the man who owned the land on what was soon to become Jamestown, and he asked the tribe to buy it. Balch and two other men went to Jamestown to look over the place. At this time there was a logging camp there but the owner had bought the property primarily for right of way and consented to sell it to them provided he could keep the deed until he finished logging in that vicinity (Gunther, 1924).

Eleven or 12 men contributed to the purchase price of $500 and the land was bought in 1874. The group soon moved from Dungeness to this location and in 1875 was well established there. Balch contributed a large percentage of the purchase price and the deed was made out in his name.

There seems to have been no difficulty in raising this amount of money. All indications are that many of these Indians saved relatively large sums of money, in most cases to be used for potlatching.

Joe Johnson, one of the men who had accompanied Balch to see the place earlier, had talked to the owner and found a good farming site. He soon cleared part of this site and planted potatoes. The rest of the people laughed and made fun of him but he had a good crop and soon all the people got together and began to clear some land. This was very difficult work as the land was full of cedar stumps which had to be burned and removed by hand (Gunther, 1924). Potatoes, oats, wheat, and turnips were planted and soon a few horses, chickens, swine and cows were acquired. Cherry, pear and apple trees were planted. Some of these may have been a gift from the Rev. Eells. Almost all of the families had well-kept gardens of some kind and some of the people planted cash crops although these were very small.

Many of the men began working regularly for wages both for the white farmers and in the sawmills. The older people still mainly fished and fishing

was still by far the most important activity. Most of the farming and the working for wages was done by younger men.

As nearly as I can discover there were between 120 and 140 persons in this group when they founded Jamestown and named it after Balch. Most of those who contributed towards the purchase price were fairly young men but it is said that many old people were attached to the group when they settled in Jamestown. In most cases these were parents and relatives of the purchasers. The fact of land ownership for the first time apparently was not perceived by them as very important, for initially everyone built more or less wherever they chose, including many who had not actually contributed. Soon, however, the land was surveyed and divided up according to the amount each had contributed towards the purchase price. No one, including non-contributors, was asked to move, however.

The village was laid out in the traditional fashion, a single row of houses with entrances facing the water. At each end of the village was a large house, one belonged to Balch, the other to a man called "Lame Jack." In between, there were several smaller houses. These houses were built with gabled roofs and more or less in the fashion of the whites instead of in the old style with shed roofs. Most of them were built with sawn lumber which they procured from a nearby sawmill. Most of the houses had windows, locks, doors, and floors.

One of the first things that occurred as a result of buying Jamestown was a change in the marriage customs. It was soon called to the attention of these new landowners, presumably by the whites at Skokomish, that if they wanted their children to inherit the land, it would be necessary for them to marry in the manner of the whites. In 1876 Eells married eleven couples in Jamestown...[see page 89].

These people were not forced to marry in the manner of the whites, nor were existing polygamous marriages broken up, but no new polygamous marriages were being permitted by the agent at Skokomish.

There was much more to Jamestown than simply buying the land and planting crops. Balch had very progressive ideas for the new community. One of the first small buildings to be erected was a jail. This jail was used for some years primarily as a punishment for drinking. Balch disapproved of drinking and quite regularly either fined heavily or jailed those who were found inebriated (Eells, 1886).

An interesting point to be noted is that as far as is known, Balch took these judicial powers upon himself and enforced them with the consent of the others. There was no Indian agent for 90 miles, no Indian policeman, and no whites to enforce law and order in Jamestown. They were, of course, subject to the law of the Indian agent at Skokomish but there seem to have been very few, if any instances of his intervention in the affairs of Jamestown. It is known that on some occasions Klallam were taken to the reservation as a punishment but there is no record of this which specifies where the individuals were from or what their offenses were.

During the first few years these Indians were not given help by the government. Eells writes:

> The Indians there had at first no help from the government because they were not on a reservation. They had, however, some worthy aspirations, and realized that if they should rise at all they must do so largely through their own efforts (Eells, 1886).

In March 1875, shortly after Jamestown was established, Balch visited the Skokomish reservation and appeared very anxious to obtain religious instruction. This was unusual in that he was not a Christian, nor had he shown much interest in Christianity prior to this time. Rev. Eells, delighted, gave him some instructions, a Chinook hymn and a few bible pictures. Balch returned to Jamestown to hold prayer meetings (Eells, 1886).

Balch did instigate some religious meetings which were held in the best-kept homes each Sunday. In 1877 the people of Jamestown began to think about building a church. This was Balch's idea but was quickly approved by the agent at Skokomish and by Rev. Eells.   Construction was started immediately. By April of 1878 the church was almost completed and was dedicated by Rev. Eells. He gives the following description of this event:

> About a 125 persons were seated in the house: 90 Klallams, 10 Makah Indians, and 25 whites. The house is small, 16 by 24 feet. It was made of upright boards, battened and white-washed. It was ceiled and painted overhead.   It was not quite done, for it was afterward clothed and papered and a belfry built in front, but it was so far finished as to be used. Although not large or quite finished, yet there were three good things about it: it was built according to their means, was paid for as far as it was finished, and was the first church-building in the county. Its total cost at that time, including their work, was about $160. Of this, $37.50 were given by white persons, mostly on the reservation, $4 were given by Twana Indians, and some articles, as paint, lime, nails, windows, and the door, came from their government annuities, it being their desire that these things should be given for this purpose rather than to themselves personally. It was the first white building in the village, and had the effect of making them whitewash other houses afterward (Eells, 1886).

A significant fact to be noted in conjunction with the building of this church is that in spite of the obvious effort and expense of building it and the large attendance at its dedication, there was not, at this time, a single Indian in Jamestown who had become a member of any church. Nor were there any who had made any effort to become members. At the prayer meeting held on the evening preceding the dedication of the church there were only five Indians in attendance (Eells, 1886). It was not until some months later that any of the Jamestown people became members and these were only two. No others joined until 1880 when four more joined (two Indians and two whites), and later in that same year two more (Eells, 1886).

In 1881 Balch and some of the others became dissatisfied with the slow progress the church was making. Their attempt to remedy this situation indicates to me that the church was a symbol of achievement, in addition to whatever other functions it may have had.

> A rather singular incident happened a year later. Some of the older Indians, including the chief, were not satisfied with the slow growth of the church; but instead of remedying affairs by coming out boldly for Christ, they chose three young men, who were believed to be moral at least, and asked them to join and help the cause along. These consented, although they had never taken part in religious services or been know as Christians. As I was not informed of the wish until Sabbath morning, I did not think it wise to receive them then, but replied that if they held out well until my next visit, in five months, I should have no objection. They were hardly willing at first to wait so long, but at last submitted. Before the five months had passed, one of them, the least intelligent, had gone back to his old ways, where he still remains, and the other two were received into the church, one of whom has done especially well and has been superintendent of the Sabbath-school. Yet it always seemed a singular way of becoming Christians, more as if made so by others than of their own free will, they simply consenting to the wishes of others (Eells, 1886).

Until 1882 the members of the Jamestown church were considered a branch of the church at Skokomish. In 1882 four new converts were made and Eells organized the Jamestown Christians into their own church. There were 11 members, nine of whom were Indians. In the fall of 1882 three more joined and seven in 1883. One of these latter was a white man over 70 years of age. Three of the Indian members accompanied Eells to Clallam Bay on a missionary tour in this year and he was highly satisfied with their help. Also in 1883 five Klallam infants were baptized, the first in the history of the Jamestown church (Eells, 1886).

In 1880 there were 600 white residents in Clallam County but the only church in the county was this one at Jamestown, built by the Klallam and with a membership composed mostly of Klallam. The deacon of the church was a Klallam. One white who lived close to Jamestown remarked to Eells in 1880, "It is a shame, it is a shame! that the Indians here are going ahead of the whites in religious affairs.   It is a wonder how they are advancing, considering the examples around them" (Eells, 1886).

Between 1878 and 1883 21 members came into the church, some of whom were whites.   There were a few others who attended services but a great many did not.   Some were known to be anti-Christian.   There was definitely a division in the village between Christians and anti-Christians.   This is attested to by Eells both directly and indirectly:

> Not all, however, of the people in the village can be called adherents to Christianity.   There is a plain division among them.   Some are members of the church, a few who are not attend church and some hardly ever go, but profess to belong to the anti-Christian party (Eells, 1886).

In discussing the deacon of the Jamestown church Eells gives an indication of how this division manifested itself:

> In 1881 two of his children died, a fact of which the opponents of religion made use against Christianity, and he was severely tried, but he stood firm (Eells, 1886).

There is no way of knowing how well these Indians actually understood Christianity.   The Klallam had undoubtedly been exposed for some time to Christianity before founding Jamestown but these exposures must have been sporadic at best.   The first services at Skokomish were little more than singing.   Later they became more serious but were carried out in such a mixture of languages that it would seem doubtful they could have been clearly understood by all.   Eell's description of one of these later services at Jamestown provides an example:

> ....The services were in such a babel of languages that their order is here given: singing in Klallam and then in English; reading of the Scriptures in English; prayer by Rev. H.C. Minckler, of the Methodist-Episcopal church, the school teacher; singing in Klallam; preaching in Chinook, translated into Klallam; singing in Chinook; baptism of an infant son of a white church member in English; prayer in English; singing in English; propounding the articles of faith and covenant in English, translated into Klallam, together with the baptism of four adults; giving of the right hand of fellowship in English, translated into Klallam; prayer in Chinook; singing in Chinook; talk previous to the distribution

of the bread in Chinook, translated into Klallam; prayer in English; distribution of the bread; talk in English; prayer in Chinook, followed by the distribution of the cup; singing in English a hymn in which nearly all the Indians could join; benediction in Chinook. A number of their white neighbors gathered in, to the encouragement of the Indians, six of whom communed with us (Eells, 1886).

In spite of this it seems that many of them took Christianity quite seriously. There were no Christians in Jamestown among those who drank to excess although some of them had drank heavily before joining the church. They attended church regularly, prayed before every meal, and outwardly at least appeared to be serious and devout Christians.

A Christmas celebration was held regularly in Jamestown. It featured a tree, singing and refreshments, all paid for and furnished by the Klallam. Many whites attended this celebration and thought it very worthwhile (Eells, 1886).

The first deacon of the Jamestown church, Billy Cook, like Balch, had a history of drunkenness and wildness. He had lived much among whites, had worked in a sawmill and cookhouse, and had once travelled to San Francisco. He spoke English quite well and it was primarily for this reason that he had been elected to lead the prayer meetings previous to the building of the church, and later elected deacon. He took his religion quite seriously and was thought by Eells to be a stabilizing influence on the others. Before he became minister of the church he was once remonstrated by Balch for drinking (see page 94).

Another very interesting fact about the Jamestown church is that although James Balch was largely responsible for its inception, and even went so far as to direct three persons to join in order to help it along, he never became a Christian. When Eells questioned him about this he replied that he was eager to join but as chief would probably do something to harm the church.

Accompanying the construction of the church in 1878 came a desire for a school. There was no provision for a school (except at Skokomish) according to the provisions of the treaty they had signed but, according to Eells, the people of Jamestown plead their case so effectively that the government provided them with a school teacher in that same year. The church building was used as a schoolhouse. Attendance fluctuated between 15 and 30. A few of the pupils walked barefooted every day from Washington Harbor to attend. Some of the residents of Jamestown boarded children at their own expense whose parents either could not or did not care to send them to school (Eells, 1886). The school teacher, of course, was white, and doubled sometimes as a Sunday school teacher. He boarded with a family on a nearby farm. By 1883, when the school teacher resigned, one of the Indians was sufficiently capable to keep the school in operation for a year until a new teacher was procured (Eells, 1886).

Once the school was established the teacher insisted that the pupils speak only English. He also attempted to teach the old people to read and write but they did not respond well and this attempt resulted in a laughable failure. Discipline was strict but the children were eager to learn and the school had a very important influence on the life of the community. It expedited the learning of English, rapidly increased the rate of literacy, and thus enabled the people to deal with whites on a more equal basis. The children studied

English, arithmetic, geography, habits of personal cleanliness, as well as parliamentary procedure and the ways of American civilization generally.

Writing a "progress report" about 1883, Eells reported that many had abandoned the old way of smoking salmon and had begun salting it. Flour, potatoes, and sugar had become indispensable to them. They also used such products as rice, beans, coffee, tea, butter, salt, lard, spices, syrup, crackers, cherries and pears. In their gardens they raised corn, peas, beans, onions, turnips, beets, carrots, parsnips, cabbages and raspberries. They had a few cows but did not use much milk.

Their houses were all built in the style of the whites and many had floors and stoves. They also had beds, tables, chairs, benches, cupboards, and a few had rugs, clocks, brooms, and looking glasses. Some of the rooms were papered and they bought sawn lumber, locks and windows. Dishes, knives, cups, forks, lamps and buckets were common. Mirrors, brushes, combs and soap were in use. Native articles for war and hunting had almost entirely disappeared. In fishing, however, they still used many of the old style articles as they saw no advantage in giving them up. They preferred their canoes to American boats but had added oarlocks to some of them. Eells reported that he had never seen an Indian in native garb. The women, however, were slow in wearing shoes. American standards were used for measuring. There were outbuildings in the form of latrines, stables, cellars and woodsheds.

Tattooing was going out of practice and the older Indians seemed to be ashamed of their tattoos. Cradling of children was still done in the old style but deformation of the head was no longer practiced. The old marriage customs had not been completely given up. A few men still had more than one wife but no new polygynous marriages were taking place. Slavery had disappeared but potlatching was still common (Eells, 1887).

Sometime between the years 1887 and 1892, Balch was killed by a white men. This occurred because of an altercation over the price of a canoe trip. Apparently Balch changed his mind and wanted more money for canoeing a white man to Port Discovery. The white refused to pay and Balch jumped overboard trying to upset the canoe. The white struck him on the head with a paddle and killed him. As far as I can discover this created little ill-feeling between Indians and whites, as most people believed it to be a more or less private affair.

There was no real successor to the chieftaincy after Balch's death. A man named Howells considered himself chief for a short time but no one paid any attention to him. Then Billy Cook tried to be chief. Cook's claim to leadership seems to have rested on the fact that he was put in charge of dispensing the government rations and was deacon of the church. Neither of these men was considered a chief by the people and they had very little effect upon the villagers.

In approximately 1885 Shakerism was introduced into Jamestown (Gunther, 1949). At first the movement involved all the members of the community, young and old alike, and they all attended services and curing ceremonies. The younger members of the community soon lost interest, but many of the older people became seriously influenced by the new religion and it was firmly established in Jamestown. The church dedicated by Eells was almost immediately forgotten and its membership was converted to Shakerism. A new church was constructed, much larger than the first one. One of the first Shaker ministers was Billy Cook, who had been the deacon of the first church. This change from one church to another had little effect upon the economic life of the community except insofar as some of the people may have missed work to attend the curing ceremonies. The Shaker meetings became very important in the social life of the people, and even many of those who were not active Shakers, including many of the younger people, attended the curing ceremonies which were held frequently. Also Shakerism stimulated much visiting back and forth between Skokomish, Port Gamble, Elwha, Washington Harbor and more distant places. The number of Shaker members who attended the regular Sunday service was much lower than the number who attended the curing ceremonies.

According to Barnet (1957) Shakerism was introduced to Jamestown by the Skokomish who had been invited there to cure Annie Newton who had been suffering from some unknown illness for an extended period of time. They were successful in curing her and in this way Shakerism gained a strong foothold quickly. It is interesting to point out that Annie Newton was the wife of Billy Cook, whose real name was Newton. Furthermore, both Billy and Annie were considered by Eells to have been the staunchest advocates of Christianity prior to this time (Eells, 1886).

There is little doubt that curing was the most important feature of this new religion to these people. The Jamestown Shakers claim to have cured many people, most of whom had been "given up by others." In extremely difficult cases messengers were sent to other communities and the Shakers there would come to help. They did not charge for this but often transportation and food were furnished by the requesting village. The most significant cures reported from Jamestown were for blindness and insanity.

In addition to curing, some of the Shakers had the power to locate lost objects. One man located lost horses regularly by shaking and then pointing out the direction where they were to be found. This same man once determined by shaking that his own son had stolen $500 he had hidden in a barrel and was able to get most of it returned.

Shakerism was inhibited in this area by pressures exerted by Rev. Eells and others until about 1891, when the implications of the Dawes Severalty Act came to be fully recognized and the Indians were given full citizenship and religious freedom (Barnet, 1957). This pressure was not felt nearly so much at Jamestown as on the reservations.

The nature of village life in the years 1875-1890 was a curious mixture of the old and the new. Along with the church, school, and jail most of the traditional customs were still represented, even though they might not have still been considered typical or normative for this period of time. There were still recognized social classes although they were breaking down and different classes did not live in separate parts of the village. Puberty rites for girls were still observed; blood money was still demanded upon occasion; people sometimes still received "songs" which gave them power, and shamans were still active both benevolently and malevolently. One man in Jamestown still had two wives; the levirate was still practiced (Balch himself had married his brother's widow sometime between 1870-1880).

Potlatching and the secret society were still maintained during this time. Eells gives an excellent account of a fairly large potlatch which featured a secret society initiation in Jamestown in 1878 (Eells, 1883). This was not he last potlatch held, however, as several were held in nearby Washington Harbor after this time. They were becoming less frequent, smaller, and less important by 1885. The last initiation of the secret society held by the Klallam was in Port Angeles in 1893 and was attended by people from Jamestown (Williams, 1916).

The most important ritual activity after this time was that performed by the Shakers. Shakerism was extremely active in Jamestown in the year 1885-1920. In approximately 1894 several new families moved to Jamestown from Washington Harbor and Dungeness and some of them soon bought land there. One of these was a Shaker minister who became very important in the movement and was seen at all the conventions. This was William Hall who had a great deal of influence on the other members of the community. The strong belief in the tenets of Shakerism and the influence of Hall greatly inhibited drinking in Jamestown and is claimed that with one exception there were no troublesome drinkers. This one exception was an old man who tried to be a Shaker and gave up drinking for a time but he failed to sustain this effort. Some of the Shakers slipped occasionally of course. When this happened, they would make a public confession and be accepted back into the fold with ceremony.

Jamestown in the years 1900-1910 was flourishing and was one of the most important Indian settlements in the area. Farming had increased in importance and three of the villagers began dairying about this time. In

1902 a modest trade sprang up. One of the Klallam who had recently moved from Dungeness and bought land in Jamestown started a crabbing industry.

He employed six men and they furnished crabs to the City of Seattle. They had a contract to furnish so many crabs a day which were taken to Dungeness by canoe, picked up there by boat, and taken to Seattle. Many of the men worked for wages on farms and sawmills. Some of the women went by canoe to a nearby cannery and supplemented the family income. A few of the men by this time hired out their teams as well as themselves and in this way earned more money. Fishing of all kinds was still by far the most important single activity.

In approximately 1910, the government built a school immediately adjacent to Jamestown. One of the teachers at about this time, Johnson Williams, was one of their own people, a man born and reared in Jamestown. Williams went to school in Jamestown and later attended the Cushman Indian School in Tacoma. He then returned to Jamestown to teach. A few other Klallam boys at this time enrolled in the Cushman school, after completing the five years taught in Jamestown.

Some of the young people learned to play the banjo, violin, and other instruments. They had dances frequently, usually in someone's home, and they danced the waltz, two-step, and the schottische. They had an excellent community baseball team which travelled to Port Gamble, Port Townsend, Skokomish, and other places to play. This activity was important to them and they took great pride in having good players and a winning team. All of the young people spoke English at this time and in some homes it was the only language spoken.

About 1910 two of the young men purchased American-made fishing boats. These were 26 feet long and aroused a great deal of pride on the part of the owners. They used these boats for commercial fishing which was beginning to be important. They furnished fish of all kinds to the canneries and made a good living.

Dungeness was still the most important town near Jamestown and the Indians from Jamestown went there occasionally for supplies. Sequim, which was to become more important still, had not yet grown very large. They travelled to Dungeness by canoe and sometimes by horse and buggy. Every Fourth of July they attended the celebration held in Dungeness which featured horse racing, games, and an elaborate Fourth of July ceremony. This was one of the big events in their year.

Up to this time the people of Jamestown still came annually for the salmon run and they speared many fish on the flats of Dungeness. This was an important source of salmon for their own use. These salmon were salted and stored in barrels. The women still returned regularly to the customary places to gather china slippers, roots, berries, and other foods; but they did not do this as often, nor gather as great a quantity as they had done in former years.

It was not until around this time that fishing laws and regulations became of any importance to the Klallam. Spearfishing was suddenly made illegal and other restrictions were enforced which closed the Dungeness River to the Indians. This interfered seriously with their economy and aroused a great deal of bitterness. Fishing laws had been enacted prior to this but the Indians had been exempt and in cases where they were not, the local authorities had simply ignored any violation. Now, however, they were enforced and this made it difficult to obtain fish for their own use. They still fished, of course, but the catch was limited. They continued to fish commercially also, but by this time preferred to sell these fish rather than keep them.

Farming had become increasingly more important but only three or four had sufficient acreage to reap any cash profit. They all depended upon their gardens, the fish, and what money they earned working out. Even with the new fishing laws they were relatively prosperous and well fed.

Some of the recently married young couples made an effort to speak only English to their children who were growing up unable to speak or understand Klallam.

The two large houses at the ends of the village had disappeared as had some of the other original buildings. These had been replaced by new ones of slightly better construction. The jail, which had not been used much after Balch's death disappeared, but there was little use for a jail. Few people drank and there were no serious crimes committed. Even if there had been, they would have come under the jurisdiction of the county. Shakerism flourished and helped to keep the older people sober and honest. By this time the young people sometimes laughed openly at the Shakers and had little interest in religion; but they too did not drink much and there were few problems of social control.

In 1917 the government dug a well for the people of Jamestown and soon running water appeared in the houses.   In 1918 the first car was purchased by one of the villagers and became very popular immediately, although there were no good roads for automobile travel.   The other villagers often rented it for rides, and they began throwing rocks and gravel in the wagon ruts to make them suitable for automobiles.   Electricity came in about this time also, and soon the first telephone.   Some new farm equipment was purchased, a phonograph, and many of the people read the newspaper when they could go to Dungeness to get one.

By this time the last of the old ways were rapidly being forgotten. Slavery and polygamy had long since passed. It was more than 25 years since the last potlatch or initiation of the secret society.   Very few items were manufactured in the traditional way.

Fishing remained throughout as the most important activity. Billy Hall, the Shaker minister, was a crab fisherman, as were several others. One man was a carpenter, several worked as farmhands, two or three farmed, and a few went every year to Puyallup to pick hops.

There were no shamans at this time, since they had been replaced by the Shakers. (Most of the shamans became Shakers when the movement started in Jamestown.) The older Indians still preferred the Shakers to the white doctors, and even the younger people did not depend upon white doctors because of the distance and expense involved.

By 1924 there were several automobiles in the village. The first washing machine appeared, and one man had installed an outboard motor on a large canoe. Dungeness had become less important and the town of Sequim was becoming more important. With better communication and transportation the village became less autonomous and more and more dependent upon the outside.

In 1921 the government school was abandoned and the children began going to school in Sequim with the whites. This did not take place without some serious objections on the part of the whites. They argued that the Indian children would introduce tuberculosis and other diseases and said very cruel and unflattering things about the Indians. Some of the Jamestown people were present at these meetings and came away with very bitter thoughts.

In some ways Jamestown was little different from most small rural communities. There were still some links with their Indian past, however; those which survived in Shakerism, a few old canoes, and what remained in the memories of the older people. The census taken in 1923 revealed that 76 lived in Jamestown. The decrease seems to have been from illness and death more than from migration although a few had married out and gone elsewhere to live (both males and females).

After 1930 Shakerism declined rapidly. The older generation was disappearing and the younger people were not interested. The young people seem to have had almost no interest in the former culture. My informants apologize for their lack of knowledge about the old people and old traditions by saying that when they were young they were not interested in the past. When the Shaker church burned just before 1940 there were only six Shakers remaining and they made no attempt to have a new church.

Five or six of the young men from Jamestown entered the armed services during the war and many of the others left the village to work elsewhere. After the war most of them returned, but by this time there was very little for them to do. The standard of living had risen, small farms were no longer a profitable occupation and there was not enough land for large farms. The majority of the younger people did not like to farm as it was easier to work for wages which were high at the moment. Fishing was not very profitable because of increased competition. Many of them were not satisfied but had difficulty finding steady jobs elsewhere. In the late 1940s five families were moved by the government to Elwha, which was now a reservation area, and were settled on farms there in an attempt to aid them. This was not successful and one of these families immediately moved to Tacoma. Those that remained made no attempt to farm but worked out as loggers and farmhands.

Jamestown in 1959 consists of 16 houses with a total population of 36. Five houses are vacant. Only one of the remaining residents came with the original group, a man now over 90 years of age. Seven of the houses are new, built within the past 10 years. These are modest, modern one-story buildings with picture windows, fairly well furnished with davenos, television sets, refrigerators, and other things you would expect to find in a slightly-less-than-average American home. Some of the old houses are still occupied, and even though their outward appearance is somewhat "shack-like" they are comfortably furnished and reasonably well kept inside.

Six of the people (three men and three women) are 70 or over, unable to work, and receive a small state pension. Nine of the men are working. One raises beef cattle and works for a nearby farmer. Three are crab fishermen who supply crabs to Port Angeles and other nearby towns. Four work on construction jobs or whatever they can find. (They do not reside in Jamestown when they find work elsewhere, but they own homes there.) One man goes to Alaska on a fishing boat each year. There are four housewives and 17 children.   The children range in age from one month to approximately 16 years.

There has been no very effective leadership in the village for approximately 20 years, but in spite of this the people of Jamestown have acted as a group upon several occasions.   In 1936 they petitioned the government for permission to use the abandoned school buildings for public meetings and for housing. In 1948 they acted as a group in opposing the remainder of the Klallam with respect to the claims case. They hired their own attorney and at present are still awaiting settlement. This action stems from a difference of opinion as to what each of the three remaining Klallam groups should receive by way of settlement and is a very interesting case. The government awarded the Klallam the sum of $400,000 in 1926; but as the Jamestown group was not on a reservation, they did not receive the same treatment and consequently their interest in the present case is different from that of the other two groups.

For entertainment (mostly movies, dancing and drinking) the people go to Sequim, Port Angeles, or other places. They do their shopping in Sequim. Only two families have gardens and these are not extensive. Jamestown might easily be said to be a suburb of Sequim, although it is four miles away and somewhat isolated still.

There are two Shakers left, both old men. They still believe strongly in their religion but never attend services of any kind as they would have to travel a great distance to find an active Shaker church. They still pray before each meal, cross themselves, and in 1958 one of them located a lost object by shaking.

None of the adult members of Jamestown attends church. The children are taken by bus to Sunday school every Sunday, however.

Only five people in Jamestown can still speak Klallam but they rarely do. With the exception of the six old people, nothing ties Jamestown to the past. All of the younger residents of the village are modernized in every way. They do not speak Klallam, nor do they desire to do so. They have no interest in the past or in their Indian ancestry. They consider themselves as part of the county, state, and nation, not as members of an Indian community.

Their problems now are those faced by most lower-class Americans. None of them is a really skilled laborer and it is difficult for them to find steady employment. The three crab fishermen would prefer doing something else,

and they occasionally do; but the crab fishing is steady during the season. The others work intermittently with the exception of one who works for a nearby dairy farmer and raises a few beef cattle.

Of those who have left the village many have married whites and are widely distributed throughout the United States. Some have married other Indians and gone to live on one or another of the reservations. Some have moved to the cities and found jobs. All of them return occasionally to visit, but they have no intention of returning permanently.

Some of those who have moved away still own land in Jamestown, which eventually will be sold. Some of the land, about 10 acres, has been taken over by the county for back taxes. Recently two small lots were sold at auction. Both of these were purchased by whites who have built summer homes on them. No doubt many more will be bought and converted into summer homes as Jamestown is in a fine location for fishing and swimming, and duck hunting in the fall. There is dissatisfaction over this. Most of the residents wish Indians had bought the lots but none could afford to do so.

Jamestown can no longer be considered a community either in spirit or activity. But the old people still living remember when it was truly a community, and speak approvingly of the "old days," when things were "different," when they worked and danced together, when they could still get a fresh salmon now and then, and when Jamestown was a symbol of their achievements.

CONCLUSIONS

There can be little doubt that the creation of Jamestown was a conscious, rational attempt on the part of this group of Indians to alleviate tensions and dissatisfactions stemming from the condition into which they had fallen....

In order to place Jamestown in a clearer perspective, let us look briefly at the events which were taking place among the neighboring Indian groups during this same period.

The Makah, a tribe directly west of the Klallam, had also signed a treaty with the whites in 1855. The history of contact until 1863 is essentially the same for these two groups. The difference lies in the fact that as the Makah were more isolated they had much less contact with white settlers. In 1863 the terms of the treaty were enforced and they began reservation life. They did not have to move from their homeland as their reservation on Cape Flattery was a smaller replica of where they had always lived. They were given an Indian agent, tools and equipment for cultivating their land and teachers and artisans to instruct them. They were under the complete control of the Indian agent. The people were treated like children and had little voice in their own affairs.

At first there were many attempts to evade the authority of the agent. People refused to send their children to school, they continued for a time to raid the Klallam, they held potlatches, secret society initiations, dances and gambling games, in spite of the fact that these were all forbidden. Soon, however, they learned, after many had been arrested and punished, to do as they were told. They were made to build houses in the manner of the whites, native curing was ridiculed, and often the agent inspected their houses and punished the women for not keeping house properly. The class system was abolished. Agents refused to recognize the traditional leaders, preferring instead to appoint others in their place.

Government employees were sent among them to teach them farming, blacksmithing and carpentry. The fact was overlooked that the land was not suitable for agriculture and that they were traditionally fishermen. In 1874 the original day school was abolished and a boarding school established a mile from the nearest village where the children were isolated from their parents. This was in line with the goal of the Indian service to break all ties with the past as rapidly as possible. Attendance at school was compulsory, and those parents who did not send their children were imprisoned.

According to Pettitt (1950) the situation among the Quileute during this period was not fundamentally different than that of the Makah. The Quileute were at first (1863) subject to the agent at Neah Bay and had no agent of their own at this time. They were more isolated than the Makah and they had no friction with white settlers until about 1880. They had experienced the administration of American law prior to this time, however, and had been punished on several occasions.

When the first school was established in Neah Bay, an order had been sent instructing the Quileute to send their children there for schooling. They did not comply but instead hid their children inland when a schooner came for them. In 1883 a schoolteacher was sent to LaPush. There is no adequate record of how willing the Quileute were to accept schooling, but there is some reason to believe that it was not eagerly accepted. From this period onward the Quileute changed fairly rapidly (at least in some ways), but not without many difficulties. There is little to indicate that they accepted Christianity in any form until Shakerism gained a wide following there in approximately 1900.

At Skokomish, where the Rev. Eells was active, the story was not significantly different. The Skokomish had come under reservation control earlier than the Makah and Quileute. Consequently they were subject to white pressures and influences earlier and were farther along in the process of change (at least in the eyes of the whites). Eells made an earnest attempt to win converts at Skokomish and was active there for many years. His church membership there, however, was never more than 19 (Barnett, 1957). It is also true that conditions at Skokomish might have been somewhat better than at Neah Bay or LaPush because of more understanding on the part of Eells and less intense pressure exerted by the agent.

It is obvious that Eells regarded the people at Jamestown as among the most "advanced" and "progressive" of Indians even when compared to those on the reservation who were directly and constantly under the supervision of whites. From reading the various writings of Eells one gets the impression that he gained much satisfaction from the achievements of the group at Jamestown. He was well aware in later years, however, that he had been largely unsuccessful in introducing Christianity to any of the Indians of Puget Sound.

From these accounts it can be seen that during the same period the reservation Indians were being forced to accept Christianity, schools, and horticulture, and were actively resisting, the people at Jamestown were making a conscious effort to change in just these ways. There were undoubtedly individuals on all the reservations who were relatively eager to change, and certainly the resistance could have been much more serious, but it is clear that the process of change was quite different for Jamestown than for any other place.

The situation on the reservation points up the difference in the process of change as it was occurring at Jamestown and at the same time offers some explanation for this difference. There is no question that the Klallam at Dungeness (as well as all the others) knew of the events taking place on the reservations. They must have both heard about the situation and witnessed it firsthand. In view of the treatment being given the reservation groups, it is small wonder the Klallam at Dungeness feared removal to the reservation. Furthermore, unlike the situation for the Makah, Quileute and Skokomish, for them this would have entailed leaving their traditional territory. It also would have involved living in direct contact with the Skokomish.

In addition to this knowledge of the consequences of being placed on the reservation, there were many other factors which combined to bring about the Jamestown movement. The Klallam that founded the community, as we have seen, were located near the town of Dungeness. Until 1850 there were no settlers in this area. From 1850 to 1874 more and more settlers came onto the northern part of the Olympic Peninsula. Because the Sequim prairie was more suitable for agriculture than the more heavily forested areas to the west and south, the settlers coming into this area concentrated more heavily near Sequim, Port Angeles, and Dungeness than in other places.

Many whites also settled in Port Townsend, which was the most important port in the area. The three largest settlements on the northern part of the peninsula were Dungeness, Port Angeles and Port Townsend, all in Klallam territory. To the east and south, around Seattle, Tacoma and Olympia, settlement was greater. Thus, although the Klallam were subject to fewer settlers than the Indians further to the east and south, they were subject to considerably more than the Makah or the Quileute, and as more and more settlers came in, their position worsened. Up to this time, however, the whites in the area of Dungeness and Port Angeles did not constitute a great majority, nor were they overwhelmingly better equipped and supplied.

We have already gained some insight into the nature of the interpersonal relations between Indians and whites from the statements quoted by Weir, Lotzgesell, and Leighton. It is obvious that the individual whites treated Indians differently, but by and large the rights of Indians were not recognized in business dealings or in simple day-to-day activities. Often white treatment was harsh and offensive. This shows up plainly in the Duke of York's remarks to Gov. Stevens at the signing of the treaty.

> ....I hope the Governor will tell the whites not to abuse the Indians as many are in the habit of doing, ordering them to go away and knocking them down (Gates, 1955).

It is clear, I think, that in the earliest years, when settlers were scarce, the Indians were not yet in a totally subordinate situation. This can be seen in the fact that in 1861, they were paid blood money by a white man, and on many occasions entered houses and gardens at will, with no regard for propriety or the presence of whites. As the number of whites increased and their position strengthened, a dominance-subordinance relationship became more firmly established; and the Indians became less able to behave as they pleased. This is, they were relegated more and more to subordinate positions.

Because of the relatively large number of Indians at Dungeness, it was also the point of greatest contact between whites and a fairly large group of Indians. In other places, such as Port Angeles, Port Townsend, Washington Harbor and Sequim, there were fewer Indians, contact was on a more individual basis, and in most cases was subject to greater control.

There were other factors which are important to understanding subsequent events. It is significant to note that the last act of violence (1869) involving the Klallam was perpetrated on the Tsimshian by the group at Dungeness. This must have contributed greatly to the white attitude towards the Indians living at this place.

Also, as we have noticed, there was a serious decrease in population in the years 1862-78. This must have been quite noticeable by 1874. It was due to smallpox and other diseases as well as intemperance, but Balch seems to have blamed it almost entirely on intemperance.

The Klallam head chief has said that five hundred Indians have been killed by the saloons of Dungeness within twenty years. This is probably an exaggeration, but not a very wide one. The diseases consequent upon licentiousness and consumption have caused the death of many (Eells, 1887a).

It is also the case that although Klallam culture had not completely broken down, it was in the process of doing so. Slavery and raiding had been given up, under terms of the treaty of 1855. Trading in Victoria had been forbidden, and polygamous marriages, although not forcibly broken up were no longer allowed. Potlatching, secret society initiations, and native curing were still widely practiced but were subject to much white criticism. The class structure of Klallam society was in the process of being broken down.

This was probably due to the decrease in numbers as well as to the attitude of the whites. Also, the whites had earlier given European names to the Indians with no regard for differences in class and treated all Indians alike. This led to claims of chieftaincy on the part of many Indians (vis-a-vis whites) who had no legitimate claim to it. This probably affected relations among Indians also and tended to help break down the class structure.

The grandiose titles given to various Indians were derogatory. At first the Indians probably did not recognize this, but surely later there must have been instances in which they did. It is also true that the next generation did not have similar names but more Americanized and less eloquent versions of them. The practice of giving "letters of recommendation" also must have ultimately been recognized by the Indians as degrading. One might imagine their reaction when some honest white or literate Indians read the truth to them for the first time.

They had always been treated as children, as if they had no rights and were incapable of exercising judgment or prerogative. This attitude can be seen very clearly in Gov. Stevens' speech to them at Point-no-Point.

At first there was much intermarriage between the settlers and the Indians. Many of the whites had Indian wives or mistresses and there was little social stigma attached to this. But this was primarily the result of biological necessity and did not imply equality between Indians and whites. As more white settlers came in, and more white women, intermarriage became less acceptable and more stigma was attached to it.

It is unquestionably true that the whites regarded the Indians as inferior and exploited them to some extent for labor and as a market for liquor. In addition, in their interpersonal relations they treated the Klallam largely as they saw fit and this must have left much to be desired from the Indians' point of view. These things seem to have been more true at Dungeness ("Whiskey Flat") than at any other place.

Attempts were made to control the sale of liquor much earlier and were much more effective at Port Townsend than at Dungeness. In fact, the Indians for a long time were forbidden by the agent at Skokomish from living at Port Townsend (Eells, 1887a). Many of the Indians had left Port Angeles by this time because of the limited opportunities for employment there after the removal of the United States Custom's house. These facts account to some extent for the presence of so many Indians near Dungeness. They also indicate, I think, that the situation at Dungeness was worse from the liquor standpoint than at other places.

The uncontrolled use of liquor was a very important factor and led to a great deal of bickering, fighting, and petty thievery both between Indian and Indian, and Indian and white. There was much personal deterioration resulting from drunkenness and this led inevitably to social and cultural disorganization and disintegration. At first, when most of the settlers were men, many of whom drank to excess themselves, Indians were a market for liquor and were not particularly chastised for drunkenness. They were, in fact, encouraged to drink by many. As more whites came into the area, bringing their wives and families, Indian drunkenness became more and more of a problem in Indian-white relations. Indian drunkenness now was a more important factor in the appraisal of status. A pattern was established whereby whites who had need of Indian labor for farming, logging, milling, or transportation, would (when possible) hire Indians known to be sober and reliable rather than those known to be heavy drinkers. This must have had some effect upon the attitude of the Indians towards drinking, and those Indians who did not drink probably looked upon those who did as an undesirable element. It is clear that all the Klallam did not drink and that there were some who disapproved of those who did.

The rapid decrease in population, the attitude of the whites, the recognition of liquor as one of the chief sources of their dilemma, the fact that the Klallams were a highly class conscious people who were now relegated to the lowest possible class, to say nothing of the general disorganization, must have become intolerable to them. These are the factors which contributed to the decisions they made from this point onward, which resulted in the formation of Jamestown and their general moral reform.

We must be somewhat cautious, however, in saying that this group suffered from the "crushing impact of European civilization" (DuBois, 1939). There were factors which tended to cushion the impact. One such factor is the relatively slow influx of settlers. Even as late as 1857 there were only 351 whites in all of Clallam county (Pettitt, 1950). It is significant that most of these were in the eastern part, nearer the Klallam than any other group, but this relatively small number is significant. Also, in Port Townsend, in neighboring Jefferson County, there were a relatively large number of whites.

Another factor to be noted is the absence of an agent or missionary. There was an agent at Neah Bay who had no jurisdiction over the Klallam. The agent at Skokomish was approximately 90 miles away and seldom visited. The Rev. Eells, as we have noted, visited them only twice a year for about a week at a time. They were under no direct pressure from an agent or a missionary to give up their old ways and were not being forced to submit as were their neighbors on the reservations. At the same time, however, there was pressure of a more indirect kind which expressed itself in white disapproval of Indian ways and outright ridicule in some cases.

As we have seen, there were no economic hardships; the Klallam were not deprived of making their livelihood in their traditional ways and in fact their wealth in goods increased; or at least they appear to have believed it had. This can be seen in the statement made by the Duke of York and another Klallam dignitary at the signing of the treaty:

...Formerly the Indians were bad towards each other, but Governor Stevens had made them agree to be friends, and I am willing we should act as he pleases. I think the more I know him, the better I will be satisfied. Before the Whites came we were always poor. Since then we have earned money and got blankets and clothing (Gates, 1955).

....I have become satisfied since I have heard you. I know now that you are our father. I shall always be the same. I was once poor but am now better off and shall always look to you for aid (Gates, 1955).

The fact that the terms of this treaty were never carried out is significant. The Klallam were not moved to the reservation as stipulated in the treaty but they were given goods periodically in the form of food and materials. There may have been dissatisfaction over this, but most certainly none of them went hungry or were any worse off economically for it.

Their natural resources were not depleted and they carried on their traditional economic pursuits without serious interruption. Added to this was the opportunity to work for white settlers, both on the farms and in the sawmills. Even when the situation was at its worst in 1873, they appear to have been economically sound.

One interesting feature of the treaties signed by various groups on Puget Sound is that they were signed in some cases long before there was any great demand for land in their particular area. As we have seen, in 1855 there were no settlers immediately near the Makah or the Quileute and only a few near the Klallam. The pressure for land and requests to the governor for treaties came from farther south and in response to this pressure treaties were signed with all tribes within Washington Territory, in spite of the paucity of settlers in many areas. There is no record of what kinds of pressures were brought to bear upon the tribes that signed the treaty of Point-No-Point but undoubtedly there were some.

The fact that the Klallam were being deprived of their land seems to have been relatively unimportant to them. This is understandable in view of the fact that they practiced no agriculture and the sea and the rivers were much more important to them. The terms of the treaty promised them freedom to travel and fish where they chose so long as they maintained permanent residences at Skokomish reservation. They seem to have been satisfied with this:

> ...We are willing to go up the canal since we know we can get fish elsewhere. We shall only leave there to get salmon. And when done fishing will return to our houses. I am glad to acknowledge you and the Great Father as our Fathers (Gates, 1955) (Duke of York speaking).

Another factor to take into consideration is that the Klallam had suffered only one serious defeat at the hands of the whites and that had been almost 50 years before. Most of the violence between Indians and whites had been farther south and east, and had not involved the Klallam directly. Furthermore, even when they attacked and slaughtered the Tsimshian in 1869 they had not been heavily punished, but merely slapped on the wrist. They were well aware, of course, that they could not overcome the strength of the whites and that resistance was futile.

Even with these cushioning factors it seems apparent that the Klallam group at Dungeness was subjected to increasing pressures from the white settlers. They were more and more subject to white control, made increasingly subordinate, ridiculed for continuing to carry on their traditions, treated in an offensive manner in many cases, and deprived of rights and status. These factors, coupled with their knowledge of conditions of the reservations and the futility of resistance must have combined to bring about their sudden reform.

SEAM-ITZA

Marian Taylor

Essentially this is a true story. My stepfather, Frank Vincent, told it to me years ago. I was too young to press for details, therefore I am not sure whether it was Frank's mother or grandmother to whom it happened. If it was his mother, it happened somewhere near Graymarsh Farm. If it was his grandmother, it happened in Port Townsend. (M.T.)

She had left no note....The little house glowed. The floors had been scrubbed, the windows sparkled and on the board table, covered with her favorite blue checked table cloth, her precious blue willowware pitcher held a few late blooming wild flowers. On the counter by the   kitchen pump were two freshly baked blackberry pies. Their aroma almost hid the faint, foreign odor of the room. Piles of freshly laundered clothes were stacked neatly on the bed near mounds of newly darned socks. Hanging at the windows were crisp, newly laundered curtains, hanging from the door !

Alexander Vincent had come to Port Townsend as a boy. He was tall; a distinguished looking man whose grandparents had fled from France during the French Revolution. Although not titled, they were aristocrats and in grave danger of death. The family fled first to England and then to America, making their home in New York State. There, the family put down permanent roots, but there was a spirit of adventure in the second generation and Alexander joined other pioneers and went west.

Seam-Itza also was an aristocrat. Daughter of the chief of the Port Townsend Klallams, she was proud of her heritage. Many strings of dentalium adorned her throat and head. Her hair was as black as Kah-kah's wing, her eye as bright as Chil-chil, the star. She carried her head proudly as became a chief's daughter. Her tiny feet and shapely legs, showing as she stepped forth in her cattail skirts, caught the eye of many a young brave. Although of marriageable age, Seam-Itza had not as yet given her heart. Her father, in no hurry to have his daughter leave the family house had at her urging refused many offers of marriage.

The stories do not tell exactly how Alexander met the lovely Seam-Itza, but he must have been deeply in love because he and Seam-Itza were married, not only in the tribal tradition, but also in the white man's way. Seam-Itza legally became Alexander's wife.   For some time the young couple continued to live in Port Townsend but finally moved to the Sequim area and settled down on part of what is now Graymarsh Farm.   Here several children, including Frank, were born.

Alexander had written many letters home describing the beauty of his bride. One thing he neglected to do, probably because it seemed unimportant to him was tell his family that he had married an Indian girl.

One day a sailing vessel dropped anchor off Port Williams. A beautifully gowned, handsome woman disembarked. After making inquiries, a team was hired and the journey to the Vincent home was made. Arriving at the little home, the woman asked the driver to wait lest there be some mistake. Seam-Itza, looking out the window, saw the beautiful white lady approaching the house. She gave a quick pat to her hair, a twist to her dress, and was ready to open the door at the stranger's knock.

The stranger smiled graciously at the little Indian woman and said, "Please tell your mistress, Mrs. Vincent, that Alexander's sister, her sister-in-law, is here to pay a visit."

Seam-Itza was delighted. Excitedly she said, "Come in, come in. I am Alexander's wife. I am Mrs. Vincent." Without a word the beautiful lady turned away, got into the wagon, and ordered the driver to leave. Seam-Itza walked a few feet into the yard and watched the disappearing wagon. She turned and walked slowly, sadly but determinedly into the house.

No one actually was witness to the events that followed. They were pieced together later. It was not Alexander who was the first to enter the little cabin. One of the sons came home from work and it was he who saw the result of his aunt's visit. He found no note. Seam-Itza could not write. He saw the pies and stacks of laundry. He saw the crisp curtains hanging at the window, and hanging from the door was Seam-Itza.

COMMENTARY:
AN ANTHROPOLOGIST'S VIEW

Joyce Morden

The beautifully written and powerful story of the Klallam woman, Seam-Itza, illustrates the clash between two different political systems and its devastating effect on human lives. Superficially, the political structure of the European aristocracy and that of the Pacific Coast Indians of North America were similar. Both were ruled by powerful men whose positions were inherited, along with their wealth, power, and prestige. In both societies greater and lesser nobility existed; some of whom were quite wealthy and powerful. The power and privilege enjoyed by members of noble families depended, in part, on currying favor with their powerful ruling relatives, and in part on social, economic and political shrewdness (and of course, luck). In both cultures nobility made the most advantageous marriages possible - to other members of noble families - in order to increase (or gain access to) power, wealth, and prestige. In both systems advantageous marriages were arranged, often without consent of the bride and groom.

But there was a crucial difference between the European aristocracy and the Klallam. European power, prestige, wealth, and birthright were passed patrilineally, through the father to his sons only. Women did not inherit wealth or power, unless there was no legitimate male heir. Women, then were noble only insofar as they were related to noble men. They could not own or pass on their status, and a man might marry a noble woman in order to gain access to her father's wealth and power, never hers.

This was not, however, true for Pacific Coastal tribes. In general, they were ambilineal, which means wealth, power, and prestige were passed either through the male or the female line. Women could, and did, inherit songs, dances, coppers, titles, power, and prestige from their fathers or their mothers, and these they possessed in their own right, so they could pass them on to their heirs. A noble man, then, would marry the daughter of a chief because she, herself, owned the rights to songs and dances (symbols of great prestige) and could pass them to her children. Intertribal marriages were arranged in order to have tribal access thereafter to a particular song or dance. So great was the prestige of these women that, in many tribes, a woman might be married many times, so that more men might have access to her wealth. Rather than the dowry a woman in Europe was required to bring to her husband's family (a symbol of the woman's economic liability), a Klallam woman's family received great gifts (bride price) from the groom's family, as she was considered an economic asset.

Just why Seam-Itza would choose to marry a white man is a mystery. Undoubtedly her father could have demanded a substantial bride price from an Indian suitor. Perhaps Alexander's aristocratic background influenced her father. Perhaps he understood that the white men were gaining power in the region, and he wanted to make an alliance. Love would not have been a particularly important factor, although it might have made Seam-Itza put pressure on her father to allow the marriage. At any rate, Seam-Itza would have considered herself, as the daughter of a chief, as good as (or better than) her husband's sister. His sister, however, even had she known of her sister-in-law's nobility, would never have considered Seam-Itza her equal. Not only did she come from a culture in which women did not have power in their own right, but she came from a culture which was extremely ethnocentric and regarded all non-Europeans as inferior, primitive, and worthless. It must have been inconceivable to her that her aristocratic brother had married a "savage."

The snub Seam-Itza received from her sister-in-law would not have been so terrible had she been a commoner or, indeed, a slave. But Seam-Itza was used to respect. I do not know if suicide to protest a terrible injustice was common among Klallams, but I do know it was frequent among other American Indians. When someone had been done a dreadful wrong, the only way one could reclaim one's dignity and at the same time heap scorn upon and publicly shame the wrongdoer was to commit suicide. It was approved of as the ultimate act of dignity and courage, and at the same time the most terrible insult to the perpetrator of the original slight. In most Pacific Coastal groups it was certainly not considered immoral.

Seam-Itza chose death with dignity to shame her sister-in-law and to assert her right to power and respect. This act, viewed from our perspective as tragic but from hers as the ultimate act of strength and defiance, illustrates the human consequences of the battle between two different cultures in which power and prestige are understood in different terms. If we are able to step outside our culture and set aside our ethnocentrism for a moment, we see in Seam-Itza's suicide the supreme act of power, dignity, strength, and courage - a triumph instead of a tragedy.

SMALLPOX SHIP

Mary Ann Lambert

Mystery has long shrouded the circumstances concerning the old grave and marker on the marshland of Dead Man's Point. To the leeward of Protection Island at the mouth of Port Discovery Bay, on the swampland beach of Rocky Point, stands a lone grave. Carved upon a bleached weather-beaten wooden cross is this inscription: "Capt. Thompson 1860." Only this and nothing more.

This isolated grave faces the Strait of Juan de Fuca, as it should, captains and saltwater being kindred spirits. In the background, tall, dark hemlock and cedar trees stand, sentinels to the man who mastered wooden ships and roamed the relentless seas. Tall razor-edged swamp grass sways with a gentle swishing noise adding to the utter loneliness of this grave and its surroundings.

The San Francisco shipping records from 1859 indicate that the bark "What Cheer," whose master was Capt. Thompson, sailed for Portland on Dec. 23, 1859. However there is no record of clearance from Portland, an indication that the ship did not stop there on this trip. It is assumed, therefore, the "What Cheer" bypassed the treacherous Columbia River bar because of her crippled manpower; smallpox had broken out among the crew soon after leaving San Francisco; already some of the sailors had died.

It is assumed that Capt. Thompson proceeded toward Puget Sound.

An old Indian who said he witnessed the burial of Cap. Thompson related the following account of the tragedy of the smallpox ship.

By the time the bark, "What Cheer," reached the Washington coast, many more sailors had died. Instead of disposing of their pox-infested garments and bedding by burning, they were cast overboard and were carried by the currents to the very door of some of the Indian villages along the beaches. The first village contaminated by the blankets and straw mattresses was the Ozett Indian village. Not realizing these salvaged articles contained death for them, the Indians put them to use, and many quickly died. In a short time the village of 400 souls became a tomb, peopled by scores of dead and the fearful, desolate living.

The few survivors fled from their devastated village through deep forest, along the Strait of Juan de Fuca, only to find their escape led them into the same dread circumstances from which they had tried to escape. The Makahs lay dead or dying everywhere. The handful who survived noticed a small ship passing. Despite a fair wind she flew no sails, which seemed strange and uncanny to the Indians. "Something is wrong," they said, not realizing it was that ship which caused their near extermination.

By the time the smallpox ship reached and passed Dungeness Spit, she had become a funeral barge. Capt. Thompson, the ship's master, had succumbed to the dread disease.

Big Ben, the Grandee, a strapping and powerful Indian living at the village of Washington Harbor, picked up a jacket from the beach; he didn't last long after donning it. So many contracted the disease and died that few were left to care for the dead. Big Ben's body was deposited in the woods back of the village until such a time as it could be properly cared for.

At this time the surrounding country - Sequim and Dungeness - was infested with roving packs of hungry wolves. One dared not venture far from the villages unless armed against this carnivorous menace.

After a time the epidemic waned. The people who survived strove to resume normalcy. Not until then was it possible to care for the body of Big Ben, the Grandee, to give him a burial befitting a chief. However, a few bones were all that was found of Big Ben's body. Every morsel of flesh had been eaten by the ravenous wolves.

The Indians say the wolves became infected with smallpox. Hundreds of these animals died.   It was not until years later that wolves became numerous, but never as many as before.

In the meantime the smallpox ship reached Rocky Point, later called Dead Man's Spit, where she dropped anchor. Capt. Thompson's body was taken ashore and burned on the only dry spot to be found on the marshland. The grave lies a few yards from high tide, parallel with the Strait of Juan de Fuca, where a sympathetic countryman erected a wooden cross to the memory of Capt. Thompson.

But what of the five or more graves at the foot of the hill, 100 yards from Capt. Thompson's? Contrary to the belief handed down that these graves also contain the bones of "What Cheer" smallpox, the five graves were there when the captain was laid to rest according to the lone Indian who witnessed Capt. Thompson's burial.

After the beach burial of its captain, the "What Cheer" faded out of existence, carrying with her into Valhalla the mystery of her fate.

However the epidemic had yet to run its course. Indian villages at Port Discovery and Port Townsend were stricken. In Port Discovery only two people were immune to the disease - a man and a woman who alone cooked and cared for more than 100 men, women, and children.

Port Townsend was next and apparently last to receive the blow. However, by this time the disease had slackened. The hardest hit was the house of Chet-ze-moka, the Duke of York's household. Lach-ka-num (Prince of Wales), the 10-months-old child of Chet-ze-moka, fell gravely ill and in a few days succumbed, or so members of his household believed.

The Duke of York placed the body of his first born, still laced tightly on the slumber board, in a large spuchoo (watertight basket) and carried it out to the smokehouse to be left there until some member of the family had recovered from the sickness to give it the burial due a prince.

Two days later Judge James G. Swan, a true friend of the Indians, came to the village to see how his stricken friends were faring. Passing the smokehouse, he was startled to hear a feeble whimper from within. Hurriedly entering the shack he found the baby Prince of Wales very much alive but weak from exposure. Judge Swan carried the baby to its mother. The Prince of Wales completely recovered, lived to a ripe old age, highly respected by the townspeople and members of his tribe.

No one seems to know what became of the smallpox boat, ironically named "What Cheer." "What Sorrow" would have been a more appropriate name.

SMALLPOX AND WOLVES

Commentary

All of the transcontinental railroad surveys ordered by Congress submitted natural history reports to the Smithsonian Institute. Under the direction of Spencer Baird, the Smithsonian prepared a report based on the expedition's findings. In the report for the route near the 47th and 49th parallels, explored in 1853-55 by Isaac Stevens, Governor of Washington Territory, Dr. George Stuckley and George Gibbs collaborated on mammals. In a section written on the coyote, Gibbs and Stuckley give the following interesting account relating to the great smallpox epidemic of 1853 which reinforces Mary Ann Lambert's story of wolves dying after consuming the diseased bodies of the "What Cheer" victims:

> In 1853, during the smallpox epidemic among the tribes north of the Columbia, the natives, frightened, left their dead unburied. These were devoured by the coyotes, who shortly became afflicted with a terrible skin disease, in which the hair fell off, and the whole surface of the body became covered by scabs and putrid sores, which, irritated by the sun, wind and sand, were a dreadful annoyance to the miserable brutes, who undoubtedly perished in great numbers (War Department, 1859).

CIRCUMSTANTIAL EVIDENCE

Mary Ann Lambert

Under the charge of Maj. G.O. Haller, Station Prairie Garrison was built in 1856 by the government of the United States to quell any uprising that might occur among the Indians of Port Townsend and vicinity.

Instead of setting a good example, however, soldiers of the garrison were poor representatives of the government. Coming to Townsend for a few days' furlough, the men immediately headed straight for one of the two dozen saloons the little seaport town boasted. As is usual with men living under routine and rigid discipline, they chose the only relaxation at hand - over-indulgence in that which gave them temporary relief...namely intoxication.

It wasn't unusual, therefore, to see these uniformed men, under the influence of strong drink, proceed to the nearby Indian village with immoral intent upon the Indian women. The beastly act was often forcibly realized by the drunken offenders...an act which, were it committed by a drunken Indian upon an innocent white woman, would in short order have resulted in an uprising of the townspeople and probable lynching of the offenders. Be it said at this point, to the credit and honor of the Indian men...very seldom, if ever, has rape upon a white woman been known.

One day two soldiers on furlough arrived in Town. (Port Townsend was spoken of as "Town" by people living on the outside). Going directly to the nearest saloon, they soon became intoxicated...so much so that they lost count of the days of their leave of absence.

One day during a lull in their drunken orgy, the absentee soldiers suddenly realized with a jolt that they had overstayed their leave. They decided to return to the garrison at once and take their medicine like good soldiers. Then came the realization that this was not the day for the "Mule Team" from the garrison to arrive in Town. No means of getting back being available at the moment, the two soldiers decided to confiscate an Indian canoe, which they proceeded to do at once.

Going to the Indian village located near Point Hudson, they found a small fishing canoe at the water's edge. Shoving it from shore and boarding it, they paddled across Port Townsend Bay toward the garrison. A strong southeast squall suddenly arose, capsizing the cranky little vessel. Both men presumably drowned.

Days passed. The two absentees failed to report at the garrison for roll call. Quite naturally the consensus of opinion was that the men had either been shanghaied by one of the many ships anchored in the bay or murdered by Indians, the latter opinion being the most plausible one.

While there was no proof that the Indians had molested the soldiers, the officers of both the garrison and Port Townsend were on the lookout for the suspected culprits.

A week after the two soldiers' disappearance an Indian youth, Tommy Shapkin, by name, was walking along the water's edge, beachcombing, when he came upon the body of a soldier which evidently had been washed ashore. The body was fully dressed in the uniform of the U.S. Army, even to the blue-visored cap still held taut by the regulation narrow patent leather chin strap.

Although the youth was startled and frightened by the first glance at the dead man lying on the beach before him, his fear was soon dispelled by admiration of the bright shiny buttons on the dead man's coat and cap. Contrary to an Indian's traditional fear and repulsion of the dead, Tommy Shapkin decided to remove the cap and jacket from the dead soldier and put them on. "Why shouldn't I? This man is dead anyway and no longer needs these things." Without much ado Shapkin removed the dead man's jacket and cap and put them on.

"What a fit!" he thought with pride. "Now I'll show those Bostons I at least am willing to adopt their way of dress."

Without realizing what he had done, Tommy Shapkin turned toward the main street of the seaport town and proudly strode, face agleam with pride and pleasure, toward his doom. He hadn't gone very far before he was completely surrounded by a jeering, hostile crowd, yelling and shouting: "Look! Look at the Siwash! Grab him, grab him! He's the son of a so-and-so who killed the soldiers." A look of consternation and fright came over the Indian boy's face as he started to run. He didn't get far. "Arrest him, arrest him!" yelled the crowd.

"No, kill him! Kill the damned murdering Siwash!" some drunken sailor shouted. "Yes! Yes! Kill him!" yelled the infuriated crowd of onlookers.

By this time Townsend's lone policeman appeared on the scene. Seizing Tommy Shapkin roughly by the arm, he shoved the frightened boy toward the high wooden fenced jail, saying loudly for the benefit of the crowd, "I'll learn you not to kill a white man, you goddamned Siwash! Get along there. Get along, I say!" at the same time booting him in the seat of his pants.

"I don't kill it, the soldier man," remonstrated Shapkin. "I find it on beach. He already dead."

"Like hell you say! Dry up before I kill you right here, you damned Siwash!"

Quickly the jail was reached. The policeman pushed the boy headlong inside, then ordered him into one of the iron cages and locked the door.

The following day the cosmopolitan population of this little seaport town, purely on circumstantial evidence, witnessed the erection of a scaffold in the jail yard upon which to hang the innocent youth, Tommy Shapkin.

On the afternoon of the second day the people began arriving. Everybody was going to the hanging except the Indians, who had not as yet heard of the events of the day before. Men and women, soldiers, sailors and Chinamen; all rubbed elbows with each other in their haste to get to the front row.

As was usual with any kind of public gathering in this small town, "Spades," the colored companion of huntsmen and boatmen, brought up the rear of this motley crowd. "Spades," whose real name was Abner J. Spates, was never in a hurry. At this particular moment he had just returned from a hunting trip; consequently his powder horn still hung over his shoulder, he held his muzzle loader in one hand, and a spotted deer hound was held tightly on leash and dragging "Spades" forward. Temporarily he diverted the attention of the crowd, who turned to see what was causing the commotion to the rear.

Then they heard the familiar voice, "What's dis here all about? Circus done come to town?" The crowd knew it was "Spades" and was satisfied.

The jail door opened. The youthful prisoner was brought forward. The excited, nervous crowd began jostling anew, all stretching their necks to get a better view of what was about to happen.

All was now in readiness. The show was about to begin.

The jail door opened. The youthful prisoner was brought forward. The excited, nervous crowd began jostling anew, all stretching their necks to get a better view of what was about to happen.

All was now in readiness. The show was about to begin.

Presently the policeman and the boy reached the foot of the gallows. Together they climbed the stairs to the platform above which dangled the hangman's sinister noose. The prisoner's hands had been hand-cuffed behind him. Tommy Shapkin was ready to be blindfolded and stood waiting.

In the meantime a chum of Tommy Shapkin, who had joined the crowd, saw his friend emerging from the jail with the policeman and surmised that something was wrong. He turned and ran swiftly back toward the Indian village. Chetzemoka (Duke of York) saw the boy running breathlessly toward him and hurried to meet him. "Come quick, come quick, my uncle!" called the boy. "Something is about to happen to Shapkin. I don't know what it is, but it's something bad! Quickly, let us run!" Without losing a second's time, this dignified chief and the youth ran swiftly until they reached the place of the hanging.

Forcing his way through the dumbfounded crowd, Chetzemoka approached the scaffold. Without a word he mounted the steps and stood beside his kinsman. Reaching into his belt the Duke of York withdrew a knife, reached up and cut the knotted noose and threw it upon the ground below. Then removing the blindfold from the boys eyes, he said, "Go, my kinsman. You are free!"

The boy dismounted from the scaffold and joined his friend. Both boys walked rapidly from the crowd without looking back toward Point Wilson.

Turning and facing the astonished crowd, Chetzemoka stood for what seemed ages, looking down upon the bloodthirsty crowd while they seemed to stand as one immovable object, petrified to the ground. Speaking in Chinook the chief said, "Friends, this is Indian country, our country. There never was a time when it was not our country. We are Klallams. Once we were a strong, proud people. Because of sickness and death we have diminished in numbers until now we are no longer a strong people. But we are a proud people. We will not be the first to spill Boston blood upon our beloved land. You Bostons are a strong people. Do you wish to be the first to spill Klallam blood upon this soil which once belonged to us? Have you no pride?"

Then descending halfway down the scaffold steps, the Duke of York with hand uplifted again spoke. "Bostons, we have been friends. Let us remain friends. If this unwise act which you were about to commit is what you call civilization, then give us back our way of life." Continuing, the chief said with profound sadness but proud demeanor, "Oh, White People, our brothers under the skin, do not let this happen again." Stepping to the ground the Duke of York wedged his way through the crowd and was gone.

The cheated populace reluctantly dispersed. Plainly they were disappointed. Unmistakably, however, they understood this great chief. Too well they respected this red man, who at a council of different tribes, by sheer courage and vision, had alone averted that which might have resulted in the complete annihilation of the white settlers of the little seaport town of Kah Tai (Port Townsend).

THE HANGMAN'S TREE

Mary Ann Lambert

This is the one exception where I have deviated from my strict focus on the Klallam people. The Chemakum aboriginal territory bounded the Klallams on the east. This case of arbitrary white "justice" is probably typical of the treatment afforded both tribes by the settlers. (J.G.)

There stands a lonely, sparsely-limbed tree, scrubby but staunch, between the southeast corner of the Port Townsend Golf Club course across the street from the site of the former Olympic View Housing Project. It can be seen by people on Blaine Street near Walker.

This ancient tree, battered by the winds as they blow across the valley, is not unlike a weather-beaten old mariner. The shallow, black top soil upon which the tree stands yields no nourishment, so it is the same size today as it was when Port Townsend was a baby....yes, even before she was born.

On one of the deformed limbs of this venerable tree a man was hanged many, many years ago. His name was Kia-a-han. A Chimakum Indian, Kia-a-han was hanged after he was falsely accused by Percival Chamberlin, a farmer living in Chimacum Valley, of killing one of his wild steers.

Percival Chamberlin lived with his Klallam wife in the valley on a large tract of homestead land, which he took up some years before. Upon this acreage and trespassing across the farms of the community roamed a herd of 20 or more wild steers belonging to Chamberlin. These animals were dangerous, a menace to those passing along the roads and fields. Frequent complaints were sent to Chamberlin, who paid no attention to them.

Becoming alarmed for the safety of their children to and from school, the farmers went to the proper authorities with their complaints: something had to be done at once about this danger. If one has never been chased by a stampeding herd of wild steers - be it large or small - then he has no idea of the existing situation in the valley at this time.

Percival Chamberlin was forced to do something so he sent word to the Indians living at Kuhn's Spit and Port Townsend to shoot on sight any roaming steer, but to report to him at once and he would claim the critter, giving the Indian some of the meat as reward for killing it.

So it happened that Kia-a-han, the Chimakum Indian, was hunting one day on the marshy outskirts of Anderson's Lake when he came upon five or six of Chamberlin's wild steers, which had gone there to graze in the tall grass.

This was an opportune time for Kla-a-han. He fired, killing one of the steers, while the others, frightened by the gunshot, fled to the underbrush of the alder bottom and disappeared.

The Chimakum hurried to the home of Chamberlin to notify him of what he had done. Without reasoning or remembering the instructions he had given about shooting his wild steers, Chamberlin flew into a rage. The Indian stood watching the white man until he calmed down somewhat, then spoke in Chinook - "Mika wa-wa kupa nesika, spus sawash nanitch mika misache mos-mos kupa kaw, klash mamock mimiloss yaka, pe chucko wa-wa mika, pe alta mika potlatch nesika tanas mos-mos muck-mcuk." Continuing, "Pe alta mika delate hyas soloy cupa nikt mamok" (You send word to the Indians, should we run across any of your wild steers, to kill them, report to you, in which event you'd give us some of the meat as reward for doing so. Now you are mad because I killed a steer. What can I now do about it? What's done is done!).

Turning on the Indian, the raving Chamberlin yelled, "I've had enough of you damned Siwashes. I'll show you who is boss around here!"

Then snatching his coat and hat from the wall pegs he hurried from the house to the barn, saddled his horse and galloped townward.

In the meantime Chamberlin's wife, who observed her departing husband, turned and spoke to Kia-a-han. "Leave at once and hide in the woods back of Station Prairie. I'll take word to your wife, tell her what has happened, also where you will be in hiding. Wait there. She will find you."

The next day a posse composed of citizens of Port Townsend was on the hunt for a fugitive cattle-rustling Indian. Many days passed. The officer in charge of the posse approached O'wo-o-ta, the wife of Kla-a-han.

"If you don't tell us where your husband is hiding, your whole family will suffer," he threatened.

Terribly frightened at this threat, O'wo-ota went at once to the hiding place of her husband to tell him what had taken place and how the life of the family was threatened if he didn't give himself up. The Chimakum didn't hesitate. Walking out of the woods to where the posse was waiting, he spoke, "Yakwa nika. Iskum nika" (Here I am. Take me.).

The Indian's hands were handcuffed behind him. With a boost he was made to mount the waiting horse. Then the long line of mounted men rode back to Port Townsend, to the tragic old tree. Kia-a-han sat upon his horse, erect, proudly, while the noose was lowered over his head and around his neck. The horse was given a hard rap on the rump, then bolted forward, leaving the Indian dangling from the limb of this gallant old tree. A fitting monument to an innocent red man.

Thereafter, Percival Chamberlin lived a not-too-peaceful life. Like a hunted animal, his ears were ever alert to the faintest sound or slightest movement. His end was something the family could never erase from its memory.

THE PRINCE OF WALES

Anonymous

To preserve the unpublished stories of Washington State's settlers, the Pioneers Project was begun in 1936 as a part of the State Department of Public Welfare old age assistance program. Elderly persons were interviewed and their stories, which might otherwise have been lost, have been preserved as part of the pioneer lore of the State. The original interviews are on file at the State Library. (J G.)

"I am 74 years old, "this wrinkled old chief told me; "they seem many years when I say them, but looking back they have passed quickly. In my time I have seen my people grow so few in number that it is hard to believe that when I was a young man they numbered thousands. The settlements of my people were scattered all along the beaches. Their fires were bright at night, and their houses were crowded together on the saltwater shores."

The father of Prince Wales, the Duke of York, was chief of the Klallam tribe of Indians, and the land and people over which he ruled reached from Clallam Bay to Port Townsend, this allotment of territory having been established by Isaac I. Stevens when Governor of Washington Territory.

Prince Wales is a native son of Port Townsend. He was born on the site of the old First National Bank, and has never traveled far from his birthplace. He speaks of his father, Duke of York, with great admiration and respect: "My father was always a warm friend of the white people; he liked them and they liked and trusted him. When he died I became chief of the tribe. I have always tried to do as he would have done, and I have many friends among the white people who have known me all my life. We have never quarreled and never will."

Old pioneers also speak highly of the Duke of York, father of the Prince, and there appears no question but that on more than one occasion serious ruptures, with possible massacres, were prevented by the capable efforts of this old-day chief of the Klallams. Prince Wales says: "The decline in number of the Indians came naturally. Perhaps the adoption of some of the practices of the whites hastened the end of Indian lives; but with everything around us changing, we couldn't remain as we had been before the coming of the white people to our beaches.

"Our people, in the olden days, lived almost entirely from the sea. They caught fish in plenty; they hunted the hair seal and the fur seal in canoes, spearing them with lances tipped with bone. Our homes on the beaches were comfortable according to our standards. But the appearance of the white people brought new diseases previously unknown to the Indians and the toll was pitifully heavy. The fires on the beaches burned less brightly as the mounds in our graveyards increased in number. The boasted benefits of civilization brought no welfare or happiness to my people, and perhaps we would have been more in number today "if we could have lived as our ancestors lived before us."

Prince Wales tells of the days when hop-picking time at Chimacum brought Indians by the thousands to Puget Sound, many coming from the British Columbia coast as far north as the border of Alaska. "Their canoes, 45 years ago, were hauled up on the beaches below Point Hudson by the hundreds, and for several weeks our people made good money picking hops."

Prince Wales has a soft voice, and his English at times is perplexing; but there is a charm in his low tones. There is something about him that indicates he is a ruler by birth, by tradition and by right. Despite his lifelong friendship, he feels that the coming of the white people brought the Indians no good. "The automobile has taken the place of the canoe," he says. "We build better homes, and dress differently - perhaps better; but I cannot say that there is among us the happiness that our fathers and mothers and their fathers and mothers knew. And I speak not as a young Indian, but as a man who has grown old."

THE CULTURAL TRANSFORMATION
OF SEQUIM PRAIRIE

Jerry Gorsline

This essay attempts to describe how the occupation of the Sequim Prairie was succeeded by whites, and the anthropological influence of each culture on the landscape. See Appendix B for data on Klallam ethnobotany and Sequim Prairie flora. (J.G.)

PART 1: A VANISHED LANDSCAPE

Most people think all of western Washington is very wet country. However, the Sequim Prairie lies in the lee of the Olympic Mountains, which block the flow of moist marine air from the Pacific to create a "rainshadow." This northeastern part of the Olympic Peninsula receives a fraction of the heavy precipitation found on the coastal slopes west of the mountains. The present-day town of Sequim has an average rainfall of 15 inches, some years as low as 10 inches. Such precipitation is marginal for forests. In fact, 12 inches per year is a figure often used to define prairie conditions.

The authors of a soil survey of Clallam County, Washington, undertaken in the 1950s, speculated on the origin of the unique dark-colored soils underlying Sequim Prairie. Observing that the prairie is situated in close proximity to former Klallam Indian village sites at Dungeness and Washington Harbor, that the parent material and moisture relations are the same as adjacent forested areas, and that the forest margins are rapidly encroaching since the prevention of fire, the authors concluded that Sequim Prairie was artificially maintained by Indians as hunting and gathering grounds by deliberate burning.

Today the town of Sequim sprawls over the former prairie. Interspersed among the tract homes and backyard farms stand the few remaining oaks, advanced in age. Their large trunks and open canopies testify to the former savannah ecology (Steelquist, no date).

The dry prairies of western Washington are the unique products of climate, geology and culture: level or gently sloping terrain underlain by coarse glacial till or ancient alluvial fans; excessively well drained, gravelly soils

wet in winter, dry in summer. These prairies were maintained by deliberate burning by native people since at least 3,000-4,000 years ago when a climatic cooling initiated reforestation, creating essentially the landscape we see today.

Since white settlement in the mid-1800s, the expanse of these prairies rapidly diminished. Only a few small conservation preserves remain today. By combining the evidence of paleobotanical research, records of early botanical surveys, observations of ethnographers, diarists, and record-keepers from the time of exploration and settlement, the following history of the Sequim Prairie from its post-glacial origins to the present day begins to emerge; a history that illustrates the dynamic interaction of culture and landscape.

PART 2: A LOST BIOME

In 1977, during a prolonged drought, a farmer in the vicinity of the Sequim prairie started to excavate a desiccated peat bog lying on his 16-acre front yard and found parts of two tusks from an ancient elephant.

Mammoths and mastodons were known to have ranged here until about 10,000 years ago, but complete skeletons are rare. This one was especially unusual. Archaeological investigation was begun and, within the first two hours of work, zoologist Carl Gustafson uncovered a fragment of rib with another piece of broken bone protruding from it which he suspected to be a remnant of a spear point. If so, this point is the oldest evidence of human activity in the Pacific Northwest. Dating from about 12,000 years ago the alleged spear point was the first direct evidence that man hunted mastodons in North America.   Subsequent excavations and pollen analysis have provided a glimpse into this lost biome, peopled by hunter-gatherers, with roaming mastodon, bison and caribou, and the plants that first occupied the deglaciated terrain (Gustafson, 1983).

Plant fossils from the Manis Mastodon site reveal a stagnant ice terrain dotted with lakes. This raw till landscape was dominated by grasses and shrubs, with patches of willow and, remarkably, a native prickly pear cactus, *Opuntia fragilis*, which, along with the warm water aquatic plant *Ceratophyllum demersum*, indicates a climate at least as warm as today, and probably drier.

Our present-day landscape is still dotted with potholes and small lakes, moraines, and terraces, all legacies of the last ice age. Carl Gustafson offers the following picture of what the environment was like around the fringe of that pond 12,000 years ago:

> The pond was choked with weeds growing in the clean, fresh water; many attached to the gravel-lined bottom. A dense tangle of cattails extended for 100 yards or more following the gentle slope of the surface to the east, south and west. To the north, the cat-tail made this a good place to wait in ambush over 11,000 years ago. High ground within 25 yards of the pond was suitable for a camp site and charcoal and bones found there suggest the people made use of that area on several occasions between 12,000 and 6,000 years ago.

> Outward from the cat-tail fringe, rolling terrain blanketed by deposits left by glaciers apparently supported shrubs, grasses and sedges. The gravelly, glacial till would not hold moisture like productive, loamy soils. Even though the climate may not have been much drier than today, water would flush through the gravel rapidly and be lost to plants growing there. Thus, the well-drained glacial deposits may be partly responsible for the presence of plants, such as cactus that normally live in still drier climates.

> The hummocks and swales of the rolling topography provided habitats for other plant species. The warmer south-facing slopes and tops of knolls may have supported rose bushes, blackberries and Canadian soapberry, along with other plants that prefer warmer environments...plants such as willows and sedges probably occupied the cooler, north-facing slopes and moist swales. Thus, we picture a mosaic of plant communities mottling the landscape surrounding the 12,000 year old pond.

> The pond probably was fed with water from nearby buried blocks of ice left as the glaciers wasted. After 12,000 years ago the ice seems to have disappeared completely and the pond was supplied by the local water table just as it is today. Along with the rising water table came forest trees - pine, spruce, hemlock, alder...Douglas-fir and western red cedar (Gustafson, no date).

PART 3: THE STRONG PEOPLE

Now the stage was set for the transformative work of culture. The Klallam, whose name means "strong people," belong to the Salishan linguistic family whose range extended from the central British Columbia Coast to northwestern Oregon and the interior Fraser and Columbia river basins.

Though archaeological evidence suggests the Salish people were, relatively speaking, recent arrivals to the Puget Sound area, the Klallam are continuous with an ancient human continuum that began in this post-glacial landscape with mobile bands of hunter-gatherers 12,000 years ago (Bergland, 1983).

Early prehistoric people left tool remains at a number of locations near Sequim. They made extensive use of native basalt as a chipped stone medium. Evidence of their subsistence patterns shows a dependence on hunting land mammals, although some shellfish, seals and fish were also taken.

Beginning about 8,000 years ago, a major adaptive shift began, from an economy based on land mammal hunting toward one based on fishing and gathering of intertidal resources. Settlement patterns shifted toward the seasonal round, taking salmon and gathering saltwater mollusks to supplement a diet of deer and elk meat. Technology evolved to include stone-ground tools and elaborate woodworking (Bergland, 1983).

By the Late Prehistoric, from 3,000 to 1,000 years ago, water transportation in the form of cedar dugout canoes was well established along the Northwest Coast.

By 1,000 years ago, the first cedar-plank houses appear at coastal sites, along with an offshore and riverine fishery, and seasonal fishing camps geared toward the production of a surplus: the beginning of the famous maritime culture of the Northwest Coast.

Cooler, moister conditions have prevailed during the past 3,000 years, giving rise to the dense closed forests of most of the Olympic Peninsula we know today. But the "rainshadow" effect persists in the lowlands and uplands of the northeastern Olympics.

Today, the Dungeness-Gray Wolf river system drains this huge area characterized by dry Douglas fir montane forest, subalpine white bark pine, and associated prairie communities on open, south-facing grassy balds and rocky outcrops, as well as many other features more common east of the Cascades. Some of the plants found in the few remaining lowland Puget Trough prairie fragments are identical to subalpine plants in the upper Dungeness. This suggests that the highlands may have served as refuges for these plants when ice sheets covered the lowlands.

In fact, there is considerable evidence that the Olympic Peninsula served as a refuge in glacial times for plants separated from others of their species far to the north, south and east (Buckingham, 1989).

These isolated populations (disjuncts), and unique forms (endemics), reveal the diversity of habitats available on the Olympic Peninsula during glacial times.

From archaeological evidence, we know prehistoric human pathways led up to the high Olympics. It may even be that some of the prairie plants that in the 19th century had such importance for the native diet, pharmacopeia, technology and religion, were first identified and used at these upland sites.

Following withdrawal of the ice sheet, and during the warmer, drier periods, such high-country plants were the most adaptable species to colonize favorable lowland sites.

It is likely the transformative work of culture in dynamic interaction with the landscape began at this point.

With natural succession and a climatic cooling the forest encroached on the prairies. This probably triggered the deliberate cultural burning of the prairies to maintain suitable habitat for species of great importance to the natives: roots and berries, tubers and bulbs, leaves and nuts, and other plant parts that provided food, medicine, tools, utensils, charms and cosmetics. These species provided the major sources of carbohydrate, the only significant source of vegetable protein in the region (acorns and hazelnuts), and numerous sources of vitamins and minerals. A conservative estimate would suggest that Sequim Prairie flora probably yielded at least 80 plants used by the Klallam for food and technology (see Appendix B).

The Salish were intimate with their floral environment. James Swan observed they had "a separate word for every plant, shrub, and flower, as our own botanists have. I noticed this among even the children, who frequently brought me collections of flowers. They readily told me the name of each, and were certainly more conversant with a difference in plants than many of our own children, and even grown people, who are too ready to class all common plants as weeds" (Swan, 1857).

These lowland prairies also served to attract game, and white settlers capitalized on this fact as well: Swan, in his 1861 account of a visit to Sequim Prairie, noted that "deer abound, and vast numbers are annually killed by settlers and hunters either for their own food or else for the Victoria market. Grouse, partridges, rabbits and squirrels are [also] very abundant....."

Explorers including Vancouver in 1792, Wilkes in 1841, and Cooper in the 1850s, all commented on the choice locations of these prairie areas near permanent water courses and salmon runs, and their luxuriant beauty in spring and early summer. Vancouver referred to "lawns" and "cleared areas" (Meany, 1957); Wilkes commented on the lupines and camas flowers "all seeming in the utmost order as if man had been ever watchful of its beauty and cultivation" (Wilkes, 1856).

Dr. James G. Cooper made first-hand observations of these prairie areas in the 19th century. He was a surgeon naturalist who had served as Army doctor at Fort Vancouver on the lower Columbia River and Fort Steilacoom at the head of Puget Sound. At a time when the transcontinental railroad project was at a political dead-lock due to sectional interests, Congress authorized surveys of the contending routes. The newly appointed governor of the Washington Territory, Isaac Stevens, headed up the northern railroad survey. Cooper was given responsibility for the field collections of natural history material. When the survey party arrived at Fort Vancouver it disbanded, but Cooper remained, collecting specimens and attempting a general ecological survey. In his 1859, report Cooper made the following comments regarding the prairies of western Washington:

> A few remarks are necessary upon the origin of the dry prairies so singularly scattered throughout the forest region. Their most striking feature is the abruptness of the forest which surrounds them giving them the appearance of lands which have been cleared and cultivated for

hundreds of years. From various facts observed, I conclude that they are the remains of much more extensive prairies, which, within a comparatively recent period, occupied all the lower and dryer parts of the valleys, and which the forests have been gradually spreading over in their downward progress from the mountains.

The Indians, in order to preserve their open grounds for game, and for the production of their important root, the camas, soon found the advantage of burning. On some prairies near Vancouver and Nisqually, where this burning has been prevented for twenty years past, young spruces are found to be growing up rapidly, and Indians have told me that they can remember when some other prairies were much larger than at present.

Records from contemporary observers testify to frequent burnings. William Fraser Tolmie, a British citizen and chief factor of the Puget Sound Agricultural Company, made these observations in his diary:

7 July 1833: Fire has today consumed all the herbage on the plain for an extent of several miles.

6 September 1834: The Weather warm and we are surrounded by a thick smoke owing to fire being put to the field behind us (Norton. 1979).

Col. I.N. Ebey, an early settler on Whidbey Island to the northeast of the Olympic Peninsula, reports on June 9th, 1852: "A great deal of smoke is to be seen on the other side which I suppose is caused by the Indians burning the woods" (Norton, 1979).

Theresa Henson, in her 1986 study on native burning practices in western Washington, notes that burning today on conservation preserves demonstrates that the key plants of the Indian diet are increased by burning, and that:

Plant diseases, pests and fleas are killed with burning. But the burns must be of low intensity. This requires small amounts of fuel. The temperature of a fire is regulated by the amount of fuel that is available for the burn. In order to keep the amount of fuel at a minimum, the

Indians had to burn at regular intervals. The intervals probably ranged from yearly burning cycles to 3-5 year burning cycles depending on the areas' soils, climate and seed sources (Henson, 1986).

If fuels were abundant at the time of burning, the fires could rise to temperatures that were lethal to plants.

PART 4: NATIVE GARDENS

The Klallam people, at the time of Euro-American contact, occupied the area along the south shore of the Strait of Juan de Fuca, from the Hoko River east to Discovery Bay, a good 80 miles of coastline measured in a straight line. Early estimates indicate they numbered approximately 2,000 and were loosely organized into bands with winter villages situated at choice locations near the mouths of rivers including the Dungeness. The first European contact was with Spanish and English explorers who penetrated these inland waters in the last years of the 17th century.

Following the explorers came fur traders, missionaries, gold seekers, and then settlers.

The prairies were the first of their lands to go. Level, relatively fertile, well-drained, unforested land was rare and just what the settlers needed for grazing and cropping. Land claims were filed by territorial settlers before treaties were made to extinguish Indian title. In 1853, two years before territorial Gov. Isaac I. Stevens conducted his treaty-making with the Puget Sound tribes, Ezra Meeker wrote in his book *Pioneer Reminiscences of Puget Sound* of a cruise on Puget Sound in search of prairie land: "We were headed for Whidbey's Island, where, it was reported, rich prairie land could be found...we spent two or three days in exploring the island, only to find all the prairie land occupied...." (Meeker, 1905).

Towns were founded on the sites of older native villages and prairies, essentially native gardens.

Olympia, Tacoma, Seattle, Bellingham, Vancouver, Victoria, Port Angeles, and Sequim were all once sites of Indian habitation.

The first settlers filed claims under either the Donation Land Law, granting 320 acres to citizens who arrived in the territory before 1850, or the Preemption Act, which made parcels up to 160 acres of land available to settlers for $1.25 an acre.

With no understanding by whites of the cultural value of the prairies, occupation followed the same pattern everywhere across the West:

> Americans reduced the complex view of the Indians to a few simple categories. The new farmers saw most native plants as simply "weeds" or "brush." Land that grew these plants was, in the words of the census, "unimproved." Land on which native plants had been eliminated and replaced by domestic plants was "improved." For all practical purposes most native plants vanished from the everyday landscape of the new settlers, disappearing into the undifferentiated flora of the prairies. The intimate and detailed knowledge of the natural world that was widespread among the Salish became a specialized realm of esoteric knowledge among the whites (White, 1980).

In 1851 white settlers first came to the area known then as New Dungeness when it was still Oregon Territory. A low, sandy cape stood at the mouth of the Dungeness River and expansive tidelands spread south along Dungeness Spit in the protected Bay. In 1853, the settlement of Dungeness was located on what was called "Whiskey Flats" at the mouth of the Dungeness River just west of the Klallam village on Cline's Spit. B.L. Madison gave Whiskey Flats its name by selling contraband liquor to the Indians there.

Of course things had already changed a lot by the time settlers moved in. Trade goods and disease spread well ahead of white settlements. Smallpox (and other diseases) had already done devastating work: the first explorers commented on the scars they saw on the people's faces. Whole villages had died off or were deserted by fleeing survivors.

As the natives tried to adapt to changing conditions there was a curious convergence of old and new techniques involving the camas bulb and the potato that symbolized the next major shift for the Klallam people.

Camas bulbs had supplied the chief carbohydrate staple in the diets of many Pacific Northwest tribes (in the form of the complex sugar *inulin*). Trappers and early settlers in the region, and explorers including Lewis and Clark, told of eating camas when they were short on food. Anthropologist Erna Gunther, who compiled an ethnobotany of the Klallam people, declared, "except for choice varieties of dried salmon there was no article of food that was more widely traded than camas." (Gunther, 1973)

The following quote from Nancy Turner's study of Coast Salish ethnobotany provides more detail:

> Among the Vancouver Island Coast Salish, aboriginal harvesting and crop maintenance practices for camas can be termed "semi-agricultural." Large areas around Victoria...were visited each year ...the camas beds were divided into individually owned plots, passed from generation to generation. Each season, these were cleared of stones, weeds, and brush, often by controlled burning. Harvesting continued over several days, with entire families participating. The soil was systematically lifted out in small sections, the larger bulbs removed, and the sod replaced. Even within the present century, families would collect four to five potato-sacks full at a time. Most of these would be used for a communal feast upon returning to the villages. (Turner, 1975)

Indians roasted the bulbs, up to 100 pounds at once, in pits lined with hot rocks and covered with soil. Early observers called these camas cooking pits "oven mounds." Leftovers from the meal were pounded into cakes and dried for snacks or winter use. Bulbs boiled like potatoes are slimy and gummy, but longer boiling reduced them to a molasses-like substance which was a special treat for native feasts.

The potato, like the horse, originated in the New World, but didn't arrive in the Pacific Northwest until brought by the Euro-Americans. Beginning in 1789, the Spanish attempted to establish settlements on Vancouver Island in British Columbia and Neah Bay in Washington. At Neah Bay the temporary settlement consisted of "a fortified site of 10 houses, ovens, corrals and vegetable gardens....With 70 seamen and 13 soldiers it is the oldest non-Indian settlement in the Pacific Northwest." (Gamboa, 1979) This was probably the earliest introduction of potatoes into the region.

In 1811 the Pacific Fur Company introduced potatoes near Astoria, on the lower Columbia River. When the Hudson's Bay Company took over Astoria they continued to farm there and also in connection with their other forts, including Fort Vancouver on the Columbia and Fort Nisqually at the head of Puget Sound. (Suttles, 1987)

Although the Coast Salish people of the Puget Sound area were described by early explorers as a hunting and fishing people, with no agricultural practices, fifty years later Wilkes found potatoes being grown by the Port

Discovery Klallam and the people of Port Townsend (Wilkes, 1856). Potato patches were established on the prairies.

Anthropologist Wayne Suttles, in his study of Coast Salish potato cultivation, makes the following observations:

> The institutions and techniques of the native food gathering societies were organized in such a way that the cultivation of potatoes was able to enter without any need for a major economic readjustment...the truth may be that potatoes were accepted quickly and readily because in part they had a cash value and thus a superior status among roots even at some distance from the posts. During the period of settlement White needs may have been a factor in increasing Native production. Buying potatoes from Indians seems to have been a common practice among settlers.

Among Coast Salish people, gathering had been done largely by women. Using digging sticks and baskets they would harvest family-owned beds of camas and other plant concentrations that made up their seasonal round. This root-gathering tradition, combined with a sedentary life, allowed the potato to slip in naturally as a supplement to the camas.

A Dungeness pioneer woman has left this picture of the Klallams tending their potatoes: "It was not unusual even as late as 1906 to see a gang of Indians digging potatoes by use of a long sharp pole which was thrust into the ground under each vine and then the bulk of the hill was thrown out on the ground surface, digging the remainder of the hill out by the use of their hands. (Lotzgesell, 1933)

PART 5:   CULTURAL TRANSFORMATION

John Donnell was the first white to settle on the Sequim Prairie in 1853, after he spent the winter in a log cabin nearby and discovered the prairie by following an Indian trail. (Keeting, 1976) At this point judging by the soil survey cited above) Sequim Prairie included about 1,500 acres.

Other settlers soon followed. Water was scarce and the few wells had to be shared. Dry land farming began with raising of grains.

In the late 1880s talk began about bringing water from the Dungeness River to the prairie. D.R. "Crazy" Callen initiated construction on the irrigation ditch that would transform the prairie. The Sequim Prairie Ditch Company was formed in July 1895, and on May 1, 1896, pioneers celebrated completion of the first ditch. Eventually up to 25,000 acres in the Dungeness Valley would come under the largest canal-sprinkler system west of the Cascades.

Dry land farming was soon replaced by pasture. Even before irrigation, a survey taken in 1880 showed the following livestock on farms in the Dungeness Valley: 220 horses, 2,890 cattle, 996 dairy cows, 1,162 swine, 565 sheep and 3,464 chickens.

Irrigation and grazing eradicated the prairie flora. Foraging swine ate all the camas bulbs. "With the coming of settlers to the Sequim Prairie, there can be no doubt about 'anthropological influence' on the prairies. Populations, successional patterns, community composition, moisture regimes, and food chains were all transformed radically by the influence of settlers, their cultivation practices and domestic animals," writes Bob Steelquist in his study of the Sequim Prairie oaks.

An early botanist, observing the effects of the "Caucasian Invasion" on the vegetation of the Olympic Peninsula, called it a major catastrophic event and compared the magnitude of its effect to that of the Ice Age. (Jones, 1936)

More than just the prairie flora was affected by this transformation. Vernon Grant, a child of ditch company days, told of first ditches: "Farmers found fish in their fields after flood irrigating. The Dungeness River was full of fish in those days and they came down the ditch when the gates were opened, and it was easy to pick up a bucket of trout." (Brown, 1982). A Clallam County official recalled that after flood irrigation in the 1940s he would go through the fields picking up dead salmon because "the cows would leave an area of grass the size of a desk around the carcass...there were hundreds every year, mostly humpies (pinks) and silvers (cohos)." (Brown, 1982)

It was not until the late 1940's that diversion screens were finally installed to protect fish.

This quote is from Bruce Brown's book on the wild Olympic salmon (Brown, 1982):

> The low dams that diverted water from the Dungeness into irrigation ditches were not equipped with ladders for salmon passage. Salmon could jump some of these at high water, but at other times they blocked all migration.
>
> Protective screens over irrigation intake pipes were even rarer. As a result, millions of salmon fry were lured into ditches, and generally perished.
>
> Elsewhere, the shrunken streams provided salmon with less area to perform the vital functions of their lives. Many salmon were unable to find a place to spawn, and of those that did, many lost their eggs when the river dropped more. Fry were limited by the lack of adequate rearing area, and all salmon, large and small, suffered from the fact that there was not as much room to run from their enemies.
>
> The water that remained heated up faster, thereby reducing the amount of oxygen it could hold and fostering the growth of salmon diseases. Warm water dulls the salmon's senses, and above 55 degrees Fahrenheit (about the temperature of cold bath water) it prevents them from spawning. Water returning from irrigation ditches was warmer still, and often contained manure, pesticides and other poisons.
>
> In good years irrigation generally took about two-thirds of the Dungeness, but during extreme droughts, virtually all the water was removed from some sections, leaving pools and trickling rivulets in a broad bed of gravel. In 1975, the Washington Department of Fisheries estimated that a dozen separate runs of wild Dungeness coho and chum salmon had been exterminated by diversions for human and agricultural use.

The occupation of the Sequim Prairie by white settlers took away premium forage and game lands from the Klallams. In grazing and plowing, they destroyed native plant resources and transformed the floral landscape with introduced species. With irrigation they effected the extinction of dozens of native salmon runs. Today's impoverished Dungeness River salmon stocks are the legacy of that time. One culture supplanted another. Whereas the Klallam culture was comparatively nondestructive and symbiotic, the settler's culture was different. For the Klallam people the landscape had a spiritual dimension: plants and animals had a religious as well as economic significance. There was an inherent ecological wisdom in the Klallam attitude that mediated their cultural interaction with the landscape. With the arrival of Euro-Americans, human nature didn't change, the culture did; and today the landscape of Sequim Prairie vividly displays this change in human values and behavior.

THE NEW FEDERALISM: FUTURE TRENDS IN INDIAN-WHITE RELATIONS

Commentary

A recent historical overview of U.S. Indian policy identified four stages in the evolution of Indian-white relations: paternalism, dependency, Indian rights, and self-determination (Prucha, 1985).

The Bureau of Indian Affairs (BIA) is the principle government agency responsible for Indian matters. The Snyder Act of 1921 authorized expenditures for many BIA activities, including health, education, employment, and administration of Indian property.

Since 1824, when it was first established as a part of the U.S War Department, the BIA has grown into an independent and heavily entrenched federal bureaucracy with almost total power over Indian lives. It was recently characterized in a Senate investigative report as "ensnarled in red tape and riddled with fraud, mismanagement and waste." (United States Senate, 1989)

Since the 1930s the reassertion of tribal self-government has brought about an increase in services initiated or administered by tribes. In 1932, the Indian Reorganization Act began a new trend which will ultimately transfer control of most federal services to tribes.

With the new federal policy of Indian self-determination first formally enunciated in 1970 by President Richard M. Nixon, the nation embarked upon the most progressive federal Indian policy in our history. This self determination policy is based on the legal recognition that Indian tribes are the basic governmental units of federal Indian policy. Today tribal powers of self-government are recognized by the Constitution, acts of Congress, treaties between the United States and Indian tribes, judicial decisions, and administrative practice and local governments.

At the national level, the Tribal Self Governance Demonstration Project (PL 638, 1975) opened an era of "new federalism," a decentralist policy restoring tribal government to the local level, into the hands of those who know and care about Indian community needs.

The concept was extended to the state of Washington with the1989 Governor's Accord which recognizes the legal rights of Pacific Northwest tribes to manage their own affairs, and formalizes a co-operative relationship between state government and tribes, with a commitment to resolve issues of mutual concern through negotiation.

Recent action by Congress approving the Self Governance Project has given the people of 10 Indian nations, including the Jamestown and Port Gamble Klallam tribes, the chance to assume many of the jobs done by the BIA. At this writing (1991) the Jamestown Klallam have begun implementing this new relationship. Ironically, the last to receive federal recognition (in 1981), they are the first to sever ties with the BIA.

Important resource and social policy questions continue to evolve from this new, cooperative relationship.

Native people have a cultural bond with the surrounding natural environment, and today, throughout their ceded lands in the state of Washington, they play a progressive role in fisheries management.

Following the Boldt decision in 1974, the Skokomish Tribe joined with the Port Gamble and Lower Elwha Klallams to form the Point No Point Treaty Council, a fisheries management cooperative designed to manage the fisheries resource in the Point No Point Treaty area. The Jamestown tribe joined this cooperative after receiving federal recognition.

An unprecedented coalition of state, tribal, sports and commercial fishing interested produced the U.S. Salmon Interception Treaty in 1984, forming an international fishery management entity essential to the survival of the fishery resource. Tribal biologists played a lead role in this process.

Treaty rights are tied to place. The tribes must protect their native stocks. If local stocks are depleted they cannot move to another area and harvest there. Tribal jurisdictional interests are forcing agencies into more complicated forms of management that will help protect the abundance of naturally-spawning salmon stocks, the basic building blocks of the Pacific salmon species.

Non-native fisheries managers would often prefer to write off many of these genetic sub-populations to manage with greater efficiency in response to market demands.

Former Klallam Fisheries biologist James Lichatowich expressed the conflict this way: "The tribes are caught between two worlds: the treaties fix them to their traditional place and its resources, but they must live in a world without a sense of place, a world whose economic engines have no concern for resources in local places, a world that is increasingly driven by markets of global scale."

Lichatowich co-authored a recent study listing 214 naturally spawning Pacific salmon, steelhead, and sea-run cutthroat stocks that are at risk from California, Oregon, Idaho, and Washington. The authors state emphatically: "It is at the stock level that conservation and rehabilitation of salmon, if it is to be successful, will take place" (Nehlsen, 1991).

Logically, some degree of tribal jurisdiction over habitat management is next. Habitat is the key. In order to protect their legal entitlement to half the salmon runs, the tribes realize it is essential to protect the forested and urbanized watersheds where salmon spawning and rearing occur. In 1980, in a decision referred to as "Boldt Phase II," the U.S. district court concluded that the treaty right to take fish necessarily includes the right to have those fish protected from man-made environmental degradation. The State of Washington is currently attempting to negotiate with tribal members to avoid litigation on this matter.

Politically, this historical dynamic has led Washington State toward a cooperative resource management strategy. The last 20 years of the fishing controversy in the Pacific Northwest could be characterized as a path from confrontation to co-management.

Today, all three Klallam tribes have achieved federal recognition and have reserved lands: Port Gamble in 1939, the Lower Elwha in 1968, and the Jamestown in 1981.

Tribal identity is still firmly rooted in territory (ceded lands), sovereignty (federal recognition), and blood (quota).

In 1982, Klallam land claims were finally paid off at the rate of one dollar per acre and the tribes each received a share of the 438,430 acres ceded on that cold January day at Point No Point.

Ron Allen, current Tribal Chairman for the Jamestown Klallam, recently declared that key issues to be addressed in the near future are enhancement of tribal economies, improved awareness of the history, culture and traditions of Indian communities, and the educational foundation for Indian youth.

Meanwhile, there is still the unresolved problem of Indian-white relations, the legacy of racism, violence and ignorance. It is my conviction that it is neither fair nor appropriate to speak of an "Indian problem" - that, in fact, today's white community needs to confront, understand, and go beyond its traditional role in the history of native-white relations. Until then, this bitter legacy will continue to poison present-day relations.

The history of this relationship must be understood not only in a general way, but in terms of our specific geographic communities, because history is rooted in place, and plays a part, along with other environmental factors, in making up the world we live and breathe. Every region and tribal history has its unique "Trail of Tears."

Finally, our society must learn to value cultural diversity. Just as diversity is essential to the health of ecosystems, so cultural diversity has to be appreciated as a positive feature of human social systems, and valued for the strength, as well as the richness and texture, that it provides. This is our "medicine for human survival." (Taylor, 1970)

Historically, American Indian Policy has wavered between two Philosophical poles: isolation or assimilation. Neither position has been achievable. Now, as always, we are faced with a *relationship*.

Jerry Gorsline
Discovery Bay, Washington

APPENDIX A: CHRONOLOGY

1774   Earliest recorded Indian-white contact on the Pacific Coast with the explorations of the Spaniard Juan Perez and the landing of Spanish sailors near the Hoh River.

1775   Bodega y Quadra's Spanish galetta "Sonora" loses landing party to Indians near the Hoh (or Quileute) River.

1787   English trading vessel "Imperial Eagle" loses longboat and crew near Hoh River.

1788   Robert Duffin encounters Klallam Indians at Discovery Bay.

1789   Captain Gray reaches Clallam Bay in the "Washington."

1790   Manual Quimper reaches Port Discovery.

1791   Spanish military post established at Discovery Bay.

1792   Sea captain and explorer Robert Gray names the Columbia River after his ship.

1805   Lewis and Clark passed by the southern end of Coast Salish territory.

1807   Simon Fraser descends the Fraser River through Salish territory.

1819   John Jacob Astor organizes the Pacific Fur Company at the mouth of the Columbia River.

1824   Bureau of Indian Affairs created in the War Department.

1825   Fort Vancouver established on the Columbia as the first trading post in the area.

1827   Ft. Langley, the first Hudson's Bay Company trading post in Salish territory, established on the lower Fraser River.

1828   The Hudson's Bay Company's launches punitive expedition against the Klallam.

1832   Nisqually House established as first trading post and agricultural settlement in Puget Sound.

1833   Nisqually House records show evidence of Klallams trading.

1837   Two Catholic priests, Fathers F.N. Blanchet and M. Memers, arrive on the lower Columbia and establish a mission on the Cowlitz River.

1841   Wilkes explores Puget Sound and reports potatoes being grown by Port Discovery Klallam.

1843   City of Victoria founded.

1844   The Oregon Territory is created with Joseph Lane as Territorial Governor.

1846   Arguments with England over the ownership of the Oregon Territory are settled when the 49th Parallel is fixed. England retains Vancouver Island.

1847   6,000 sheep and 2,000 cattle recorded at Nisqually.

1848   Gold is discovered in California bringing thousands of settlers to the West.

1849   Bureau of Indian Affairs transferred to Dept. of Interior from the War Department.

1851   First settler arrives in Port Townsend and finds approx 500 Indians living on the beach just above high tide. Pioneers meet at Cowlitz Prairie and ask Congress to create a separate territory north of the Columbia River.

1852   Settlement of Dungeness area begins at Whiskey Flats.

1853   President Fillmore signs a bill creating the Washington Territory, a 193,071 square-mile area, including the present state of Washington, northern Idaho and western Montana. Olympia is chosen as the capital city and Isaac Ingalls Stevens as governor. By now, 3,965 pioneers have settled in the area; first settlers occupy land on the Sequim prairie; sawmills in operation at Port Gamble and Port Ludlow.

1853   Klallams murder the master and steward of the "John Adams."

1855   Point no Point Treaty concluded; Gibbs' census shows 926 Klallams.

Nisqually House records show evidence of Klallams trading.

1857   Dungeness lighthouse constructed; Catholic Oblate Fathers establish headquarters at Esquimalt.

1859   James Swan's Port Townsend census shows 300 whites and 200 Klallams; the ship "What Cheer" unleashes a smallpox epidemic on the Olympic Peninsula.

1860   March 31, James Swan took a census of the Indian camp at Point Hudson, counting 18 houses with Chemakum families and 14 Klallam lodges.

1862   Census shows 1,300 Klallam.

1869   Dungeness massacre, last intertribal warfare involving Klallams.

1871   Superintendent of Indian Affairs in Washington Territory bans "Indian doctoring"; Congress abolishes the practice of making treaties with Indian tribes. Hereafter, Congress would deal with Indians by passing legislation, with or without tribal approval.

1873   Catholic priests establish mission on Cowlitz River.

1875   Jamestown established.

1878   Census show 597 Klallam; last Klallam potlatch held at Jamestown.

1882   Shaker Church established in South Sound.

1885   Shaker Church established at Jamestown.

1887   General Allotment Law (also known as the Dawes Act) passed, dividing communally held tribal lands into separate parcels, and authorizing the sale of "surplus" parcels to white farmers.

1888   June 21st, Chet-ze-moka dies.

1893   Last Klallam secret society initiation held at Port Angeles.

1900   May 18th, James Swan dies.

1900   U.S. Indian population reduced to less than 300,000 due to disease and warfare; approximately one million Indians were living in what is now the United States when Europeans first arrived on this continent.

1910   Fishing laws and regulations exclude Klallam and close the Dungeness River to their fishing.

1921   Snyder Act authorizes the Bureau of Indian Affairs to administer programs "for the benefit, care, and assistance of federally recognized Native peoples."

1924   Indian Citizenship Act declares Indians to be U.S. citizens.

1934   Indian Reorganization Act passed, prohibiting further allotment of tribal land and beginning a trend of transferring control of federal services to tribes reorganized under the act.

1939   Port Gamble Klallam achieves federal recognition.

1968   Lower Elwha Klallam achieve federal recognition.

1970   September 18, United States v. Washington suit filed against the State of Washington over the degree to which the State could regulate and restrict the off-reservation fishing rights of the Treaty Indians, and whether existing state laws and regulations were discriminatory against the Indians.

1974   February 12th U.S. District Court Judge George Boldt renders his decision against the State of Washington and in favor of Indian Treaty Rights.

1974   The Skokomish Tribe joins with the Port Gamble and Lower Elwha Klallams to form the Point No Point Treaty Council, a fisheries management cooperative, to manage the fisheries resource in the Point No Point Treaty Area.

1975   U.S. Ninth Circuit Court of Appeals affirms Judge Boldt's decision in U.S. v. Washington; Indian Self Determination and Education Assistance Act of 1975 increases extent of tribal control over federal Indian programs and opens the era of "new federalism."

1980   Orrick Decision: U.S. District Court rules that (1) hatchery fish were to be included in the allocation between treaty and non-treaty fishermen, and (2) that the treaty right to take fish necessarily includes the right to have those fish protected from man-made environmental degradation.

1981   Jamestown Klallam achieve federal recognition.

1991   Jamestown Klallam begin implementing self governance under PL 638.

APPENDIX B:
KLALLAM ETHNOBOTANY
The Relationship between a
People and their Floral Environment

The following plants were part of the native Sequim Prairie vegetation and were utilized by the Klallam people for food, medicine, cosmetics and charms; ceremonies and games; dyes and perfumes; fumigants and flavorings; detergents, tanning agents and tools; scents and repellents; fuel and boatbuilding; bedding and shelter; carving material; mats, boxes, nets and bindings.

My authority for the species list is Nelsa M. Buckingham, an expert regarding the Olympic Peninsula flora, and co-author of Vascular Plants of the Olympic Peninsula, Washington (1979). Nomenclature is from Hitchcock, et al., Vascular Plants of the Pacific Northwest (1969).

My authority for the ethnobotany is Dr. Nancy J. Turner, Curator of Ethnology, British Columbia Provincial Museum. Her two volume work on use of plants by British Columbia Indians is considered definitive. Where she indicates a plant had cultural utility for Salish coastal people I have included it here.

T = Plants in British Columbia Indian Technology; F = Food Plants of British Columbia Indians (Turner, 1975, 1979).

Species	Common Name	Usage
Abies grandis	Grand fir	T
Acer macrophyllum	Big leaf maple	T,F
Achillea millefolium	Yarrow	T
var. californica	Yarrow	T
var. lanulosa	Yarrow	T
Allium acuminatum	Tapertip onion	F
Allium cernuum	Nodding onion	T,F

	Red Alder	T,F
Amelanchier alnifolia	Serviceberry	T,F
var. *semiintegrifolia*	Serviceberry	T,F
Anaphalis margaritacea	Pearly everlasting	T
Apocynum androsaemifolium	Spreading dogbane	T
ssp. *pumilum*	Spreading dogbane	T
var. *tomentellum*	Spreading dogbane	T
Arbutus menziesii	Madrona	T
Arctostaphylos uva-ursi	Kinnikinnick	T,F
Athyrium filix-femina	Lady-fern	T,F
var. *cyclosorum*	Lady-fern	T,F
Berberis aquifolium	Shining oregongrape	T,F
Bromus sitchensis	Alaska brome	T
var. *sitchensis*	Alaska brome	T
Calypso bulbosa	Fairy slipper	F
var. *occidentalis*	Fairy slipper	F
Carex species	Sedges	T
Castilleja miniata	Indian paintbrush	T
var. *dixonii*	Scarlet paintbrush	T
Camassia quamash	Camas	F
ssp. *azurea*	Camas	F
Cirsium edule	Indian thistle	F
Claytonia perfoliata	Miner's lettuce	F*
Claytonia sibirica	Siberian springbeauty	F*
Corylus cornuta	Hazelnut	T,F
var. *californica*	Hazelnut	T,F
Crataegus suksdorfii	Suksdorf's hawthorn	F
Delphinium menziesii	Menzies' larkspur	T
ssp. *menziesii*	Menzies' larkspur	T
Deschapmsia cespitosa	Tufted hairgrass	T
Dryopteris expansa	Spreading wood-fern	T
Elymu s glaucus	Blue wildrye	T
var. *glaucus*	Blue wildrye	T
Elymus mollis	Dune wildrye	T
Epilobium angustifolium	Fireweed	T,F
ssp. *angustifolium*	Fireweed	T,F

Equisetum arvense	Common horsetail	T,F
Equisetum telmateia	Giant horsetail	T,F
Fritillaria lanceolata	Rice-root fritillaria	F
Fragaria vesca	Wood strawberry	F
ssp. *bracteata*	Wood strawberry	F
Fragaria virginiana	Broadpetal strawberry	F
ssp. *platypetala*	Broadpetal strawberry	F
Galium aparine	Goosegrass	T
Galium triflorum	Small bedstraw	T
var. *pacificum*	Small bedstraw	T
Gaultheria shallon	Salal	F
Holodiscus discolor	Oceanspray	T
var. *discolor*	Oceanspray	T
Juncus effusus	Common rush	T
var. *gracilis*	Common rush	T
Lillium columbianum	Tiger lily	F
Lomatium nudicaule	Pestle parsnip	T
Lomatioum utriculatum	Pomo-celery	F
Mahonia aquifolium	Shining Oregongrape	T,F
Mahonia nervosa	Dull Oregongrape	T,F
Malus fusca	Western crabapple	T,F
Mentha arvensis	Field mint	T
var. *villosa*	Field mint	T
Oemleria cerasiformis	Indian plum	F
Opuntia fragilis	Prickly-pear cactus	T
Philadelphus lewisii	Lewis' mockorange	T
var. *gordonianus*	Lewis' mockorange	T
Physocarpus capitatus	Pacific ninebark	T
Poaceae species	Grasses	T
Polystichum munitum	Swordfern	T,F
Populus balsamifera	Black cottonwood	T,F
ssp. *trichacarpa*	Black cottonwood	T,F
Potentilla pacifica	Pacific silverweed	F
Prunus emarginata	Bitter cherry	T
var. *mollis*	Bitter cherry	T
Pseudotsuga menziesii	Douglas fir	T
var. *menziesii*	Douglas fir	T
Pteridium aquilinum	Bracken	T,F

var. *pubescens*	Bracken	T,F
Quercus garryana	Garry oak	F
Ribes divaricatum	Coast black gooseberry	T,F
var. *divaricatum*	Coast black gooseberry	T,F
Ribes lacustre	Swamp gooseberry	F
Ribes lobbii	Gummy gooseberry	F
Ribes sanguineum	Red flowering current	F
var. *sanguineum*	Red flowering current	F
Rosa gymnocarpa	Woodland rose	T,F
Rosa nutkana	Nootka rose	T,F
var. *nutkana*	Nootka rose	T,F
Rubus leucodermis	Western Blackcap	F
var. *leucodermis*	Western Blackcap	F
Rubus parviflorus	Thimbleberry	T,F
var. *parvifiorus*	Thimbleberry	T,F
Rubus spectabilis	Salmonberry	T,F
var. *spectabilis*	Salmonberry	T,F
Rubus ursinus	Pacific blackberry	T,F
Salix lasiandra	Pacific willow	T
var. *lasiandra*	Pacific willow	T
Salix scouleriana	Scouler willow	T
Sambucus cerulea	Blue elderberry	T,F
var. *cerulean*	Blue elderberry	T,F
Sambucus racemosa	Red elderberry	T,F
ssp. *pubens*	Red elderberry	T,F
var. *arborescens*	Red elderberry	T,F
Satureja douglasii	Yerba buena	F
Shepherdia Canadensis	Russet buffalo-berry	F
Spiraea douglasii	Douglas' spirea	T
ssp. *Douglasii*	Douglas' spirea	T
Symphoricarpos albus	Snowberry	T
var. *laevigatus*	Snowberry	T
Trifolium species	Clovers	F
Typha latifolia	Cat-tail	T
Urtica dioica	Stinging nettle	T,F
ssp. *gracillis*	Stinging nettle	T,F
var. *lyallii*	Stinging nettle	T,F
Vaccinium parvifolium	Red huckleberry	F

*Claytonias are not in Turner but surely they were eaten.

Note: not all the plants listed are "prairie" species. Some, such as Pacific silverweed, Cat-tail and Red huckleberry, grew on the margins of Sequim prairie or in wetlands encompassed by the prairie.

BIBLIOGRAPHY

AFSC (American Friends Service Committee). *Uncommon Controversy: Fishing Rights of the Muckleshoot, Puyallup and Nisqually Indians.* Seattle: University of Washington Press, 1970.

BANCROFT, HUBERT HOWE. *History of Washington, Idaho, and Montana 1845-1889.* San Francisco: The History Company, Pubs., 1890.

BARNET, H.G. *Indian Shakers.* Carbondale: Southern Illinois University Press, 1957.

BERGLAND, ERIC O. *Summary Prehistory and Ethnography of Olympic National Park, Washington.* Seattle: National Park Service, 1983.

BLANHET, FRANIS NORBERT. *Historical Sketches of the Catholic Church in Oregon during the past forty years.* Portland: Catholic Sentinel Press, 1878.

BROWN, BRUCE. *Mountain in the Clouds: A Search for the Wild Salmon.* New York: Simon & Schuster, 1982.

BROWNE, J.R. *Crusoe's Island.* New York: Harper & Brothers, 1864.

BUCKINGHAM, NELSA M. *The Uniqueness of the Olympics.* Unpublished MS, 1991.

BUCKINGHAM, NELSA M. and EDWARD L. TISCH. *Vascular Plants of the Olympic Peninsula, Washington.* Seattle: College of Forest Resources, University of Washington, 1979.

CARLSON, ROY. "Chronology and Culture Change in the San Juan Islands." *American Antiquity* 25, 1960.

CASTILE, GEORGE PIERRE. *The Indians of Puget Sound: The Notebooks of Myron Eells.* Seattle: University of Washington Press, 1985.
"The Indian Connection: Judge James Wickersham and the Indian Shakers." *Pacific Northwest Quarterly,* Vol. 81, No. 4·, 1990.

COLVOCORESSES, LT. GEORGE M. *Four Years in a Government Exploring Expedition.* New York: Cornish, Lamport & Co., 1852.

COOK, S.F. *The Epidemic of 1830-1833 in California and Oregon.* Berkeley: University of California Press, 1953.

COOPER, J.G. "Botanical Report." *Explorations and Surveys for a Railroad Route from the Mississippi River to the Pacific Ocean.* Washington, D.C.: War Department. Vol. 12, Part 2, 1859·

COWELL, RAY T. "History of Port Townsend." *Washington Historical Quarterly,* Vol. XVI, No. 4, 1925.

CROSBY, ALFRED W. *The Columbian Exchange.* Westport: Greenwood Press, 1972.

DAVENPORT, T.W. "Recollections of an Indian agent." *Oregon Historical Quarterly,* Vol. 1, 1907.

CURTIS, EDWARDS. *The North American Indian.* Vol. IX. Norwood: Plimpton Press, 1913.

DILLON, RICHARD H.J. *Ross Browne: Confidential Agent in Old California.* Norman: University of Oklahoma Press, 1965.

DRUCKER, PHILIP. *Indians of the Northwest Coast.* New York: McGraw Hill Book Company, 1955.

DuBOIS, CORA A. "The 1870 Ghost Dance." *Anthropological Records*, 3:1. Berkeley: University of California Press, 1939·

ECKROM, J.A. *Remembered Drums: A History of the Puget Sound Indian War*. Walla Walla: Pioneer Press, 1989.

EELLS, MYRON. "The Potlatches of Puget Sound" *The American Antiquarian*, Vol. V, No.2, 1883.

    Ten Years Missionary Work at Skokomish. Boston: Congregational Sunday School and Publishing Society, 1886.

    "The Twana, Chemakum and Klallam Indians of Washington Territory." *Smithsonian Report*. Washington. D.C.: Smithsonian Institute, 1887.

ERMATINGER, C.O. "The Columbia River Under Hudson's Bay Company Rule." *The Washington Historical Quarterly*, Vol. V, No. 3, 1914.

ERMATINGER, FRANK. "Earliest Expeditions Against Puget Sound Indians." *The Washington Historical Quarterly*. Vol. I, No. 2., 1907.

FARRAR, VICTOR. "Journal of Occurrences at Nisqually House." *The Washington Historical Quarterly*, Vol. VI, No. 3, 1915.

    "The Diary of Colonel and Mrs. I.N. Ebey." *Washington Historical Quarterly*. Vol. 7, 1916; Vol. 8, 1917.

FAY, R.C. "Report No. 85." *Report of the Commissioner of Indian Affairs for 1858, 1858*.

GAMBOA, ERASMO. "Washington's Mexican Heritage." *Columbia*, Fall 1989.

GATES, CHARLES M. "The Indian Treaty of Point No Point." *Pacific Northwest Quarterly*, Vol. 41, No. 2, 1955·

GIBBS, GEORGE. "George Gibbs Journal." *Documents Relating to the Negotiation of Ratified and Unratified Treaties with Various Indian Tribes, 1801–1865*. Washington, D.C.: National Archives. Record Group 75, 1854.

    Report on the Indian Tribes of the Territory of Washington. Washington, D.C.: War Department. Pacific Railroad Report, Vol. I, 1855.

    Alphabetical Vocabularies of the Clallam & Lummi. New York: Cramoisy Press, 1863.

    "Tribes of Western Washington and Northwest Oregon." *Contributions to North American Ethnology*, 1:1 57-242, 1877.

GRANT, W. COLQUHOUN. ESQ. *Description of Vancouver Island, 1857*. London, 1857.

GREGORY, V.J., ET AL. *With Pride in Heritage: History of Jefferson County*. Port Townsend: Jefferson County Historical Society,1966.

GUNTHER, ERNA. Unpublished field notes, 1924.

    "Klallam Ethnography." Seattle: *University of Washington Publications in Anthropology* 1 (5), 1927.

    "The Shaker Religion of the Northwest." *Indians of the Urban Northwest* (ed. M.W. Smith) New York: Columbia University Press, 1949.

    "Vancouver and the Indians of Puget Sound." *Pacific Northwest Quarterly*, Vol. 51, No. 1, 1960.

    Ethnobotany of Western Washington: The Knowledge and Use of Indigenous Plants. Seattle: University of Washington Press, 1973.

GUSTAFSON, CARL E. *The Manis Mastodon Site: An Adventure in Prehistory.* Privately printed pamphlet. No date.
  "Late-Glacial Vegetation and Climate at the Manis Mastadon Site, Olympic Peninsula, Washington." *Quaternary Research 1,* 1983.

HANCOCK, SAMUEL. *Trip Across the Plains, from Independence, Missouri to Portland, Oregon, 1860.*

HASTINS, LOREN B. *Journal of L.B. Hastings.* Unpublished manuscript of trip on the Oregon trail in 1847 housed at The Beinecke Rare Book and Manuscript Library, Yale University, Princeton. Microfilm copy available at the Washington State Historical Society, Tacoma.

HENSON, THERESA R. *Indian Burning Practices in Western Washington.* Unpublished, 1986.

HOWAY, F.W. "Some Remarks upon the New Vancouver Journal." *The Washington Historical Quarterly,* Vol. VI No. 2, 1915.
  "The Introduction of Intoxicating Liquors amongst the Indians of the Northwest Coast. *"British Columbia Historical Quarterly.* Vol. VI., No. 3, 1942.

JONES, GEORGE NEVILLE. *A Botanical Survey of the Olympic Peninsula, Washington.* Seattle: University of Washington, Publications in Biology, Vol. 5, 1936.

KANE, PAUL. *Wanderings of an Artist Among the Indians of North America.* Toronto: The Radisson Society of Canada Limited, 1925.

KAPPLER, CHARLES J. "Treaty with the S'Klallam, 1855. *"Laws & Treaties, Vol II.* Washington, D.C.: Government Printing Office, 1904.

KAUTZ, FRANCES. "Extracts from the Diary of Gen. A.V. Kautz." *The Washington Historical Quarterly,* Vol. I., 1900.
  "Extracts from the Diary of Gen. A.V. Kautz," *The Washington Historian.* Vol. II, 1901.

KEETING, VIRGINIA. *Dungeness: Lure of a River.* Sequim: Bicentennial Book Co, 1976.

KELLOGG, GEORGE ALBERT. *A History of Whidbey's Island.* Seattle: The Shorey Book Store, 1934.

KROEBER, A.L. *Cultural and Natural Areas of Native North America.* Berkeley: University of California Publications in American Archaeology and Ethnology, No. 38, 1939.

LAMB, KAYE W. *The Voyage of George Vancouver, 1791-1795.* Vol. 1. London: The Hakluyt Society, 1984.

LAMBERT, MARY ANN. *The House of the Seven Brothers.* Port Townsend: Port Townsend Pub., 1960.
  Dungeness Massacre and Other Regional Tales. Port Townsend: Port Townsend Pub., 1961.

LAURIDSON, G.M. and A.A. SMITH. *The Story of Port Angeles.* Seattle: Lowman and Hanford Co., 1937.

LAUT, AGNES C. *The Overland Trail: The Epic Path of the Pioneers to Oregon.* New York: Frederick A. Stokes Co., 1929.

LEIGHTON, CAROLINE. *Life at Puget Sound, 1865-1881.* Boston: Lee & Shepard, 1884.

LOTZGESELL, MRS. GEORGE. "Pioneer Days at Old Dungeness." *Washington Historical Quarterly,* 24: 264-270, 1933.·

MARTIN, DOUGLAS DALE. *Indian White Relations on the Pacific Slope, 1850-1890.* PhD Thesis. Seattle: University of Washington, Department of History, 1969.

McCURDY, JAMES G. *By Juan de Fuca's Strait.* Portland: Metropolitan Press, Pubs., 1937.

McDONALD, LOIS HALLIDAY. *Fur Trade Letters of Francis Ermatinger, 1818-1853.* Glendale: The Arthur H. Clark Co., 1980.

McDONALD, LUCILLE. "Events of 1853 at Port Discovery." Seattle: *Seattle Times,* Magazine Section, April 6, 1958.

Swan Among the Indians: Life of James G. Swan, 1818-1900. Portland: Binfords & Mort, Pubs., 1972.

MEANY, EDMOND S. "Northwestern History Syllabus," excerpts from *The Washington Historical Quarterly,* April, 1912 to October, 1916.

Vancouver's Discovery of Puget Sound. Portland: Binford & Mort, 1957.

MEARES, JOHN. *Voyages in 1788 and 1789 from China to the North West Coast of America.* New York: De Capo Press, 1790.

MEEKER, EZRA. *Pioneer Reminiscences of Puget Sound.* Seattle: Lowman & Hanford, 1905.

MOONEY, JAMES. *The Aboriginal Population of America North of Mexico.* Washington, D.C.: Smithsonian Miscellaneous Collections, 1928.

MORGAN, MURRAY. *Puget's Sound.* Seattle: University of Washington Press, 1979.

NEHLSEN, WILLA, ET AL. "Pacific Salmon at the Crossroads: Stocks at Risk from California, Oregon, Idaho, and Washington." *Fisheries,* Vol. 16, No. 2, 1991.

NORTON, HELEN H. "The Association Between Anthropogenic Prairies and Important Food Plants in Western Washington." *Northwest Anthropological Research,* 13:2, 1979·

NUNIS, DOYCE B., JR. *The Hudson's Bay Company's First Fur Brigade to the Sacramento Valley. Alexander McLeod's 1829 Hunt.* Fair Oaks: The Sacramento Book Collectors Club, 1968.

OWEN, GIFFORD P. *Appraisal for S'Klallam Indian Lands, 1859. 1969*

PETTITT, GEORGE. *The Quileute of LaPush, 1775-1945.·* Anthropological Records. Berkeley: University of California Press, 1950.

PRUCA, FRANCIS PAUL. *The Indians in American Society.* Berkeley: University of California Press, 1985.

RICHARDS, KENT. *Isaac I. Stevens: Young Man in a Hurry.* Provo: Brigham Young University Press, 1979.

RUBY, ROBERT H. and JOHN A. BROWN. *Indians of the Pacific Northwest.* Norman: University of Oklahoma Press, 1981.

SCHWANTES, CARLOS A. *The Pacific Northwest: An Interpretive History.* Lincoln: University of Nebraska Press, 1989.

SEEMAN, BERTHOLD, F.L.S. *Narrative of the Voyage of the H.M.S. Herald during the Years 1845-51 Under the Command of Capt. Henry Kellett, R.M., C.B.; Being a Circumnavigation of the Globe and Three Cruises to the Arctic Regions in Search of Sir John Franklin.* Vol. I. London: Reeve & Co, 1853.

SIMPSON, PETER. *City of Dreams.* Port Townsend: Bay Press, 1986.

SIMPSON, PETER and HERMANSON, JAMES. *Port Townsend: Years That Are Gone.* Port Townsend: Quimper Press, 1979.

SIMPSON, SIR GEORGE. *Narrative of a Journey Round the World during the years 1841 and 1842,* Vol. II. London: Henry Colburn, Pub., 1847.

SNOWDEN, CLINTON A. *History of Washington: The Rise and Progress of An American State.* Vol III. New York: The Century History Co., 1909.

SMITH, LESLIE H. *Soil Survey of Clallam County, Washington.* Washington, D.C.: U.S.D.A., 1951.

SPERLIN, D. B. "Washington Forts of the Fur Trade Regime." *The Washington Historical Quarterly,* Vol. VIII, No. 2, 1917.

STARLING, E.A. "Report of E.A. Starling, Agent for Puget Sound." Henry R. Schoolcraft, Ed., *Information Respecting the History, Conditions and Prospects of the Indian Tribes of the United States,* Part IV. Philadelphia: Lippincott, Grambo and Company, 1854.

STEELQUIST, ROBERT. *Distribution, Abundance and Age Classes in Quercus Garryana of the Sequim Prairie, Olympic Peninsula, Washington.* Unpublished. No date.

SUTTLES, WAYNE. *Coast Salish Essays.* Seattle: University of Washington Press, 1987.

SWADISH, MORRIS "The Linguistic Approach to Salish Prehistory." *Indians of the Urban Northwest.* Edited by Marian Smith. New York: Columbia University Press, 1949.

SWAN, JAMES G. *The Northwest Coast.* New York: Harper & Bros. Pubs., 1857. Articles in *San Francisco Bulletin,* 10 May and 19 May, 1859. *Sequim Prairie, Washington Territory.* The Washington Standard, 1861. *Almost Out of the World: Scenes from Washington Territory, the Strait of Juan de Fuca, 1859-1861.* Tacoma: Washington State Historical Society, 1971.

TAYLOR, HERBERT C. "Aboriginal Populations of the Lower Northwest Coast." *Pacific Northwest Quarterly.* Vol. 54, 1963.

TROTTER, F.I. *Unpublished Interviews and Manuscripts.* Olympia: Washington Pioneer Project, 1936. *Told By The Pioneers.* Olympia: Washington Pioneer Project, 1937.

TURNER, NANCY J. *Food Plants of British Columbia Indian Indians.* Victoria: British Columbia Provincial Museum, 1975 *Plants in British Columbia Indian Technology.* Victoria: British Columbia Provincial Museum, 1979.

UNITED STATES SENATE. *Report of the Special Committee on Investigatons of the Select Committee on Indian Affairs.* Report 101-216. Washington, D.C., 1989.

WAR DEPARTMENT. "Botanical Report." Vol. 12, Part 2. *Explorations and Surveys for a Railroad Route from the Mississippi River to the Pacific Ocean.* Washington, 1859.

WEIR, ALLEN. "Roughing it on Puget Sound in the Early Sixties," *The Washington Historian,* Vol. I, No. 2 & 3, 1900.

WHITE, RICHARD. *Land Use, Environment and Social Change: The Shaping of Island County, Washington.* Seattle: University of Washington Press, 1980.

WILKES, CHARLES. *Narrative of the U.S. Exploring Expedition During the Years 1838-1842.* 5 Vols. New York: G.P. Putnam & Sons, 1856.

WILLIAMS, JOHNSON. "Black Tamanous, The Secret Society of the Clallam Indians," *The Washington Historical Quarterly,* Vol. VII, No. 4, 1916.

WINTHROP, THEODORE. *The Canoe and the Saddle.* Tacoma: John H. Williams, 1913.

EDITOR'S BIOGRAPY

Jerry Gorsline has lived on the Olympic Peninsula since 1975. He also edited *Rainshadow: Archibald Menzies and the Botanical Exploration of the Olympic Peninsula* (Jefferson County Historical Society 1992) and co-edited with Finn Wilcox *Working the Woods, Working the Sea: An Anthology of Northwest Writings (*Empty Bowl Press 2008).